I AM A MONUMENT

I AM A MONUMENT

ON *LEARNING FROM LAS VEGAS*

Aron Vinegar

The MIT Press   Cambridge, Massachusetts   London, England

MIT Press books may be purchased at special quantity discounts for business or sales promotional use. For information, please email special_sales@mitpress.mit.edu or write to Special Sales Department, The MIT Press, 55 Hayward Street, Cambridge, MA 02142.

This book was set in Baskerville and Univers by the MIT Press. Printed and bound in the United States of America.

Library of Congress Cataloging-in-Publication Data
Vinegar, Aron.
 I am a monument : on Learning from Las Vegas / Aron Vinegar.
    p. cm.
 Includes bibliographical references and index.
 ISBN 978-0-262-22082-8 (hardcover : alk. paper)
 1. Venturi, Robert. Learning from Las Vegas—Criticism, textual. 2. Architectural writing—United States. 3. Book design—Massachusetts—Cambridge—History—20th century. I. Title.
 NA2540.V56 2008
 720.9793'135—dc22
                                    2007045988

10 9 8 7 6 5 4 3 2 1

Extra vagance! it depends on how you are yarded.

—Henry Thoreau, *Walden*

CONTENTS

ACKNOWLEDGMENTS

This book is dedicated to Amanda Boetzkes. She read every single word of it with care and attention as if it were her own. But most importantly I treasure our intellectual exchanges and will think about them long after this book's completion. I feel very fortunate to have her as an interlocutor. I am grateful for the following individuals who have helped me by discussing theoretical issues at stake in the book, reading chapters, and/or giving me the opportunity to present this material in various public forums: Mike Cadwell, Roger Conover, Whitney Davis, Lisa Florman, Michael Golec, Jeff Kipnis, Christian Kleinbub, Rob Livesey, Steve Melville, Jose Oubrerie, Will Straw, David Van Zanten, and Bronwen Wilson. As friends and colleagues, Michael Golec and I have talked long and hard about *Learning from Las Vegas*. A special thank you to Roger Conover whose enthusiasm and support for this project were unwavering. It was a pleasure to work with him on this book. I am grateful to my editors Paula Woolley and Matthew Abbate for their precision and insight, and to Yasuyo Iguchi for the sensitive design of this book.

My research was generously funded by a Social Sciences and Research Council of Canada Postdoctoral Fellowship, and by a Richard H. Tomlinson Postdoctoral Fellowship. I would like to thank the chairs of my departments at Ohio State University for their support: Mark Fullerton, Myroslava Mudrak, Andrew Shelton, Jose Oubrerie, and Rob Livesey. I received generous support for this work from Dean Karen Bell and the College of Arts, Ohio State University. The following individuals were kind enough to talk with me about Muriel Cooper and issues of design covered in chapter 5: Roger Conover, Mario Furtado, Michael McPherson, John Matill, Wendy Richmond, David Small, Sylvia Steiner, Ed Allen, Cynthia Ware, Dietmar Winkler, and Carl Zahn. I learned a lot from their expertise and insight. Needless to say, the interpretations advanced in this book are my own. I am particularly grateful to Sylvia Steiner for producing the typographic grid that Muriel Cooper used for the first edition of *Learning from Las Vegas* (see figure 5.13). Vincent Scully graciously allowed me to reproduce his unpublished introduction to *Learning from Las Vegas*, which appears in the appendix. Thanks to Bob Calhoun, who assisted me with the images for this book, to Bill Whitaker, the director of the VSBA archives at the University of Pennsylvania, who helped me find the archival material I needed, and to John Izenour, who faciliated my use of images from *VSBA*. I am very grateful to my mother, Wendy R. London, whose example of hard work and commitment I have always admired.

And finally a special thank you to Bob Venturi and Denise Scott Brown who wrote the book that this book is about. They took the time to talk with me during a very pleasant and informative afternoon in Manayunk. I am not sure if they will like this book (nor am I sure they won't). Whatever the case, it is written in admiration and respect for both their thought and their unthought.

ABBREVIATIONS

AAFAL   Avery Architectural & Fine Arts Library, Columbia University
AAUP   Architectural Archives, University of Pennsylvania, gift of
         Robert Venturi and Denise Scott Brown (also referred to in
         the text as the "VSBA archives")
LLV   *Learning from Las Vegas* (used only in the endnotes)
VSBA   Venturi, Scott Brown and Associates, Inc.
VSBI   Robert Venturi, Denise Scott Brown, and Steven Izenour

Citing the authors of *Learning from Las Vegas* has always been a difficulty for anyone writing on that book. Although the book is coauthored by Robert Venturi, Denise Scott Brown, and Steven Izenour, it has often seemed unwieldy to cite all three names, and thus very often their authorship is abbreviated in some way, such that either one or two names get left out; in the former case it is always Steven Izenour, and in the latter, Steven Izenour and Denise Scott Brown. The abbreviation VSBI is an attempt to acknowledge all three authors. However, I have not always used this abbreviation throughout the book, employing, at times, the blanket term "authors" instead. The writing of the text of *Learning from Las Vegas* was primarily the work of Venturi and Scott Brown, so often when I am citing specific passages from the book I have used Venturi and Scott Brown rather than VSBI. I can't claim any hard-and-fast rule for when I have decided to use one form of reference or the other; I have simply relied on my judgment in each case.

I AM A MONUMENT

INTRODUCTION

From its initial publication in 1972, *Learning from Las Vegas* by Robert Venturi, Denise Scott Brown, and Steven Izenour, was immediately recognized as a semi-nal statement in the history and theory of architecture and, soon after, hailed as one of the defining texts of postmodernism. As such it played an exemplary role in early theorizations of the postmodern condition by such figures as Fredric Jameson, Charles Jencks, and Andreas Huyssen. Its influence was deeply felt both within the architectural scene and far beyond its particular institutional and professional boundaries. Simply put, the role that *Learning from Las Vegas* played in identifying and theorizing postmodernism shifted architecture to the center of cultural debates, a place from which it has never departed.

Yet its categorization as an exemplary postmodernist text has rendered the book too easily grasped. In Andreas Huyssen's thoughtful essay "Mapping the Postmodern," one reads: "One of the most telling documents of the break of postmodernism with the modernist dogma is a book coauthored by Robert Venturi, Denise Scott Brown, and Steven Izenour and entitled *Learning from Las Vegas*."[1] Similarly worded statements can be found in most serious texts on postmodernism. One might argue that *Learning from Las Vegas* quickly became what Fredric Jameson has termed a "vanishing mediator": a sunken neutral term that operates as a catalyst, enabling an exchange of energies to take place between two terms—in this case, modernism and postmodernism—and then disappearing once its function is over.[2] Thus, its position in a movement from the old (modernism) to the new (postmodernism) has foreclosed the possibility of coming to terms with *Learning from Las Vegas* in and of itself. Instead of acknowledging how the book is in excess of these terms, we seem to opt for repressing our anxieties toward it, converting it into what Richard Rorty has called a "neutral framework," a privileged terrain that legislates the appropriate terms of any debate. One can therefore sympathize with Venturi and Scott Brown's rigorous opposition to any unproblematic categorization of their work as postmodern, including the drive to subsume it into the pastiche-like, historicizing modes of architectural production that their work has been accused of initiating.

By most accounts, the debates about modernism and postmodernism are now seen as primarily historical; that is to say, they are not seen as live debates. Some regard *Learning from Las Vegas* as an important historical document, but one now rendered obsolete by the conditions of globalization. From this perspective, the book's historical locatedness has become a testament to its outdatedness. I believe this may be true of some books, but not this one. An untimely book is never outdated because its untimeliness is already of a piece with its arrival. As I argue in chapter 1, although it seems obvious enough, it is worth stating that *Learning from Las Vegas* is a departure "from" the actual city of Las Vegas. Learning is not only indebtedness "to" something but is also a leave-taking, a form of departure and displacement. Thus, any account of *Learning from Las Vegas* will have to begin and depart from the book itself.[3] In other words, we need to pay close attention to *Learning from Las Vegas* as a *book*: an amalgam of words and images arranged on pages that establish certain rhythms and divisions of text and argument.

It has been argued that postmodern theorists such as Huyssen and Jameson overemphasized the effect of *Learning from Las Vegas* on architecture, and it was rather Venturi's *Complexity and Contradiction in Architecture* (1966) that was most influential.[4] But *Learning from Las Vegas* is, in fact, more relevant than it has ever been. As a jointly written endeavor, it quickly led to revealing issues about star power, sexism, gender, and collaboration within the production of architectural knowledge.[5] Those in the nascent fields of material culture and American studies recognized the book as an allied effort to pay attention to the ordinary vernacular of our urban environments, with an eye to the implications that anthropology, sociology, and urban psychology might play in this endeavor. *Learning from Las Vegas* was an early attempt to come to grips with "urban sprawl," and the different ethical, aesthetic, and representational sensibilities required to register these changes.

It was then, and still is, the starting point for any consideration of architecture and urbanism within information- and consumer-driven economies, and of the changing status of the architect within this nexus. I hope my book makes clear that the relevant inheritors of *Learning from Las Vegas* are not primarily "historicist postmodern architects," but rather architects and theorists such as Rem Koolhaas, MVRDV, and Herzog and de Meuron who are exploring the intersections between information, mood, and materiality, not to mention the influence of Venturi and Scott Brown's engagement with humor, gesture and community. Furthermore, while their work is often taken as a foil to Peter Eisenman's, *Learning from Las Vegas* brushes against his writings on surface and sign in ways that transcend mere contrast. Simply put, this book reconfigures some of the given genealogies of modern and contemporary architecture.

Learning from Las Vegas also resonates with those pursuing work on "mediated envelopes" and the relationship between the generic and specific, and it is a precursor to the recent interest in affect, mood, and atmosphere in architectural criticism and practice. Its approach to the high/low divide resonates with the recent drive toward visual culture in which these "boundaries" are supposedly erased, and there are many more connections to be explored with allied movements in pop art, minimalism, op art, and photo realism.

Learning from Las Vegas's currency in architecture schools has little to do with its centrality in historical debates about postmodernism, and more to do with its pragmatic lessons in diagramming and its use as a pedagogical model for studios interested in producing manifestos with research. This makes some sense, as the book emerged out of a third-year studio at the Yale School of Architecture, beginning in the fall of 1968, devoted to exploring the new phenomenon of urban sprawl and "the Strip," with Las Vegas as its focus.[6] The first three weeks of the studio were devoted to library research, followed by four days in Los Angeles, ten days in Las Vegas, and several weeks spent after their return working up the "raw material" into the large-scale schedules, plans, photographs, and films shown on January 10, 1969, at the final "multi-media presentation." Their attempt to account for the tangible yet difficult-to-represent atmospheric qualities in our ordinary environment using diverse graphic and verbal techniques is still fresh today, and remains an inspiration for those directly engaged in architectural practice and pedagogy. However, this relevance and topicality have often tended to obfuscate the book in other ways.

The pervasive concentration on the book's pragmatic, empirical, and disciplinary-bound voice all but ignores the other voice with which it tarries: the skeptical one. To overemphasize the former would be to tell only half the story. To make a rough analogy, it would be like talking about Thoreau's trenchant empiricism, manifested in his interest in the ordinary in *Walden*, without also hearing his transcendental and skeptical tones. In this regard, it is worth reflecting on Stanley Cavell's observation: "The transcendental and empirical crossing; possibilities shudder from it."[7] Disciplinary knowledge is intrinsic to how knowledge matters for us: knowledge is framed in particular ways, and that framing counts. But it can't be bought at the price of reducing the breadth and scope of a text whose implications are more than disciplinary. Simply put, I am attempting to bring into relief another way of thinking about the importance of *Learning from Las Vegas*.

Skepticism and the Ordinary

In this book I argue that *Learning from Las Vegas* demonstrates a full-scale engagement with skepticism and the ordinary. And where better to explore these concepts than in a book about Las Vegas, a city that, according to many, is the scene of sensory overload, illusion, and deception? In its most basic sense, skepticism is about radical doubt: Do we exist? Do others exist? Can we communicate at all? At its furthest extreme, skepticism manifests itself in nihilism: the radical denial of shared meaning altogether. By contrast, the voice of the ordinary lies in that realm of our involvement in the world and with others that acknowledges the common life and language that we share. I am suggesting that *Learning from Las Vegas* enacts an interminable play between skepticism and the ordinary. The voice of the ordinary operates in the book as a counterweight to the skeptical voice that tends to drive out our share in the words we inherit.[8] These two voices converse throughout *Learning from Las Vegas*, and my book accounts for their dialogue. I am by no means claiming that Venturi and Scott Brown *intended* to exemplify the struggle with skepticism when they wrote *Learning from Las Vegas*, merely that the resultant book does so.

My theoretical framework draws on Stanley Cavell's interpretation of skepticism and on the rich philosophical tradition that he is engaged with. For Cavell, skepticism is not fundamentally triggered by our perceived lack of knowledge of the world, as it has traditionally been cast. Rather, it is related to how we respond to and take responsibility for that world. Cavell's key term for this thought is "acknowledgment," a word that is meant not as an alternative to knowledge but rather as an interpretation of it.[9] That is to say, we make claims about the world and others in it, and that world and those others, in turn, make claims on us that we can either acknowledge or avoid. Thus, skepticism often manifests itself in our modes of ignoring what we already know.[10] The "ordinary," by contrast, is precisely that region that is closer than we "know," and thus it demands acts of acknowledgment and acceptance. Refusing such acts is also a possibility. But the persistence of this choice—whether to acknowledge or avoid—just points to the fact that skepticism is a standing threat never overcome once and for all. And indeed, Cavell's major claim is that skepticism cannot be refuted, although we can, and in fact must, reconceive its truth. When I raise the issue of skepticism, then, I am less concerned with addressing issues of doubt and belief—what we commonly think is at stake in skepticism—than with articulating how *Learning from Las Vegas* explores core architectural issues about the relationships between the inner and outer, expression and inexpression, transparency and opacity, responsiveness and avoidance, which are precisely the issues that drive the skeptical dilemma.

Acknowledgment places a strong emphasis on issues of receptivity and responsiveness, and the kinds of mood and attunement that disclose our affective relationship to the world. As an initial proposition, I would say that *Learning from Las Vegas* is an acknowledgment of the ordinary and the authors' mode of tarrying with skepticism. I am thus emphasizing *Learning from Las Vegas*'s responsiveness to the ordinary *as* the manifestation of its critical ambitions.

Skepticism is a way of *subliming* our language out of ordinary usage such that our voice in words is thrown into question. This leaves open the question of whether the use of words, let's say in billboard advertising, is a prime example of the use of ordinary language or is more indicative of a skeptical drive in which our words are pushed to a region where they are out of reach of our participation in them. I want to be clear: "ordinary" does not refer merely to words that are widely used, to vernacular architecture, or to our everyday consumer culture. It can refer to *anything* in the world we might take an interest in. Thus my interest in the ordinary in *Learning from Las Vegas* is not just about the everyday words we encounter and use in our daily lives, but also involves questioning why people speak the way they do, and how our investment in words, and architecture, is constitutive of the way we live, mean, and love, or avoid doing so.[11]

In championing the commercial vernacular of Main Street, with the Las Vegas Strip as its most extreme manifestation, Venturi and Scott Brown contrast the "ugly" and "ordinary" with modern architecture's "heroic" and "original" emphasis on space.[12] By linking skepticism and the ordinary, my account offers an alternative way of thinking about the "ordinary" in *Learning from Las Vegas*, as well as in the milieu of visual culture and cultural studies, where there has been an explosion of interest in this topic that, as far as I can tell, pays little heed to Cavellian and Wittgensteinian accounts of the ordinary.[13]

This is not to suggest that a serious engagement with skepticism is isolated to the philosophical realm—far from it. Cavell has written numerous books and essays addressing manifestations of skepticism in film, theater, literature, and opera. What is striking is that he often illustrates the struggle with skepticism through crucial references to architecture. In fact, most of the exemplary scenes that illustrate skepticism in his writings—Descartes in his garret sitting by the fire; David Hume emerging from his chamber to play a game of backgammon with his friends in the parlor; the opening scene of the builders in Wittgenstein's *Philosophical Investigations*; Ralph Waldo Emerson writing "whim" on the lintel of a door; Socrates' passage on "our city of words" in the *Republic*— all rely on metaphors of architecture and urbanity.[14] I suspect that Cavell uses these examples precisely because architecture is one of the privileged sites that reveal the overlapping of the two fundamental, yet asymmetrical, aspects of the threat of skepticism: the uncertainty of knowing the world out there—what is commonly called external-world skepticism (material)—and skepticism about other minds (mental). One way to think about this overlapping in architecture is to couple Walter Benjamin's claim that architecture is a *kleine Welt*—that it exemplifies, in a compressed and bounded way, the external world and our relationship to it *as such*—with Wittgenstein's assertion about the impression one gets from good architecture: "that it expresses a thought. It makes one want to respond with a gesture."[15] *Learning from Las Vegas* is intimately involved in exploring the relationship between the inner and the outer, expression and inexpression, transparency and opacity, that external world and other minds skepticism feeds on. But I want to be explicit here: I am not projecting a theoretical perspective onto *Learning from Las Vegas* that is somehow more profound than the book I am writing about. In place of a long explanation of why this is so, I simply want to agree with Jean-Luc Nancy that "philosophy is neither 'high' nor 'profound': it holds itself strictly at the height of things, the world, and man. And it does not adopt any 'point of view' on them, neither from above nor from below."[16] My way of approaching *Learning from Las Vegas* is simply the one that I believe is most responsive to what it is voicing.

One deleterious outcome of interpreting *Learning from Las Vegas* as simply a postmodern text has been its exposure to a particular kind of Adornian criticism.[17] Such readings have clouded our understanding of the book's subtle but trenchant analysis of the impact of commodity culture and media on language and architecture, and its critical role in determining how, or even if, it is possible to have a voice in talking about these effects at all. In essence, these accounts of *Learning from Las Vegas* posit that the book exemplifies an ironic toleration and passive acceptance, even an unabashed embrace, of the culture industry. This species of criticism emerged almost immediately after the book was published, and continues to be the dominant mode of criticism of it to the present day. Of course, a sophisticated Adornian approach to *Learning from Las Vegas* does not necessarily have to come to these conclusions, and I remark at various points how such a reading might actually intersect with my reading and, thus, come to a quite different evaluation of the text than that provided by traditional criticisms.

A strict adherence to critical theory–based interpretation obscures the subtle aversive criticism that *Learning from Las Vegas* demonstrates, and which can easily be misinterpreted as uncritical collusion with the culture industry. Approaching *Learning from Las Vegas* from the implications of its skeptical voice thus radically undermines three dominant and erroneous characterizations of the text: that it is a playfully ironic postmodern approach to architecture; that it maintains a straightforward equation of architecture with unproblematic communication; and that it is complicit with the culture industry. In other words, the book is much more *critically* and *ethically* charged than has previously been assumed. But it is a bit of a risk to spell out these two words without specifying that I am rethinking what those categories (sensibilities? approaches?) might mean in regard to architecture, the urban environment, and community. As an initial claim, I would suggest, then, that *Learning from Las Vegas* finds a particular way of negotiating a relationship between responsiveness and responsibility.

Chapter and Verse

In the first chapter, I initiate my approach to *Learning from Las Vegas,* concentrating on how it begins in a mood of wonder that suspends or delays the fall into orientation, knowledge, and communication. The way the authors abide in wonder and delay the fall into simply knowing is enabled, I argue, by their ambivalent attitude toward their "object" of study. In a sense this chapter is an extended analysis of a specific passage at the beginning of the book about being "turned around" or "lost" in the convoluted highway system in postwar America, where the simple crossroad has transformed into the knotted cloverleaf. I argue that this passage, and a related print by the artist Alan D'Arcangelo which the authors use to buttress their point, function as an aporia—a literal twisting or blocking in the text—that stymies the "drive" for the fast lane toward orientation and knowing. This analysis sets up my interpretation of the book in terms of skepticism and develops through close textual and figural readings, which I position against the characterizations of the book as simply equating architecture with meaning and unhindered communication.

Chapter 2 introduces the issue of "meaning" in *Learning from Las Vegas.* Vincent Scully once suggested that the power of Venturi's craft was his ability to transcend abstract formal manipulation and deal with meaning itself, which I take to mean not only the rich possibilities of historical reference but also unobstructed communication and signification. In fact, *Learning from Las Vegas* is precisely the opposite: it is one of the clearest demonstrations of the difficulty of identifying any criteria by which to differentiate shared meaning from noise or chatter. This topic is explored through an analysis of three canonical images from the book: a "neon" sentence that is reproduced from photographs of commercial signage near the beginning of the book; the imprinted, glassine dust cover that originally bound the first edition; and the famous Tanya billboard photograph on the cover of both the first and second editions. Throughout these analyses I suggest that there are two major voices at play in the text: one that takes an extreme, skeptical stance in its erasure of context and the denial of shared meaning; and the other, equally insistent, that argues for the recovery of context and meaning through our "ordinary" language. This chapter and the following one are also intended to be a deliberate challenge to the dominant Adornian readings of *Learning from Las Vegas,* which argue that the treatment of mass culture in the book provides predigested "schema" for easy consumption.

My third chapter examines the well-known comparison of the Duck and the Decorated Shed, which Venturi and Scott Brown introduced in order to dramatize and exemplify their arguments in the book. Rather than taking their interpretation of the Duck and the Decorated Shed as a concrete discussion about discrete and stabilized ontologies "out there," we should see them as exemplary of a particular mood or attitude in which the world is "colored" *as* Duck- or Decorated Shed-like. I argue that the comparison explores the skeptical problem of knowing "other minds," a problem that is deeply involved with the relationship between the inner and the outer, opacity and transparency, expression and inexpression. The Decorated Shed exemplifies the radical disjunction between interior and exterior, while the architectural Duck demonstrates a hyperexpressive continuity between the inner and the outer. These contrasts are brought out in Venturi and Scott Brown's fascination with the concept of deadpan humor, which, I claim, elaborates the fantasy of expression and inexpression aired in the Duck and the Decorated Shed.

One of the most notable facts about the Decorated Shed is that a sign with the word "EAT" is prominently displayed next to it. I interpret this coupling less as a semiotic "sign," which would be an indication of Venturi and Scott Brown's initiating a "linguistic turn" in architectural theory (a standard interpretation of their work), and more as an attempt to explore our "primitive" needs: a taking stock of what we need from life in terms of what we are now getting or not getting from it. What exactly are we willing to put in our mouths, or in the mouths of others? And what are we willing to release from them? Sometimes what we eat—or speak—nourishes us; sometimes it leaves us unsatisfied, hungering for something else. I take the deliberate lack of context in which the word "Eat" is presented in the Decorated Shed diagram as a provocation for the reader to acknowledge that it is up to us to find the criteria for that word and the context in which it would become meaningful. I see this as an allegory of skepticism that prompts us to ask what having a voice in architecture means at a time when it is not clear what voice, if any, architecture might have in relation to the increasing informatization of society. Taking the cliche seriously, the Duck and the Decorated Shed pose the question: What is food for thought?

In the fourth chapter I explore one image in depth: Venturi and Scott Brown's "recommendation for a monument," which is a Decorated Shed with a blinking sign on top that reads, "I AM A MONUMENT." At first glance, this image seems to be an exemplary expression of *Learning from Las Vegas's* brand of postmodern irony, its fundamental concern with architecture as representation or spectacle, its initiation of a text-based approach to architecture, and its seamless equation of signs, signification, and meaning. It has certainly been taken in these ways. I try to demonstrate that the "I Am a Monument" proposal puts into question all of these characterizations. It is more about evidencing the force of imaging; showing the *work* of re-presentation; suggesting ways that text, matter, and image touch on each other without claiming that any one subtends or veils the other; and opening up the possibility of meaning beyond signification, with an emphasis on the phatic rather than the semantic. In this way it fosters the conditions for encounter and community. Simply put, the "I Am a Monument" proposal explores how one might "make sense" in architecture that links its aesthetic and material possibilities with its social and political dimensions.

One might say that the authors' "recommendation for a monument" makes a "claim for community" that, precisely because it is a claim, is not grounded in any given community that already exists "out there." Rather, this claim raises the possibility of how the "I" relates to the "we," which is always the pressing question in any critique of the monument. The words "I Am a Monument" literally give voice to that claim. It is a claim that is equally vulnerable and bold, compelling each some*one* to engage in what Cavell calls an "arrogation of voice": to speak representatively *for* community from our own singularity. In other words, the "I" in the "Monument" proposal is not a fixed or stable "I," but rather a personal pronoun operating as "shifter," which can be understood only by reference to the context in which it is uttered. It encourages us to voice our claim to community in saying "I Am a Monument," and thus calls forth a "concatenation of speech acts" that is no stronger or weaker than the linking of other I's who might participate in its claims for community (or ignore those claims, as the case may be). The authors thus propose a conception of architecture that is attuned to the multiplicity of the city in which absolute singularity and endless commonality are our ordinary condition. The title for this chapter—"A Monument for Everyone and No One"—suggests this condition. In this chapter the reader will notice that my interest in the work of Jean-Luc Nancy comes to the fore and begins to resonate with Cavell in my thinking about *Learning from Las Vegas*. Nancy and Cavell are rarely read together, and are by and large overlooked in architecture circles, but I have found them to be mutually illuminating.

Chapter 4 poses the following question: Can Venturi and Scott Brown's "I Am a Monument" proposal, which they describe as a "stupid, blinking sign," be compared to the "blinking eye" (read: empty, content, vacuous, stupid) of Nietzsche's speech on the Last Man in the prologue to *Thus Spoke Zarathustra*? I argue that this is a standing risk in their work but that *Learning from Las Vegas* cannot be reduced to this scenario. I connect blinking—the opening and closing of the eye—to the skeptical question about acknowledging or avoiding the ordinary world we must attempt to live and communicate in. Instead of the "happiness" of Nietzsche's last man, I argue that *Learning from Las Vegas* is a serious investigation of what Cavell calls "aversiveness": the pursuits of happiness within the actual world with an eye to its eventual transformation. It is the rhythm and patterning of this blinking that count, and that this chapter attempts to account for. This blinking is not isolated to the "recommendation for a monument," but rather permeates the way *Learning from Las Vegas* as a book "blinks." This, in turn, is inseparable from the design of the book, its particular rhythm, texture, and patterning, the way we move through its pages.

The last chapter is about the design of the first and revised editions of *Learning from Las Vegas*. A serious conflict arose between Muriel Cooper, the head of the design department at the MIT Press, and Denise Scott Brown and Robert Venturi over the design of the first edition, published in 1972. Venturi and Scott Brown felt that Cooper's "Swiss style" design was inimical to the philosophy of the book, while Cooper felt she was doing justice to the material. Scott Brown was convinced that Cooper had given them a "Duck." Cooper was sure that that was what they wanted all along.

At the heart of these disagreements were not simply differences in design philosophy, but also issues of skepticism that I track throughout this book. I am not claiming that issues of design are the superficial "signs" of "deeper" issues of skepticism, but rather that *Learning from Las Vegas*'s engagement with skepticism is inseparable from its particular distribution and materialization of thought on a page. In its disposition of words and images, its tracing of lines, its practice of spacing and repartitioning of surface, design draws out the visible and thinkable, and thus materializes what a sensible communicability might look like.[18] In other words, design, in its most basic sense, is concerned with "forms of life." Likewise, skepticism is about our "attunement in criteria"—the mood and modes of our shared interests and concerns, and our ability to embrace or repudiate them. It is revealing that one of the primary targets of *Learning from Las Vegas* is what Venturi and Scott Brown call "total design" and its correlative, "total control," which involve issues that are at the heart of the skeptical dilemma.

If mood brings about a world, then the first and revised editions are, in many ways, worlds apart. Yet, in their very distance from each other, they are intimately connected. One might say they are abandoned *to* each other. Scott Brown's design of the revised edition is what established the book's fame, and it has been the most influential version of it. But, like all important books, *Learning from Las Vegas* contributes to its own misreading; the view that it is the "manifesto" of postmodernism is due, in no small part, to its design, which has inevitably colored its reading and its "readability." The lesson to be learned from this is not to presume a correct reading of the book, or books, but rather to find our own point of departure "from" *Learning from Las Vegas*. And that can only begin and end with reading both books together again.

As an appendix to this book, I have included a facsimile of Vincent Scully's unpublished introduction to the first edition of *Learning from Las Vegas*. This introduction was never included in either the first or the revised edition, but it is an interpretation that resonates with the authors' own interpretation of their project, despite Scully's reservations about the book. My reading of *Learning from Las Vegas* differs from Scully's insofar as I question his emphasis on the book's investment in "symbolism" as well as the humanistic and mythic subtext to his introduction, but it resonates with his interest in issues of fact, flatness, and plasticity. In other words, Scully's introduction provides a strong reading of the authors' work that provides a useful counterpoint to mine, or a kind of yardstick for the reader to take a measure of my reading of *Learning from Las Vegas*.

On Reading

Stanley Cavell has noted that American culture has the tendency to overpraise and undervalue its achievements.[19] If I understand him correctly, this statement suggests that the inflation of its important achievements is not always matched by impassioned and serious accounts of them. That is to say, important books in our culture often go underread or unread, yet that fact hardly means that people don't read them or think highly of them. To my mind, a major point of this book is to suggest that we need to pay more attention to the texts that have counted deeply for us in art and architectural history and theory—reorienting our sensibilities, and shifting our attentions and dispositions to the world and the way it matters for us. The very nature and existence of a "book about a book" might strike those in art history, theory, and criticism as odd. This is perhaps less the case in architecture, where there has been an increasing interest in issues of architectural publication and dissemination. In art history the emphasis has tended to focus on issues of "writing" as such, and not on books per se. Whereas other disciplines such as literary criticism and philosophy are more willing to pay attention to the books that have mattered to them, books about books are not usually written in art and architectural fields. That is a shame, particularly when we claim that it is often through print and digital media that ideas circulate in our field. My claim, however, is that we should be willing to engage in "readings" of those texts, rather than merely putting those books into "context," historical or otherwise.

Simply put, this book is a "reading" of *Learning from Las Vegas*. What do I mean by "reading"? First and foremost, reading requires a patient receptivity to what the text is saying, as if in a conversation to which one adjusts one's responses.[20] This kind of attentiveness, however, does not entail taking *Learning from Las Vegas* at its word. In a sense this kind of reading demands what is pejoratively called "reading in." "Reading in" is usually taken as an accusation of reading something that is not there in the text. But all that is there in *Learning from Las Vegas* is the text in front of us, and our reading can't be anything but a response to it.

Of course there is a healthy fear in the accusation; that is, that texts, like people, "mean more than you know." Thus, the accusation, as Cavell notes, might entail a fear of beginning to read in the first place—and it often does.[21] But if most robust texts are underread, presumably they require some "forcing," that is, an "interrogation to match their arrogation."[22] At times this might involve "following the inspiration otherwise than we find it followed; the author may or may not be glad."[23] I believe all good reading is involved in such interrogation. (The question is, of course, always the tone and truth of that forcing.) I think Venturi put this very nicely in the preface to the second edition of *Complexity and Contradiction*: "Should an artist go all the way with his or her philosophies?"[24] Or in the words of Thoreau: "*Extra vagance!* it depends on how you are yarded."[25] All I can say here is that I have attempted to provide a complete reading of *Learning from Las Vegas*, in the sense of seeing one interpretation through to the end, and for me reading—I prefer that to "reading in"—is essential to knowing what that end is.[26]

The question of intention can cloud the fact that writers also write more than they *know*.[27] This, to my mind, is a particularly live issue when it comes to the work of Venturi and Scott Brown. At times, their uncritical devotees and unforgiving critics have not demonstrated a sufficient respect for and acknowledgment of the *unthought* dimensions of their writing. I kept in mind a passage from Heidegger while writing this book: "To acknowledge and respect consists in letting every thinker's thought come to us as something in each case unique, never to be repeated, inexhaustible—and being shaken to the depths by what is unthought in his thought. What is unthought in a thinker's thought is not a lack inherent in his thought. What is *un*-thought is there in each case only as the un-*thought*. The more original the thinking, the richer will be what is unthought in it."[28] This meditation led me to the decision not to base my interpretation, or reading as I call it, on the authors' own interpretation of what *Learning from Las Vegas* might mean or what they "intended" by it.

Of course this decision leaves me open to criticism that I haven't "gotten it right." To this, I would recall Venturi's aphorism: "Trust your intuitions over their ideology." This idea is partially taken back in another of his aphorisms: "Beware of Ideology: don't go too far with your own ideas."[29] How far is "too far"? Whom can you trust?

1 APPROACHING LAS VEGAS IN WONDER AND AMBIVALENCE

The way up is the way down.

—Heraclitus, *Fragment 60*

Beginning in Wonder; Abiding in Ambivalence

If for Ralph Waldo Emerson the point of wonder in every landscape was the meeting of the sky and earth, then for Venturi and Scott Brown it was the disorienting "skyline of signs" in Las Vegas.[1] Denise Scott Brown described their first visit to Las Vegas together in 1966: "We rode around from casino to casino, dazed by the desert sun and dazzled by the signs, both loving and hating what we saw, we were jolted clear out of our aesthetic skins" (figure 1.1).[2] The fact that Venturi and Scott Brown continue to repeat their inaugural moment of wonder in numerous articles and interviews does not negate the import of this passage. Precisely the opposite: their concerted staging of wonder is clearly meant to perpetuate it as a "melodrama of instruction."[3] The risk of wonder, then, is the possibility of it becoming an "empty formula of pedantry."[4] The question has always been, can the "Ah!" continue to flourish in the "Aha!"?[5] Nothing less is at stake than our capacity for experience, and for that experience to count in further accounting.

1.1 Robert Venturi and Denise Scott Brown in Las Vegas; by permission of VSBA, Inc.

The English word "wonder" captures the connotations of both the exhilaration and provocation that initiate primordial questioning. Stanley Cavell, echoing many others, has suggested that philosophy begins in wonder (*thaumazein*): "it is philosophy's power to cause wonder, or to stun—to take one aside—that decides who is to become a philosopher."[6] A "wondrous" experience is not merely one among many, but a kind of rebirth that can initiate a lifelong love and labor. For example, Cavell says of the "revelatory effect" of studying with the ordinary-language philosopher John Austin at Harvard in 1955, "He hit me like a ton of bricks. It was as if a wall fell on me."[7] Most interesting projects, not just philosophical ones, start in wonder. Art historian Michael Fried writes of being "knocked on his heels" by his first encounter with Anthony Caro's sculpture, and notes, "When I first saw *Midday* and *Sculpture Seven* in Caro's garden I felt I was about to levitate or burst into blossom."[8]

Cavell's and Fried's experiences point not only to the exhilaration of wonder, but to another important dimension: the condition of being literally thrown off balance; a state of disorientation and "not knowing" that precedes the "a-ha Erlebnis" that marks the *fall* into orientation, meaning, and "learning from."[9] If bodily orientation is the phenomenological basis of meaning as such—think of being firm, upright, grounded, centered—then one must entertain the possibility that philosophical problems might also begin with disorientation.[10] The mood of wonder is precisely this dis-position. In the thrall of moods, we are transported or, better yet, "moved" by them. We are always "in" a mood; it is never "in" us, nor do we "have" such and such a mood. We can never master mood, nor can we separate ourselves from moods. "Mood Assails," in the words of Heidegger.[11] In moods, we are exposed, vulnerable, and open to the world; affected, touched, and struck by things. And wonder, as we know from Plato and Aristotle, is the mood that "begins" in perplexity (aporia). As Cavell specifies, "one can take the idea of not knowing one's way about, of being lost, as the form specifically of the *beginning* or *appearance* of a philosophical problem."[12]

Wonder is the first of all the passions, as Descartes argued, because we experience it before we can have any idea as to whether the object is agreeable to us at all.[13] This ambivalence is intrinsic to Venturi and Scott Brown's encounter with Las Vegas: "both loving and hating what we saw, we were jolted clear out of our aesthetic skins." In the strict Freudian sense of the term, ambivalence is defined as "the simultaneous existence of love and hate towards the same object."[14] Ambivalence is Venturi and Scott Brown's attempt to prolong their state of wonder through the oscillating rhythms of love and hate. As Scott Brown affirmed in an article published in 1976, "We recommended learning (note, *learning*, not loving—at most we recommend a hate-love relationship) from Las Vegas."[15]

In his first book, *Complexity and Contradiction in Architecture*, Venturi had characterized this kind of ambivalent relationship as "both-and" rather than "either-or,"[16] noting that he borrowed the phraseology from the literary critic Cleanth Brooks's account of John Donne in *The Well Wrought Urn* (1947): "But if Donne could have it both ways, most of us, in this latter day, cannot. We are disciplined in the tradition of either-or, and lack the mental agility—to say nothing of the maturity of attitude—which would allow us to indulge in the finer distinctions and the more subtle reservations permitted by the tradition of both-and."[17] It shouldn't surprise us to find that the oppositional and exclusionary "either-or" is contrasted with the paratactic/conjunctive "and" in Freud's writings on dreams, ambivalence, the unconscious, and the primary process (all characterized by simultaneity, lack of negation, and exemption from mutual contradiction). No doubt Venturi's long and close friendship with Philip J. Finkelpearl, an English professor at Vassar, played a role in Venturi's introduction to the work of the New Critics such as Cleanth Brooks and William Empson, both of whom straightforwardly acknowledged their debt to Freudian psychoanalytic thought in their writings.[18]

The direct references to the New Critics are explicit and abundant in *Complexity and Contradiction*. In fact, fifteen of its fifty endnotes refer to them.[19] In *Learning from Las Vegas* these voices are more fluidly integrated into the text, the Freudian implications of ambivalence are acknowledged, and the explicit references are mostly to T. S. Eliot and the critic Richard Poirier's writings on him. I see this difference as marking a shift in emphasis from the earlier work of the New Critics to the contemporary writings of Poirier, Marshall McLuhan, and Northrop Frye who were linking Eliot's and Joyce's work to the rhythms, sensations, and vocabularies of mediated urban life (more on this in chapter 2). For example, ambivalence is woven into urban issues in Poirier's account of Eliot's struggle with words and meaning in the clichés of the city's language, and through the Dutch architect Aldo van Eck's concept of the "twin phenomenon," which *Learning from Las Vegas* uses in addition to "both-and" to suggest that what are considered polar opposites are really "inextricably intertwined at every level in the city."[20]

Although Charles Jencks was also heavily influenced by the New Critics, his pithy and influential characterization of postmodern architecture as a strategy of "double coding"—a mingling of high and low culture, and the mixing of styles past and present—doesn't capture the pitch of this "both-and."[21] "Double" suggests a duality, either as a possible binary, or as a "contradiction" in the sense of a Hegelian *Aufhebung*. Further, the word "code" is too suggestive of a semiotic approach, implying that this code—evidently some sort of architectural "language"—might be deciphered or unlocked by the right key, some meaningful interpretation, even though the code is doubled.[22] Further, whether or not it was Jencks's intention, his terminology was taken in a substantive sense: *the* style of postmodernism as a mixture of styles, with its concomitant hermeneutics of irony that would recognize these incongruities.

Although ambivalence is never named in *Learning from Las Vegas*, the text is suffused by it through and through, and it opens up a reading that veers away from a semiotic hermeneutics, toward what is really a question of mood and attunement.[23] Freud was always at pains to emphasize this distinction by consistently writing "emotional ambivalence" or "ambivalent attitude" rather than simply "ambivalence." The kind of "fundamental attunement" that Scott Brown describes is what enables any orientation or affect whatsoever to happen without suggesting an external Archimedean point that would fix us in relation to that world. This is to say that mood colors the way we are in the world, and thus disposes us to the very possibility of having anything that we might call an experience of that world. Venturi and Scott Brown's ambivalent attitude toward

Las Vegas reveals to us how that particular portion of the world mattered to them, and the color of that mattering.

The references here to mood and "fundamental attunement" have been worked out most thoroughly in the work of Heidegger, beginning in *Being and Time* and continually expanded and refined in his subsequent work.[24] The recent explosion of interest in mood and affect in architectural criticism and theory has entirely overlooked this material in favor of Deleuze's notion of affect. But Heidegger is more relevant than ever—the interest in Deleuze should have alerted us to this fact—and deserves to be heard again in a different way, with an attention to his writings and the most sophisticated work being done in philosophy.[25] For Heidegger, mood can't be reduced to the realm of psychological "feelings" or any anthropological understanding of "lived experience." We are not displaced into moods; the disposition displaces us. The essential character of mood is that it "displaces us into such and such a relation to the world, into this or that understanding or disclosure of the world."[26] Simply put, moods make a world—a particular configuration of sense—come about.

My emphasis on wonder and its manifestation as ambivalence in *Learning from Las Vegas* would require a modification of Fredric Jameson's astute observation that one of the characteristic conditions of postmodernism is the "waning of affect."[27] Jameson's influential remark would seem to accord with Heidegger's claim in *Being and Time* that the gray everyday of the "they" is characterized by a pallid lack of mood and indifference to everything.[28] In Heidegger's later work, such moods take on historical referentiality, as they appear to do for Jameson; each finds his era is always tinged with a shade of gray.[29] But the key point here is that the waning of affect is itself a mood. As Heidegger notes, there is no escaping mood: we can only leave one mood for another.

Wonder modifies precisely that mood that is characterized as a pallid lack of mood. That is to say, indifference can be shaken and give way to another tone of being-in-the-world. Heidegger's major claim about wonder is that it lets the familiar appear as unfamiliar, and thus plunges the human being into the "aporia" (perplexity) that Aristotle speaks of in the *Metaphysics*. Heidegger argues: "Wonder does not divert itself from the usual but, on the contrary, *adverts* to it, precisely as what is the most unusual of everything and in everything."[30] Unlike the mood of the gray everyday, wonder is not characterized by indifference. Rather, it strikes us by the fact that the object does matter, yet one does not know precisely the mode of this mattering.

Ambivalence (loving and hating) marks Venturi and Scott Brown's way of acknowledging that condition of wonder. Through their ambivalent attitude in *Learning from Las Vegas* we are exposed to their affective response to that city, not merely their "knowledge" of it. Cavell reminds us that skepticism might not be fundamentally about our despair over the lack of certainty of our knowledge; that our fundamental relation to the world might not be one of knowing at all. If skepticism is not so much a matter of knowledge, but rather a matter of acknowledgment—how we respond to the world or avoid doing so—then moods are intrinsic to skepticism because they disclose our affective relationship to the world.[31] In short, Las Vegas was Venturi and Scott Brown's "fairy catastrophe," a powerful term that Le Corbusier used to describe his response to Manhattan: "That is the phrase that expresses my emotion and rings within me in the stormy debate which has not stopped tormenting me for fifty days: hate and love. For me the fairy catastrophe is the lever of hope."[32] But the ambivalent nature of *Learning from Las Vegas* has often been difficult for critics to register in a nuanced way, and thus the consistent temptation is to split the book into a "good" or "bad" object, to put it in Kleinian terms.[33]

Some cultural critics, mostly from the perspectives of critical and postmodern theory, would implicitly identify the book with their full-blown nihilistic interpretations of America, Las Vegas, and the culture industry.[34] Other critics took the authors' evaluation of the Las Vegas Strip as "almost all right" in a Panglossian light, too easily converting it to mean simply "all right." In between the two extremes, Venturi and Scott Brown were most often branded as liberal ironists embracing a witty but ultimately innocuous and possibly reckless cultural pessimism, which manifested itself in mere visual ambiguity, and carrying with it a formal excuse for aesthetic and moral irresolution. Manfredo Tafuri's accusation of their "facile ironies" comes to mind.[35] The exemplary image of their "playful irony" is, of course, the ironic Ionic column in the Allen Memorial Museum at Oberlin College (figure 1.2). But I have a hunch that what made the book so infuriating was its courting the extremes of love and hate without occupying either position or their middle ground.

This state of affairs is best captured in the graffiti that the pop artist Ed Ruscha saw scrawled in the ruins of an abandoned hotel structure near Glassell Park in Los Angeles: "FUCK THE WORLD . . . AND FUCK YOU IF YOU DON'T LOVE IT."[36] I take this as a more prosaic formulation of the real stakes of skepticism as outlined by Stanley Cavell: that there are endless specific succumbings to the conditions of skepticism and endless specific recoveries from it, and between the temptations of excessive despair and false hope is a quest for the ordinary and its perspicuousness.[37] That is to say, we can neither accept a nihilism that implies that skepticism is solvable, albeit negatively, in our acceptance of its will to nothingness, nor can we accept the alternative route of falling in love with the world—skepticism's denial. Both positions bespeak a love of the world that can never be quit or requited.

VSBI evidence their involvement with skepticism and the threat of nihilism in *Learning from Las Vegas* through the erasure of context and the denial of shared meaning, but also through the possible recoveries of shared meaning

1.2 Venturi, Scott Brown and Associates, ironic/Ionic column, Allen Memorial Museum, Oberlin College, 1973–1977, photograph by Tom Bernard; by permission of VSBA, Inc.

and context. This rhythm of submission to and then recovery from skepticism is at the heart of *Learning from Las Vegas*. The important point about the book is that it tarries with skepticism but does not defeat it. Skepticism is of a piece with the human condition and it can never simply be overcome or negated. If its overcoming is part of our lives, then the accomplishment of some of its criteria is also a human task.[38]

Learning "from" Las Vegas

Despite the italicized word "learning" in Scott Brown's passage quoted above—"We recommended learning (note, *learning*, not loving—at most we recommend a hate-love relationship) from Las Vegas"—I think the key word here is the destinal preposition "from," as in "learning *from* Las Vegas."[39] This crucial "from" has been overlooked in both positive and negative evaluations of *Learning from Las Vegas*. Although it seems obvious enough, it is worth stating that *Learning from Las Vegas* is a departure from the actual city of Las Vegas. Las Vegas was always gone, from the beginning of the book's title.[40]

We need to take Robert Venturi's question at the end of his first book *Complexity and Contradiction* quite literally: What "slight twist of context" will make an "almost all right" Main Street and Route 66 "all right"?[41] *Learning from Las Vegas* is that "slight twist of context." I take it that his question is exactly that, a question: it is not meant to imply that Main Street can ever be made "all right"; that is, "correct," "true," "straightened out," or aesthetically beautiful. We are always involved in its "twisting" or "turning." Answering the question definitively would be to leave the question once and for all. Instead, *Learning from Las Vegas* keeps the quotation marks perpetually oscillating, leaving us wondering about the "almost."[42] Learning is not only indebtedness "to" something but is also a leave-taking, a form of departure and displacement. A (re)turning "from" Las Vegas. *Learning from Las Vegas* is that double take.

In fact, the word "from" in the title of the book functions much like the word "abandonment" in Cavell's lexicon, with its connotations of enthusiasm, ecstasy, leaving, relief, quitting, going onward, release, shunning, allowing, delivering, trusting, suffering, and binding.[43] And isn't one of the primary qualities of wonder that its mode of attunement is marked by a compelling attachment to an object that simultaneously throws us back *from* it? In wonder, "this retreating and self-restraining . . . is at the same time forcibly drawn to and, as it were, held fast by that from which it retreats."[44] Being taken aback is how our mode of attachment in wonder is *addressed*. As Scott Brown put it: "Facing the implications of Las Vegas in our work is proving much more difficult than describing Las Vegas."[45] That is to say, Las Vegas is not so much a city of legible signs—as VSBI sometimes argue—as it is a primal scene in which they are confronted with intractable enigmatic signifiers "from" which they can never really leave, and which they are perpetually going-on-from in their lifelong elaboration of our urban predicament.[46]

This "from" is testament enough to the continuing relevance of the book over and above its historical importance as a supposed inaugural text of post-modernism. Thus, when critics claim that *Learning from Las Vegas* was the first book to mark out many of the salient dimensions of the so-called postmodern condition—consumerism, the emphasis on information, the disjunction between inside and outside, the attention to surface over depth, and so forth—but say that now the book is out of date because of the digital turn, global capitalism, etc., they seem to willfully ignore this "from."[47] As I put it in the introduction, somehow the book's locatedness has become an argument about its outdated-ness. But *Learning from Las Vegas* is an untimely text; it was never of its time to begin with. Dismissing the text because of changing historical conditions would be akin to citing the irrelevance of Benjamin's *Arcades Project* to contemporary theoretical interests because actual shopping conditions have changed. All this is to say that *Learning from Las Vegas* is never simply a reflection of what is "out there." Rather, it is what Deleuze and Guattari term "an a-parallel evolution of the book and the world," and such a text always has the potential to become a "rhizomatic book." I don't hesitate for a moment in claiming that *Learning from Las Vegas* is the first rhizomatic book in architecture: a book written in slogans, with an eye to "pop analysis," and constituted by a "logic of the AND."[48]

If anything, *Learning from Las Vegas* seems more "relevant" than ever. In fact, its currency in architecture schools seems to have little to do with its centrality in "historical" debates about postmodernism, and more to do with its pragmatic lessons in diagramming and its pedagogical model for design studios.[49] It was, of course, Venturi and Scott Brown's desire to find the "graphic means" to describe urban sprawl and the strip that inaugurated their interest in new techniques for registering not only the quantity but the quality of these urban phenom-ena: "It is extremely hard to suggest the atmospheric qualities of Las Vegas, because these are primarily dependant on watts, animation, and iconology."[50] Their attempt to register the dynamism and density of tangible, yet difficult-to-represent, atmospheric qualities through complex and diverse graphic means and verbal techniques resulted in the highly charged first edition of *Learning from Las Vegas* (figure 1.3).

The authors appear to take seriously the analogy to an "electric charge" in Freud's original German word *Besetzung*, translated by the pseudo-Greek word *cathexis* and loosely defined as the libidinal energy of emotional attachment to some object, person, or idea.[51] Perhaps we might think of *Learning from Las Vegas* as a "blocking" of these energies and attachments; a binding of their text through intensive acts of displacement and fixation.[52] But neither a pragmatic/

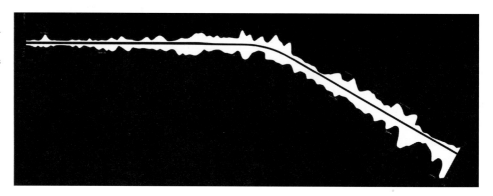

empirical account of the book's graphic relevance to present concerns about diagramming nor a straightforward discussion of the book's supposed relation to its "context," then or now, will account for that "binding" itself. We need to account for the logic of the book, which includes these other concerns but can't be reduced to them.[53]

What then is the implication of VSBI's claim, in the revised edition of 1977—which they described as "stripped," "newly clothed," and "desexed" (what a book!)—that "Las Vegas is not the subject of our book"?[54] (For a more in-depth account of these issues, see chapter 5.) At face value, the statement is pretty clear: the authors were worried that, in an act of subreption, readers would mistake the object of their study—the city of Las Vegas—for their subject—the so-called symbolism of architectural form. But we need to be careful here. As in Kant's theory of the sublime and Freud's understanding of instinct, the object is contingent but by no means arbitrary. No matter how "withdrawn" our "investment" (substitute "disinterested" for the former and "cathexis" for the latter, if you like) is *from* the object, it could not exist without it. The object always offers a return on our investment. Let's call it "interest."[55] As Venturi and Scott Brown emphasized, it was always a matter of "addressing" the object of their subject(ivization). To repeat: "Facing the implications of Las Vegas in our work is proving much more difficult than describing Las Vegas." *Learning from Las Vegas* is simply that "address," with all the connotations of destination, voice, direction, relation, instruction, writing, attitude, stance, and attention that word entails. It is their mode of dis-*placing* themselves in the world and in relation to us, the readers of their book.

I can imagine the authors insisting that this is "our city," both the city "as built," Las Vegas, and "our city of words" that is the book *Learning from Las Vegas*. Socrates' reference to the ideal state as "our city of words" in the *Republic*, at the end of Book IX, refers not to an actual city but to an eventual one that needs to be built.[56] But built out of what? Out of words and deeds. Socrates calls the reader to enter into conversation about the actual and eventual city, mediated through the written words they are reading.[57] And so does *Learning from Las Vegas*. Venturi and Scott Brown's brand of criticism is best thought of as an extension of such conversation.[58] It is an invitation to read and be read by others, and it is meant to proceed more by reorienting our sensibilities, and redirecting our interests, than by provoking modes of "argumentation."[59] (Certainly, at times the tone of their voice is polemical and hectoring, but then that is of a piece with their brand of conversation.) One might interpret their call to readers as a call for a conversation that is also a conversion, an act we are already participating in as we "turn" the pages in front of us.[60]

Thus it doesn't seem quite right to say, as some have, that *Learning from Las Vegas* initiated a "linguistic turn" in architectural theory. Of course, the contemporary characterization of the book as initiating such a shift in architecture is not meant as a one-to-one equation with the linguistic turn in philosophy outlined by Richard Rorty.[61] Nor could it, as Venturi and Scott Brown clearly were not interested in conducting a strict semiotic investigation of architecture. That characterization is meant in a much looser sense to suggest the general shift from the "material to the cerebral," to a period of high theory in architecture, and toward a general textual approach to architecture with an emphasis on reading (i.e., semiotic decoding).[62] I for one do not believe that Venturi and Scott Brown are committed to the stance that there is a "veil" of language that separates us from the world and that needs to be decoded.[63] Heidegger stated that "language is language"; that is, language is neither propped on some deeper foundation nor is it the prop for any other phenomenon.[64] Words aren't everything and they aren't nothing. Venturi and Scott Brown are modestly ambitious: they are inclined to initiate, and at times provoke, a conversation about architecture and the city in our abandonment to the words we write and read. They are calling for new "readers" of the city, and the reading they are engaged in cannot be reduced to semantics, semiotic decoding, or even isolated to the linguistic realm at all; it is a reading that is achieved by asking a question and going on "from" that question, not by seeking an answer.

The Cloverleaf

When Wittgenstein writes, "A philosophical problem has the form: 'I don't know my way about,'" we are seriously mistaken if we assume that disorientation can be *solved* or brought to an *end* by finding the right way back.[65] Which way would be right? Forward? Back? As Venturi put it: "There is perversity in the learning process; we go back to go forward, down to go up."[66] In fact, it is perverse enough to sound like Heraclitus's "the way up and the way down are the same," which is the second epigram to T. S. Eliot's *Four Quartets*, a text that figures prominently in *Learning from Las Vegas*.[67] A preposterous scene of instruction if there ever was one!

In an early essay, "The Meaningful City," Scott Brown diagnosed the condition of modern disorientation as a case of urban *agnosia*, "in which the individual perceives with his senses but cannot give meaning to what he perceives."[68] What was initially explored as a neurological/pathological condition—most poignantly by Oliver Sacks—is now our "ordinary" urban condition.[69] Venturi and Scott Brown tackle this problematic in the opening pages of *Learning from Las Vegas* in their account of the disorientation experienced in the everyday car culture of the highway in postwar America: "A driver 30 years ago could maintain a sense of orientation in space. At the simple crossroad a little sign with an arrow confirmed what was obvious. One knew where one was. When the crossroads becomes a cloverleaf, one must turn right to turn left, a contradiction poignantly evoked in the print by Alan D'Arcangelo. But the driver has no time to ponder paradoxical subtleties within a dangerous, sinuous maze. He or she relies on signs for guidance—enormous signs in vast spaces at high speeds."[70] D'Arcangelo's print *The Trip* accompanied this passage, and appeared as figure 1 in the article "A Significance for A&P Parking Lots, or Learning from Las Vegas" (1968), the precursor to the first part of *Learning from Las Vegas* (figure 1.4).[71] In it, a bold orange arrow points left, but within its staff a stenciled yellow symbol of a hand with an extended finger points in the opposite direction. Here I am reminded of a passage in Wittgenstein's *Philosophical Investigations*: "a person naturally reacted to the gesture of pointing with the hand by looking in the direction of the line from finger-tip to wrist, not from wrist to finger-tip."[72] Has the very act of pointing here become an incoherent activity? Pointless? Can we rely on signs for guidance and orientation, as the authors seem to suggest? Do we rely on signs only when we don't know our way about?[73] Can we be *certain* that signs will guide us in the right direction, as opposed to abandoning us to the uncertain criteria for differentiating between being lost and being found? It seems signs can always point to the "doubt" we assume they are meant to assuage. (Isn't wonder, after all, the basic disposition that transports us into the in-between condition of "not knowing the way out or in"?)[74]

I take the point raised about D'Arcangelo's *The Trip* in the opening scenes of *Learning from Las Vegas* as one of the most astute commentaries on Paul Klee's words on the "directedness" and "reach" of the arrow in his *Pedagogical Sketchbook*: "The father of the arrow is the thought: how do I expand my reach?"[75] Must we always assign a target or an aim for an arrow to make its mark? Do such arrows bring us closer or farther from our need? Perhaps the world is nearer than we think, and any arrow would surely overshoot its mark. Scott Brown expressed it this way: "this pop city, this *here*, is what we have."[76] The cloverleaf passage suggests that we are "implicated" in the world, and that it is not simply over *there*. VSBI equally show that the point of an arrow can be deadly, as Coleridge's ancient mariner discovered: "With my cross-bow I shot the Albatross . . . instead of the cross, the Albatross about my neck was hung." An arrow swift and sure might entail deadening ourselves to the possibilities of the world in trying to get it nearer to us at any cost.[77]

The authors seem to prefer a mode of Emersonian "indirection," which runs counter to the active directness of attempting to bring the world closer to us at any cost.[78] (This would begin to problematize the word "approaching" in the title to this chapter.) In their words: "We think the more directions that architecture takes at this point, the better."[79] This passage suggests that we need to lose ourselves before we can find ourselves; it acknowledges that loss is constitutive of finding a way in and for architecture. Unlike their contemporary Kevin Lynch, who saw the apocalyptic consequences of being lost in his influential book *Image of the City*—"the very word 'lost' in our language means much more than simple geographical uncertainty; it carries overtones of utter disaster"—*Learning from Las Vegas* at times suggests that being lost might be a necessary condition "at this point."[80] Las Vegas is the place that exemplifies the desire to *risk* being lost, to be at a loss, as internal to the human condition.

To repeat: there is an attempt in *Learning from Las Vegas* to *delay* the fall into orientation and meaning by abiding with the conditions of ambivalence and disorientation. The "cloverleaf" in the passage quoted above is an aporia—the "perplexity" of which Aristotle relates to wonder in his *Metaphysics*—that stymies the "drive" for the fast lane toward orientation and knowing. I take it that the sentence quoted earlier—"Facing the *implications* of Las Vegas in our work is proving much more difficult than describing Las Vegas"—is meant to suggest not only that architecture is meant to begin in the mood of wonder but that it must delay the *Aufhebung* of not knowing by knowledge, through a continual "folding," "turning," and "twisting" precisely *as* their mode of acknowledging that task.[81] That is their way of sustaining the upsurge of "inexplicability" in wonder.

The cloverleaf passage in *Learning from Las Vegas* recalls the "gnarly stag's horn" illustrated in Gregory Cullen's influential book *Townscape* (1961), an image meant to exemplify the eye's sudden switching from the rectilinear aspects of the city to being "entangled in a bunch of intricacy and wonder."[82] Caught in such a knot, we might heed Scott Brown's words of wisdom which come in the form of an imperative *and* a question: "Slow down—where do we go from here?"[83] In a similar vein Cavell observes, "genuine philosophy may begin in wonder, . . . it continues in reluctance."[84]

Evenly Distributed Attention (a "Non Directive Attitude")

VSBI's counter to a rush to judgment is their emphasis on "withholding judgment," or what, in their more poetic moments, they call "judgment with a sigh." Scott Brown characterized it as a receptive, "non-judgmental, non-directive attitude" in her article "On Pop Art, Permissiveness, and Planning."[85] *Learning from Las Vegas* describes it as "looking nonjudgmentally at the environment," which might provide a "way of learning from everything."[86] In the article, Scott Brown acknowledges the source of this receptive approach to "*existing* conditions," "this pop city, this *here*," in psychoanalytic thought and technique: "Perhaps Freud in our time initiated facing the unfaceable. The words 'non-judgmental,' 'permissive,' and 'non-directive' relate first to psychiatry."[87]

Scott Brown is registering a desire on the part of some urban and environmental theorists to find a way out from, or at least a significant modification of, the dominant Gestalt-oriented psychology that also happened to be the primary inspiration for Venturi's early understanding of "perceptual context" in the 1950s. In the hands of many urban critics and theorists, Gestalt principles were unable to produce adequate descriptions, criticism, or creative approaches to the new type of urban form in America: sprawl. The "good gestalt" patterns—the emphasis on simple, compact, coherent, and clearly bound "significant" shapes or figures cut out from "insignificant" or "mere" background—were not readily apparent in places like Las Vegas.[88] As Venturi and Scott Brown put it, "the Las Vegas Strip eludes our concepts of urban form and space, ancient or modern."[89] In *Learning from Las Vegas*, the authors suggest that an overemphasis on "good gestalt" results in the "rigid order of the urban renewal project" or the fashionable "'total design' of the megastructure."[90] The purported "aim" of their Learning from Las Vegas studio was a "nonjudgmental investigation" of these new urban phenomena, and "to begin to evolve techniques for its handling"; let's say seeing Las Vegas through the Nolli plan of Rome, and the Nolli plan of Rome through Las Vegas, and both through the shifting configurations of a Victor Vasarely painting (figures 1.5, 1.6).

In contrast to Gestalt psychology, psychoanalytic techniques of "free floating attention" (often called "evenly distributed attention") on the part of the analyst, and the corollary demand on the analysand to engage in "free association" during the analytic encounter, subscribed to a mode of dispersed attention, and a desire to delay selection or criticism, in order to pay attention to everything.[91]

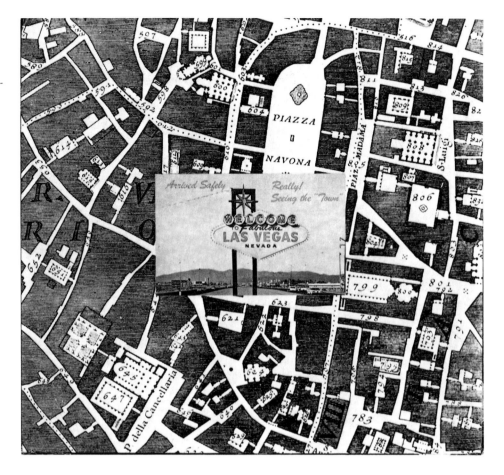

1.5 Nolli's map of Rome (Giovanni Battista Nolli, *Nuova pianta di Roma data in luce da Giambattista Nolli*, Rome, 1748), in *Learning from Las Vegas*; © 1977 Massachusetts Institute of Technology, by permission of the MIT Press.

Freud writes:

We must make no effort to concentrate the attention on anything in particular. . . . For as soon as attention is deliberately concentrated in a certain degree, one begins to select from the material before one; one point will be fixed in the mind with particular clearness and some other consequently disregarded, and in this selection one's expectations or inclinations will be followed. This is just what must not be done; if one's expectations are followed in this selection, there is the danger of never finding anything but what is already known. . . . All conscious exertion is to be withheld from the capacity for attention, and one's "unconscious memory" is to be given full play.[92]

1.6 Victor Vasarely, painting, Galerie Denise René, Paris, reprinted in *Learning from Las Vegas*; © 1972 Massachusetts Institute of Technology, by permission of the MIT Press.

The architect and urban anthropologist Amos Rapoport's 1967 essay "Complexity and Ambiguity in Environmental Design," co-written with the cognitive psychologist Robert E. Kantor, draws together many of the critiques of Gestalt psychology, from psychoanalytic thought, the New Critics, Jane Jacobs, and Venturi's first book, in order to offer some desirable techniques for investigating complex urban environments. Not surprisingly, Rapoport turns toward Anton Ehrenzweig, the psychoanalytic theorist of visual perception, to suggest what kind of vision might be conducive to picking up on the ambivalence in our environment: "Unconscious vision is wider in its focus and is thus more capable of scanning the many complications of a problem. He [Ehrenzweig] cites Paul Klee's insistence that the artist *disperse* his attention over figure and ground at the same time, apprehending both equally."[93] As Rapoport notes, Ehrenzweig suggests that one might consciously achieve this condition by "nourishing an effort to make . . . vision intentionally vague" and "to push vision towards an unfocused state."[94] Of course the risk is that the desire to elucidate the shape and order of the seemingly chaotic nature of the "not obvious order" of the Las Vegas Strip might come too close to what Ehrenzweig ultimately wanted: to support the supposed attempts by modern artists to "project an articulate gestalt into the gestalt-free elements of art form (*secondary gestalt elaboration*)."[95] It is evident that *Learning from Las Vegas* risks pushing Gestalt order ever deeper into our urban environments rather than dispersing our attention over its surface textures.

But what interests me here is that "dispersion" or "distraction" is the English word used to translate the German *Zerstreuung* in Horkheimer and Adorno's account of the impoverished condition in which we consume products of the culture industry: "The products of the culture industry are such that they can be alertly consumed even in a state of distraction."[96] It is also Heidegger's way of characterizing our "entanglement" in the "everydayness" of *they*; our attempt to look for ways in which our dispersion may be further dispersed in the world (figure 1.7).[97] But distraction might not be *merely* frivolous, or simply the mode of attention in which we passively consume products of the culture industry. For example, we know that distraction is internal to attempts to recover from the "intense" condition of skepticism. David Hume's account of exiting his chamber (and hence the straits of skepticism) into a game of backgammon with his friends is by no means meant simply to mark a *fallen* condition into a state of relaxation and distraction.[98] Venturi and Scott Brown's interest in the "deadpan" as both a technique and a disposition—exemplified for them in Ed Ruscha's photographs and art books—is directly related to their attempt to disperse attention in order to evoke an equanimity and responsiveness that might point the way to "a new vision of the very imminent world around us."[99] I will return to this idea in more depth in chapter 3.

Keeping within the realm of critical theory—even though a weak version of it has always clouded our understanding *of Learning from Las Vegas*—we might also consider Walter Benjamin's fascinating use of the word *Zerstreuung*. For him, it primarily means a "loosening of vision and attention."[100] In an article on Benjamin and cinema, Miriam Hansen has suggested that new developments in the figurativeness of language due to film and advertisement ("a blizzard of changing, colorful, conflicting letters") initiated a shift from the book into the public space of the street, which required a different kind of reading. This new *Bilderschrift* (visual writing) was also increasingly becoming a *Wandelschrift*

1.7 "Fremont Street casino entrance," Learning from Las Vegas studio, Yale University, in *Learning from Las Vegas*; © 1972 Massachusetts Institute of Technology, by permission of the MIT Press.

(a mobile and moving writing), which in turn made reading a more tactile, distracted experience.[101] VSBI continually emphasize that the Las Vegas signs are not merely "pop art" but also "pop literature." And, no less important, this reading of the urban script is predicated on issues of sensory and emotional impact. As Benjamin asked rhetorically, "What, in the end, makes advertisements so superior to criticism? Not what the moving red neon sign says—but the fiery pool reflecting it in the asphalt."[102] Thus it is never just the words or meaning that count in advertising, but rather the "color" of those words, their "profane illumination."

For Freud, and for many inspired by psychoanalytic theory and technique, a loosening of perception, dispersal of attention, and modes of ambivalence were attempts at overcoming ways of acting, meaning, and seeing that conflicted with normal modes of concentration that tended to isolate phenomena. This approach jibes well with *Learning from Las Vegas*'s trenchant critique of the purist and exclusionary strains in modern architecture, such as the emphasis on space as the essential ingredient, the opposition to mixing styles, the demand for an overly rigid order, and the criticism of the inclusive and messy nature of the Strip.[103] In a key passage of his essay "Inhibitions, Symptoms, and Anxiety,"

Freud discusses the drive to "isolate" in the processes of obsessional neurosis, and its relationship to normal modes of consciousness and directed mentation:

Motor isolation is meant to ensure an interruption of the connection in thought. The normal phenomenon of concentration provides a pretext for this kind of neurotic procedure: what seems to us important in the way of an impression or piece of work must not be interfered with by the simultaneous claims of any other mental processes or activities. But even a normal person uses concentration to keep away not only what is irrelevant or unimportant, but, above all, what is unsuitable because it is contradictory. . . . Thus, in the normal course of things, the ego has a great deal of isolating work to do in its function of directing the current of thought. And, as we know, we are obliged, in carrying out our analytic technique, to train it to relinquish that function for the time being.[104]

This emphasis on the ties that bind is of the utmost ethical import for *Learning from Las Vegas*, as Scott Brown was at pains to explain to Kenneth Frampton: "our point is that architects tend to oversimplify relationships in the city; that Las Vegas is an object lesson in complex relationships."[105] Thus there seems to be an ethical continuity from Venturi's 1950 M.F.A. thesis, "Context in Architectural Composition," to *Learning from Las Vegas* that is best captured in a passage from Emerson's poem "Each and All" quoted in the thesis: "All are needed by each one; Nothing is fair or good alone."[106] In Jean-Luc Nancy's words, "The city hardly allows one to utter 'I am' but rather 'I am in it.'"[107] We might call this VSBI's critique of the "paralysis" of the modern movement, if we take that word to mean that all binds have been unknotted or cut, and thus nothing holds or advances. Perhaps *Learning from Las Vegas* recalls for us that "the bind and the knot are necessary in order to take a step."[108] Is this what "meaning in architecture" means to them?

2 OUR CITY OF WORDS

When I talk about language (words, sentences, etc.) I must speak the language of the everyday. Is this language somehow too coarse and material for what we want to say? *Then how is another one to be constructed*—And how strange that we should be able to do anything at all with the one we have!

—Wittgenstein, *Philosophical Investigations*

Meaning Itself

Vincent Scully once suggested that the power of Robert Venturi's craft was his ability to transcend abstract formal manipulation and deal with meaning itself.[1] I am not sure what "meaning itself" is exactly, but certainly this statement illustrates the preoccupation during this period with "meaning in architecture," to take the title of a well-known book published in 1970.[2] Apart from the sophisticated work on the relationship between semiotics, structuralism, and architecture, the concern with meaning was more generally focused on the apparent lack of meaning in modern architecture, and the view that architecture was an (abstract) expression of its function, structure, or space. According to Venturi and Scott Brown, "meaning [in modern architecture] was to be communicated, not through allusion to previously known forms, but through the inherent physiognomic characteristics of form."[3]

Urban theorists at the time were deeply engaged in a generalized polemic about the chaotic nature of the exploding American metropolis in the late 1950s and early 1960s. At times, this led to binary arguments about chaos versus order—the "chaoticism" of the increasing spread of billboard advertising and urban sprawl—which tended to cleave apart the serious and the frivolous, splitting meaning off from the supposedly nonmeaningful as if scraping icing from a cake. The archetypal example of this polemic is Peter Blake's book *God's Own Junkyard* (1964), which exemplified the conditions of chaos and order in postwar America by juxtaposing an image of a "chaotic" commercial main street (Canal Street in New Orleans) with the pristine neoclassical order of Thomas Jefferson's campus for the University of Virginia (figures 2.1, 2.2). Blake claimed, "The two American scenes . . . document the decline, fall, and subsequent disintegration of urban civilization in the United States."[4] This apocalyptic tone marked many of the debates about urbanism at this time.

Venturi ends his first book, *Complexity and Contradiction in Architecture*, by roundly criticizing the validity of the comparison as such, not to mention Blake's chiliastic conclusions. Instead, Venturi concentrates on deconstructing the binary structure on which the comparison is predicated, emphasizing the

2.1 Canal Street, photograph by Wallace Litwin, in Peter Blake, *God's Own Junkyard*, 1961, reproduced in *Complexity and Contradiction in Architecture*; © 1966 Museum of Modern Art, New York.

"acknowledged dualities" within each image and not just between them.[5] What Blake overlooks in his book is that one can never separate the "serious" communicative task from what the philosopher John Austin calls the "etiolations of language."[6] *Learning from Las Vegas* demonstrates that the signscape of Las Vegas is merely the hyperbolization of the fact that *all* utterances are vulnerable to deception and insincerity. As Venturi and Scott Brown note: "Manipulation is not the monopoly of crass commercialism."[7] Any drive to firmly demarcate the "manipulative city of kitsch" (in Kenneth Frampton's words) from what Socrates in the *Republic* calls "our city of words"—the ideal rather than the actual city—is a deception in its own right.[8] Venturi and Scott Brown avoid the temptation to relegate these false alternatives to their separate domains, a move that Blake rushes into head on. Consider, for example, the closing lines of his book *The Master Builders*: "The alternatives are architecture or Disneyland, civilization or chaos."[9] Talk about either/or!

In contrast, Venturi and Scott Brown seem to be saying that the task of the critic of "culture" is not to carve out meaning from chaos but to undo meaning in an environment that is perhaps too "meaningful." It would seem that Venturi and Scott Brown were in fear not of chaos but of naked meaning, "meaning itself." Venturi quotes August Heckscher: "Chaos is very near; its nearness, but its avoidance, gives . . . force."[10] But how do they tarry with chaos yet somehow avoid it? One might say they demonstrate a "decreative impulse," a term that literary critic Richard Poirier uses to characterize Eliot's poetic enterprise in "T. S. Eliot and the Literature of Waste," an essay that is directly referred to three times in *Learning from Las Vegas*.[11] Poirier relates this impulse to Eliot's and Joyce's "extraordinary vulnerability . . . to the idioms, rhythms, artifacts, associated with certain urban environments or situations."[12] At times these idioms, rhythms, and artifacts overtake Eliot's voice. Evidently the decreative impulse is meant to *risk* a loss of voice; to withhold it as a mode of possible recovery and a reassertion of voice. In *Learning from Las Vegas*, this impulse involves deploying excess as a technique of analysis. As Steven Izenour noted, "If we have any philosophy of exhibit design at all, it's one of a kind of overload; we walk a thin line when it comes to boggling people's minds by offering lots of choices through juxtaposition—and maybe sometimes we fall over" (figure 2.3).[13] That seems to be a risk they are willing to take.

Venturi and Scott Brown end the first section of *Learning from Las Vegas* with this excerpt from the "East Coker" section of the *Four Quartets*:

That was a way of putting it—not very satisfactory:

A periphrastic study in a worn-out poetical fashion,

Leaving one still with the intolerable wrestle

With words and meanings. The poetry does not matter. . . . [14]

"The intolerable wrestle with words and meanings" in Eliot's poem refers not to the traditional sense of the "meaning" and "reference" of words *apart* from our voice in them, but rather to what those words mean for us in saying them.[15] The words may be worn out, but they are all we have, and their poetry—that institution, practice, or way of contextualizing them—will not ensure the "point" of saying those words, nor tether them to the circumstances in which they are said *now*. To return to the language of Venturi and Scott Brown, it is architecture's task to search for a practice of "inclusion," rather than to perpetuate a "pure" language of modern architecture set over and above the "impure" city that we happen to occupy. Their task is not to create a private, ideal language of architecture, but to locate our ability to mean within the ordinary language and practices we are already engaged in. Similarly, when Poirier characterizes Eliot's "skepticism about his own poetic enterprise" in terms of his drive to "dislocate, if necessary, language into his own meaning," he does not imply that Eliot is trying to secure his own private meaning over and against a public one.[16] After all, as Wittgenstein observes: "When I talk about language (words, sentences, etc.) I must speak the language of the everyday. Is this language somehow too coarse and material for what we want to say? Then how is another

2.3 Institute of Contemporary Arts exhibition, University of Pennsylvania, Philadelphia, 1992–1993; courtesy of VSBA, Inc.

one to be constructed—And how strange that we should be able to do anything at all with the one we have!"[17] This everyday language might be "somehow too coarse and material," but for Venturi and Scott Brown it is all we have to build with, and there is no other place to find what we want to say or do: "Meeting the architectural implications and the critical social issues of our era will require that we drop our involuted, architectural expressionism and our mistaken claim to building outside a formal language and find formal languages suited to our times."[18] The preoccupation with an architectural "poetry" of tastefulness and total design results in what they characterize as a condition of "deadness," a word they use more than once in the text.[19]

Certainly, there is much in *Learning from Las Vegas* to suggest that the authors believe we can carve out a space for unhindered communication from the everyday din of Las Vegas without too much struggle: "How is it that in spite of 'noise' from competing signs we do in fact find what we want on the strip?"[20] But do we really find what we want? As Tom Wolfe entitled his famous essay on Las Vegas, "Las Vegas (What!) Las Vegas (Can't Hear You! Too Noisy) Las Vegas!!!"[21] Can noise or static be so easily suppressed? Can chatter be so easily converted into meaningful communication? According to Peter Fenves, "Chatter anticipates essential speaking. Not only does chatter refer back to the discovery of loss; it also anticipates recovery while at each interval displacing and reinscribing the terms in which 'discovery' and 'recovery' are cast."[22]

The difficulties in parsing out chatter from "meaningful" communication—indeed, the fact that there are no strict criteria for differentiating them—are encountered in *Learning from Las Vegas* before one even opens the book: the glassine dust jacket designed by Muriel Cooper for the first edition (figure 2.4) consists of slogan-like section headings from the book printed in large, black letters that continue over onto the back cover.[23] The title *Learning from Las Vegas* on the second line of the jacket is set in red lettering and is thus picked out from the "black noise" of the rest of the dust-jacket text. Through the semiopaque jacket, we can see a color reproduction of the famous "Tan Hawaiian with Tanya" billboard, the gold stamped title "LEARNING FROM LAS VEGAS" (in all caps), and the names of the authors, all printed on the cloth cover (figure 2.5). The large gold lettering of *Learning from Las Vegas* on the cloth cover is overlaid by the black text on the glassine dust jacket, creating a palimpsest of sorts.[24] Although the title in red on the jacket is picked out from the surrounding typeface, it is in turn challenged by the gold embossed title of the cloth cover, seen through the layer of black lettering. If the title is supposed to point to a literal "scene of instruction," a "Learning from . . . ," it seems to be undermined by its own doubling or "contra-diction." The title is itself a repeated slogan no different from the surrounding section headings.

The cover of *Learning from Las Vegas* is a litany of monotonous one-liners divorced from any thick explanatory before and after; a parody of aphorism, it is all highlights and abbreviation in lieu of either brevity or completeness.[25] Skepticism's presence, according to Cavell, is marked by repeated attempts to erase context. Insofar as skepticism removes "our access to context, to the before and after, the ins and outs, of an expression," it is certainly that skeptical condition that Venturi and Scott Brown acknowledge.[26] And after all, advertising is precisely that mode of information, as Adorno has argued, that is "wrenched from all context."[27] This erasure of context, however, is not restricted to the mere cover of a much richer interior text; it is basic to the very conditions of the business of practicing architecture.[28] As Venturi noted: "We architects can travel 3,000 miles for a three-quarter-hour interview where we have to be sloganeers and showmen rather than thinkers and doers."[29]

The fact that Venturi and Scott Brown disavowed "the latter day Bauhaus design" of the first edition, preferring the second edition's stark title in black letters against a pale blue cover, without the "black noise" of the slogan-like section headings, does not make the dilemma go away (more on this issue in chapter 5) (figure 2.6).[30] One can't simply remove the first edition's dust jacket and neatly align those chapter headings on the contents page of the revised edition and be done with it. When we open *Learning from Las Vegas*, either the first or revised edition, we are still confronted with the task of reading, interpreting, meaning, and making in the face of such erasures of context.

A Significance for A&P Parking Lots, or Learning from Las Vegas. Commercial Values and Commercial Methods. Billboards Are Almost All

Here is a plea for a proper architectural humanity and humility, as well as a plan to accommodate the desires and values of ordinary people, who are too often dragged along on architectural ego trips and uplift programs. It is also a realistic examination of the American vernacular environment as it is and a reexamination of the goal of

the architect. The challenge is clear and forthright. Articles based on material in this book have already caused a great deal of controversy and rethinking. But at the present uncertain point in the development of the Modern movement, it's a useful controversy that could result in a firmer sense of future direction and closer accommodation to social realities.

Right. Architecture as Space. Architecture as Symbol. Symbol in Space before Form in Space: Las Vegas as a Communication System. The Architecture of Persuasion. Vast Space in the Historical Tradition and at the A&P. From Rome to Las Vegas. Maps of Las Vegas: Las Vegas as a Pattern of Activities. Main Street and the Strip. System and Order on the Strip, and "Twin Phenomena." Change and Permanence on the

LEARNING FROM LAS VEGAS

Robert Venturi   Denise Scott Brown   Steven Izenour

2.4 Glassine dust jacket for the first edition of *Learning from Las Vegas*; © 1972 Massachusetts Institute of Technology, by permission of the MIT Press.

LEARNING

FROM

LAS VEGAS

Revised Edition

Robert Venturi   Denise Scott Brown   Steven Izenour

2.6 Paperback cover for the revised edition of *Learning from Las Vegas*; © 1977 Massachusetts Institute of Technology, by permission of the MIT Press.

Neon Words . . . and Sentences?

How should we read the sequence of astonishing images in the section entitled "Symbol in Space before Form in Space: Las Vegas as a Communication System" in the first edition of the book? Images 3 to 6 are a sequence of small cropped photographs of Las Vegas signs at night, that read together produce the sentence, "Welcome to Fabulous Las Vegas, Free Aspirin—Ask Us Anything, Vacancy, Gas" (figure 2.7).[31] The neon signs are literally translated into that proper sentence on the adjacent page (figure 2.8). Venturi and Scott Brown are suggesting that these neon sentences are not only "pop art" but also "pop literature." In fact, the sentence is reminiscent of Tom Wolfe's pop literature, contemporary practices of "found" poetry, and T. S. Eliot's writing, with its mix of "Sweeney and Latin."

Consider the words of Eliot's character Eggerson from his play *The Confidential Clerk:* "He has a heart of gold. But, not to beat around the bush, He's rather a rough diamond."[32] Or those of Gerty MacDowell in James Joyce's *Ulysses*, which Marshall McLuhan has described as "a mosaic of banalities that reveals the effect of these forms in shaping and extending our lives."[33] Venturi and Scott Brown were well aware of these early modern strategies of reusing ordinary language: "We say our buildings are 'ordinary'—other people have said they are ugly and ordinary. But, of course, our buildings in another sense are extraordinary, extra-ordinary. . . . Literary critics have known about this all along, that is, about the use of clichés, the use of common, everyday language which makes the literature of Eliot and Joyce, for instance, *extra*-ordinary."[34] In sympathy with critics such as McLuhan, Poirier, and Frye, Venturi and Scott Brown underline the stakes and possibilities involved in our "subjection" to mass media culture and the reign of the cliché.[35]

One is always in the position of a painter like Robert Rauschenberg whose very first brush stroke takes place on a canvas already primed with newspaper, a "gray map of words."[36] Thoreau puts the dilemma this way: "It is difficult to begin without borrowing."[37] Whether an axe to hew logs for a house or a pen to cleave words on a page, we are all borrowers and lenders. It is significant, then, that Part I of *Learning from Las Vegas* begins with an epigraph from an essay by Poirier on Eliot; with an aphorism by a critic on a poet writing about words as always already spoken for: "Substance for a writer consists merely not of those realities he thinks he discovers; it consists even more of those realities which have been made available to him by the literature and idioms of his own day and by the images that still have vitality in the literature of the past. Stylistically, a writer can express his feelings about this substance either by imitation, if it sits well with him, or by parody, if it doesn't."[38] I am not concerned with the references to mimesis and parody in this passage—in the sentence immediately

WELCOME TO FABULOUS LAS VEGAS, FREE ASPIRIN – ASK US ANY-THING, VACANCY, GAS.

2.7 Neon sentence, "Welcome to Fabulous Las Vegas, Free Aspirin—Ask Us Anything, Vacancy, Gas," Learning from Las Vegas studio, Yale University, in *Learning from Las Vegas*; © 1972 Massachusetts Institute of Technology, by permission of the MIT Press.

2.8 "Welcome to Fabulous Las Vegas, Free Aspirin—Ask Us Anything, Vacancy, Gas," Learning from Las Vegas studio, in *Learning from Las Vegas*; © 1972 Massachusetts Institute of Technology, by permission of the MIT Press.

following, Poirier veers away from such concerns—but rather with the fact that it highlights the importance of what Venturi and Scott Brown call "receptivity." If architects are "Johnnies-come-lately on the scene," as Scott Brown writes, then their *responsibility* is not to speak first, but to listen and learn.[39]

Of course an emphasis on affective passivity can always call forth a response that architects are then abdicating the Kantian creative/critical role of schematizing the manifold of perception, for its passive, and predigested, easy consumption. In Horkheimer and Adorno's words: "The active contribution which Kantian schema still expected of subjects . . . is denied to the subject by industry. It purveys schematism as its first service to the customer."[40] This was precisely Tomás Maldonado's early critique of *Learning from Las Vegas*, encapsulated in his claim that "Las Vegas is a not a creation *by* the people, but *for* the people."[41] These words are unusually harsh for such a quintessentially American book. Are they *just* words?

But doesn't Venturi and Scott Brown's "receptivity" undermine the "inability to leave anything beyond itself untouched," which Adorno identified as the "monopolistic compulsion" characteristic of mass culture?[42] If so, they are creating room for thinking about how we touch and are touched by ordinary language rather than how we grasp or are grasped by meaning. I sense this in Scott Brown's provocative question: "what makes the city 'mine'?"[43] Assuming that Venturi and Scott Brown's stake in the neon sentences is the fact that all our words and sentences were never solely "ours," I wish to acknowledge this as the absolute starting point for locating our share in those words. What words bind us together, willingly or unwillingly?[44] They are perhaps driving us to investigate, in the spirit of Thoreau, "by what degree of consanguinity *They* are related to *me*, and what authority they may have in an affair which affects me so nearly."[45]

Might not Venturi and Scott Brown be "taking a reading" of these words? One of their favorite artists, Ed Ruscha, described words in terms of temperature: "Words have temperatures to me. When they reach a certain point and become hot words, then they appeal to me."[46] Although Venturi and Scott Brown also "take the temperature" or check the intensity of electrified words and signs in the city, they are equally interested in "cold words"; instead of boiling them, they drain the lifeblood out of them, in order to verify at what "degree" they enter into that cold, lifeless region that Horkheimer and Adorno have identified with the "mood" of advertising:[47] "The layer of experience which makes words human like those who spoke them has been stripped away, and in its prompt appropriation language takes on the coldness which hitherto was peculiar to billboards and the advertising sections of newspapers. Countless people use words and expressions which they either have ceased to understand at all or use only according to their behavioral functions, just as trademarks adhere all the more compulsively to their objects of choice the less their linguistic meaning is apprehended."[48] But as J. M. Bernstein has pointed out, this coldness is not merely a condition that is imposed; rather, it is a task that is "affirmed against its imposition as the unavoidable means of undoing that imposition."[49] This thought is also raised by Cavell in his use of the term "subliming," inspired by passages in Wittgenstein that relate it to a craving to speak in purity or in ideal terms outside of our "language games" and the "everyday."[50]

Subliming—in contrast to the term "sublimation," the scientific definition of heating a substance in order to convert it from its solid state into a vapor or gas without an intermediate liquid stage—drives us to those polar regions where we find it difficult to move because we are frozen in the ideal realm where words are lodged apart from our share in them. We might think that the language of advertising is a way of having words circulate in our world of exchange and exhibition value, but instead it leads to their paralysis. Paradoxically, we need to put words into *further* circulation so that we can begin to have the exchanges we want with them. Wittgenstein pointed to this paradox: "We have got on to slippery ice where there is no friction and so in a certain sense the conditions are ideal, but also, just because of that, we are unable to walk. We want to walk: so we need *friction*. Back to the rough ground!"[51]

Although advertising signage might appear to be a manifestation of "ordinary" language, it is more precisely indicative of that drive toward skepticism, in which words are pushed to a region where they are beyond the reach of our participation in them. The task of driving them there, however, is a necessary one, as the life of words occurs to us only *after* we have seen language as a collection of signs separate from us.[52] Wittgenstein's sentence, "Every sign *by itself* seems dead," is immediately followed by the question, "*What* gives it life?"[53] Notice that it is the "What" that is italicized, as if to remind us that it is not "the life" that is at stake but rather the "what." What have we done to take away that life? What can be done to give it back? Need we be reminded here that these are also Venturi and Scott Brown's concerns, best exemplified in the title of their 1976 Bicentennial exhibition at the Renwick Gallery, "Signs of Life: Symbols in the American City"?

(No) Vacancy

If indeed, as Venturi and Scott Brown suggest, there is a perversity in the learning process in which we go down to go up, and back to go forward, then we could equally read the "Vacancy" sign in bright orange neon, and the barely discernible, unlit "No" directly above it ready to be activated at a moment's notice, as emblematic of the plenitude or voidness of meaning in *Learning from Las Vegas* (figure 2.7).[54] The often abrupt, even precipitous movement between the plenitude and paucity of meaning in *Learning from Las Vegas* is exemplified in this image. We could think of this movement in terms of two dominant voices discernible in the text (though there are others): one taking an extreme skeptical stance in its erasure of context and the denial of shared meaning; and the other, equally insistent, arguing for the recovery of context and meaning.[55] For example, in constructing the grammatical *written* sentence out of the "primitive language" of the neon signs, the authors radically insert "context" into the discontinuous and paratactic words/images: a comma here, a dash there, the omission of "Nevada" in the first image, a period to put an end to it all. It is as if their interest in the Las Vegas "Strip" lies not only in that burlesque show, but also in "stripping" criteria for meaning and context in order to explore the very conditions of possibility for communication as such.[56] In *Learning from Las Vegas*, the layer of experience that Adorno claims makes words human, and that is absent from the cold language of billboards, has been *stripped* away. One might say that Venturi and Scott Brown are "strippers" in a melodrama of meaning what we say. As Venturi put it: "I am an exhibitionist: I go around exposing my doubts."[57]

It has always struck me that the neon sentence looks like one of those cliquéd ransom letters seen in old movies where the letters and words are ripped and pieced together from different typefaces and print media. Are we common criminals who need to steal our language back? Or have we always already had it stolen from us—willingly? Are we victims of meaning? Are Venturi and Scott Brown suggesting—in the spirit of T. S. Eliot's dictum, "Immature poets imitate, mature poets steal"[58]—that architecture is a mug's game, a rogue's gallery? We might read this sequence of images like Adorno's characterization of the telegram: its "mutilated language [is] condensed to carry the maximum information combined with the urgency of delivery imparts the shock of immediate domination in the form of immediate horror."[59] Certainly Adorno's description of the telegram calls to mind Venturi's aphorism about Las Vegas: "The city of signs spewing the vital if vulgar iconography of now—terribilità verging on orribilità."[60] The potential ambivalence, violence, and urgent delivery of such signs are all exemplified in the "Tan Hawaiian with Tanya" billboard image.

"Tan Hawaiian with Tanya"

Critics have been particularly dismissive of the "Tan Hawaiian with Tanya" that is prominently displayed on the cover of both editions, posing *provocatively* for the book as a whole (figures 2.5, 2.6, 2.9). As Neil Leach bluntly put it: "A tanned bikini-clad figure is used to promote a suntan lotion, in a poster that blatantly exploits female sexuality."[61] But are Venturi and Scott Brown really claiming, to quote Thoreau, that "we are a race of tit-men, and soar but little higher in our intellectual [and sexual] flights" than ogling half-clothed figures on advertising billboards?[62] Can we in all credulity assume that Venturi and Scott Brown were oblivious to the fact that instruction sometimes requires provocation? In a book that traffics in commodified words and images, they are all too aware of the price, not to mention the value, of those words and images.[63] One certainly can't accuse them of being agoraphobic: they aren't afraid to mingle in the spaces of exchange, where words, goods, money, and sexual temptation circulate.[64] After all, in our agora there are no strict criteria for differentiating between works of art that are "ascetic and shameless" and the products of the culture industry that are "pornographic and prudish."[65]

The Tanya image begins to look more critical if we consider it in terms of the constant skeptical project of "stripping" away criteria in *Learning from Las Vegas*. VSBI ask us, the readers, to acknowledge the difficulty of identifying any

2.9 "Tan Hawaiian with Tanya" billboard, Learning from Las Vegas studio, in *Learning from Las Vegas*; © 1972 Massachusetts Institute of Technology, by permission of the MIT Press.

scene of instruction at all, or any scene of instruction we would want to identify with. For example, the billboard is planted in the desert sharply perpendicular to the Strip, in an abrupt transition between "nature" and "culture." However, gender plays a role in accomplishing that transition. The outline of the reclining Tanya figure echoes the contours of the mountains in the background, as if calling attention to the very ideology that subtends such advertising images. (Venturi and Scott Brown also refer to this liminal space between desert and Strip as a "zone of rusting beer cans.")[66]

There is another striking image in Scott Brown and Venturi's 1969 essay "The Bicentennial Commemoration 1976" that brings the Tanya image into the constellation of issues I am talking about (figure 2.10).[67] It consists of schematic rectangular buildings with large signs tethered to them or near them, like cartoon speech balloons (more on tethering and speech balloons in chapter 3). The signs read, "EXIT," "PROCESS," "LOVE & LEARN," "SOUVENIR." Although the "LOVE & LEARN" sign is referred to as such in the text of the article, what we *see* and *hear* in this image is "LOVE & LEAR," as the adjoining sign occludes the *N*.[68] The authors subtly, and ambivalently, couple love and learn with love and leer (lear), and thus prompt the question: Should we "learn from" or "leer at" the billboard architecture of the "strip"? Venturi and Scott Brown comment, "If the commercial persuasions that flash on the strip are materialistic consumption and vapid subcommunication . . . it does not follow

2.10 "Bold Signs in the City," in Robert Venturi and Denise Scott Brown, "The Bicentennial Commemoration 1976," *Architectural Forum* (October 1969); courtesy of VSBA, Inc.

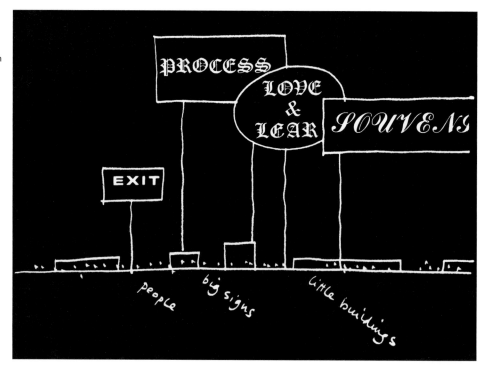

that we architects who learn from their techniques must reproduce the content or the superficiality of their messages."[69] As Cavell has noted, it is precisely the movements between "distrusting and entrusting words, investments and withdrawals" on which skepticism lives.[70]

If the bikini-clad image adorning the front cover of the book provides a striking contrast to Venturi and Scott Brown's loving and learning from Las Vegas, it also confirms that both profane and profound messages are found in the city. Like "love" and "glove," the ultimate weapon of the Blue Meanies in the Beatles film *Yellow Submarine*, sometimes they are separated by a mere hair's breadth.[71] But the skeptical dilemma in *Learning from Las Vegas* is really brought to the fore through the "indiscreet" comparison between the Duck and Decorated Shed.

3 OF DUCKS, DECORATED SHEDS, AND OTHER MINDS

. . . purely impenetrable thickness and the idea purely penetrated by itself are two abstractions—
two extremities of separating abstraction, and something like the face-to-face of stupidity and
madness, and the utter loss of sense.

—Jean-Luc Nancy, *Hegel: The Restlessness of the Negative*

The Modernist Drive for Expressive Transparency

One of the primary critiques of modernism that *Learning from Las Vegas* was
engaged in was the dialectic between inside and outside and the assumption
that the exterior expressed the interior.[1] As Rem Koolhaas explains in his book
Delirious New York: "In Western architecture there has been the humanistic assumption that it is desirable to establish a moral relationship between the
two, whereby the exterior makes certain revelations about the interior that
the interior corroborates."[2] Let's call this the modernist drive for "expressive
transparency." In contrast, VSBI stress the contradiction between the inside
and outside, drawing upon examples from premodern eras, as well as American roadside architecture with its "false fronts," combination of styles (with
"Moorish in front and Tudor behind"), and the diremption of the big sign from
the boxlike generic building behind it. *Learning from Las Vegas* attempts to make
sense of and go on from a situation in which a certain postwar modernist legacy
of architecture was breaking down.

The drive for expressive transparency in modern architecture, and *Learning from Las Vegas*'s response to it, are intimately related to the skeptical dilemma about knowing "other minds"—a problem that is deeply involved with the relationship between the inner and outer, transparency and opacity, expression and inexpression. As Cavell has put it: "At some stage the skeptic is going to be impressed by the fact that my knowledge of others depends upon their *expressing themselves*, in word and conduct."[3] If skepticism about other minds, our ability to know the other, depends on an interaction between the inner and outer—upon the expressive capacities of a body and our willingness to acknowledge or avoid those capacities—then architecture's deeply rooted investment in the metaphorics of the body, and its preoccupation with the relationship between the interior and exterior, would suggest that it is one of the privileged domains in which skepticism about other minds is dramatized. A shorthand way of thinking about the dilemma of other minds—the mode of skepticism at stake in this chapter—is roughly marked out by Walter Benjamin on the one hand, and by Venturi and Scott Brown on the other. In a well-known passage from his essay "Surrealism: The Last Snapshot of the European Intelligentsia," Benjamin advocates the transparency of the modernist building and its ability to express: "To live in a glass house is a revolutionary virtue par excellence. It is also an intoxication, a moral exhibitionism we badly need."[4] Venturi and Scott Brown argue that internal to this logic of "moral exhibitionism" is the potential—already latent in Benjamin's passage—for architecture to twist itself into a full-blown *theatricality* in which the "expressive aim has distorted the whole."[5] Thus, postwar modernism's theatricality was thwarting its own attempts to express.

Fantasies of Absolute Expression and Inexpression in the Duck and Decorated Shed

This dialectic between expression and inexpression is taken up with a vengeance in the by now infamous contrast—what Venturi and Scott Brown call an "indiscreet comparison"—between the Duck and Decorated Shed in *Learning from Las Vegas* (figure 3.1). And it is this comparison that enacts the skeptical dilemma about knowing other minds. Venturi and Scott Brown's definitions are worth quoting in full:

1. Where the architectural systems of space, structure, and program are submerged and distorted by an overall symbolic form. This kind of building-becoming-sculpture we call the *duck* in honor of the duck-shaped drive-in, "The Long Island Duckling," illustrated in *God's Own Junkyard* by Peter Blake.

2. Where systems of space and structure are directly at the service of program, and ornament is applied independently of them. This we call the *decorated shed*.

73. "Long Island Duckling" from *God's Own Junkyard*

74. Road scene from *God's Own Junkyard*

HIGHWAY

DUCK

75. Duck

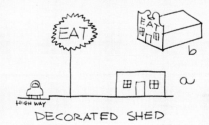

DECORATED SHED

76. Decorated shed

3.1 Top: "Long Island Duckling" and road scene (photograph by Standard Oil Co.), reproduced from Peter Blake, *God's Own Junkyard*, by permission of Henry Holt; bottom: diagrams of the Duck and the Decorated Shed. In *Learning from Las Vegas*; © 1977 Massachusetts Institute of Technology, by permission of the MIT Press.

As they note, "The duck is the special building that *is* a symbol; the decorated shed is the conventional shelter that *applies* symbols. . . . We think that the duck is seldom relevant today, although it pervades Modern architecture."[6]

The two photographs reproduced from Peter Blake's *God's Own Junkyard*, and the diagrams below them that illustrate the comparison, demonstrate that there is no hard and fast separation between the Duck and the Decorated Shed. The "Long Island Duckling" is also "conventional," insofar as the photograph includes the adjacent signs indicating that the Duckling sells game hens and turkeys as well as broiled and roasted ducks.[7] Moreover, we can see what look like two sheds behind the duck, and so we could interpret the Duck as a conventional "sign" in its own right that is applied to the sheds in back.[8] Although the free-standing Duck is described as a "building-becoming-sculpture," at various points in *Learning from Las Vegas* the authors also emphasize the sculptural qualities of the big neon signs in Las Vegas. Early images of the Duck and Decorated Shed diagrams, appearing in their articles before *Learning from Las Vegas*, are drawn at the same scale and with the same thickness of line (with the exception of the windows), as if to suggest that the curving, expressionistic lines of the Duck are the result of a twisted morphing of the shed, or vice versa (figure 3.2). Further blurring the distinction, both the Duck and the Decorated Shed are concerned with the function of eating (a point to which I will return). Most

3.2 Duck and Decorated Shed, in Robert Venturi, "A Significance for A&P Parking Lots, or Learning from Las Vegas," *Architectural Forum* (March 1968); courtesy of VSBA, Inc.

importantly, both the Duck and the Decorated Shed are deeply concerned with issues of voice. In the diagrams the Duck and the Decorated Shed have two window-eyes and a door-nose, but no mouth. The issues of voice and expression— giving expression to voice and voice to expression—are dominant concerns in this chapter and in chapter 4. I simply note here that in the Decorated Shed the mouth or voice seems to be displaced onto the adjacent sign, and in the Duck to the slightly open animal beak in the diagram, in contrast to the closed beak in the photograph. Simply put, *Learning from Las Vegas* makes it abundantly clear that many buildings throughout history should be seen as both Duck and Decorated Shed (though of course the authors' sympathies are with the Decorated Shed for its relevance *now*).[9]

What is even more telling of the skeptical dilemma is that the Duck and Decorated Shed diagrams render both types of building with a "face": the two windows and central door strike one as schematic eyes and nose (figures 3.1, 3.2).[10] There could be no better testament that skepticism about other minds is central to these images than the inclusion of eyes, the supposed windows to the soul and the canonical location and bearer of expressiveness in figural art and natural human interactions. This is reminiscent of a striking passage in *The World Viewed* where Cavell describes "a mood of nothing but eyes, dissociated from feeling."[11] Notice, however, that the dark, thicker line used to render the windows/eyes on the Duck makes them look more expressive than the ones on the Decorated Shed. And the overall "facedness" of both the Duck and the Decorated Shed is remarkably close to Cavell's claim that in material-object skepticism, "the body . . . becomes a thing with senses, mostly eyes, disconnected from the motive power of the body."[12] It would seem that, despite their apparent opposition, both the Duck and the Decorated Shed share an overarching proposition: if there is a "disconnection" between eyes, body, feeling, and voice, then perhaps we need to rethink that condition in order to see how we might reconfigure our *sense* of what architecture is and can be.

By beginning with the similarities between the Duck and the Decorated Shed instead of their differences—with their indiscreteness, one might say—I am suggesting that we are better served by understanding the comparison as voicing a certain *fantasy* of expression and/or inexpression. In calling it a fantasy, I mean that it is an interpretation of reality, and not simply a state separate from reality. As Cavell puts it, "Fantasy is precisely what reality can be confused with. It is through fantasy that our conviction of the worth of reality is established; to forgo our fantasies would be to forgo our touch with the world."[13] This fantasy suggests a particular atmosphere, mood, or attitude in which the world is colored *as* Duck- or Decorated Shed-like. Rather than taking the authors' comparison as simply a concrete discussion about discrete and stabilized ontologies "out there," we should see the Duck and Decorated Shed as categories—

one might say historical a priori categories—under which different stretches of response are evaluated.[14] If we approach the comparison from this angle, how we respond to architecture—how we permit it to count for us in specific ways—is inseparable from what architecture *is* at any given time.

In other words, the Duck and the Decorated Shed are not "tired tropes"; they do not simply repeat the ontology of architecture involved in other well-known comparisons, such as Nikolaus Pevsner's famous opening line in *An Outline of European Architecture*: "A bicycle shed is a building; Lincoln Cathedral is a piece of architecture."[15] But neither do Venturi and Scott Brown abandon an interest in the "ontology" of architecture. Rather, they modify it with an attentiveness to the historical and affective dimensions that are perpetually redefining what it is and what it can do.[16] It is our mode of acknowledgment or avoidance of that acknowledgment—a certain category of *response*, perhaps a "confusion, an indifference, a callousness, an exhaustion, a coldness"—that inflicts the status of "duckdom" on *any* building whatsoever.[17] It would appear that the Duck and the Decorated Shed operate as highly mobile, supple, and chiasmatically entwined terms—and at crucial points, each incorporates the other in order to survive.

Crawford Manor and Guild House: Plasticity and Flatness

In arguing against the "modernist" Duck's attempt to exude meaning independently of convention, Venturi and Scott Brown are drawing on art historian Ernst Gombrich's argument about the "physiognomic fallacy"—primarily read through Alan Colquhoun's article "Typology and Design Method," published in 1967.[18] At the heart of this argument is the critique of any kind of direct expression that could bypass the conventional use of signs. In his essay "Expression and Communication," Gombrich tabulates a set of binary concepts to make this clear: on one side, expression, emotion, symptom, naturalness; and on the other, communication, information, code, convention.[19] Venturi and Scott Brown take up Gombrich's criticism of the argument that "shapes have physiognomic or expressive content which communicates itself to us directly," in order to question the supposed ideology of certain strands of modern architectural functionalism.[20] Adhering pretty closely to Colquhoun's interpretation of Gombrich, they critique high modernism's belief that form is the logical expression of operational needs and techniques, which, in turn, is wedded to a mystical belief in the intuitive process. The result was, according to Colquhoun, Venturi, and Scott Brown, a biological determinism inextricably linked with a permissive expressionism. The words and phrases used to describe the Duck are indeed revealing: overarticulated, dramatic, stridently distorted, overstated, twisted, violently heroic and original, and extraordinary.[21]

Venturi and Scott Brown's characterization of the Duck as a "building-becoming-sculpture" highlights the fact that issues of sculptural plasticity and modulation carry the weight of this hyperbolic expressionism. As Scully noted in the unpublished introduction to the first edition of *Learning from Las Vegas*, VSBI are involved in flattening out the "sculptural forces" of late and postwar modernist facades.[22] Venturi and Scott Brown no doubt had the late work of Le Corbusier and its legacy in mind; they must also have recalled Le Corbusier's early fascination with issues of plasticity, and his well-known claim in *Towards a New Architecture* that the prime achievement of the Parthenon was due to the sculptor Phidias rather than the architects Iktinos and Kallikrates. A major thrust in the comparison between the Duck and the Decorated Shed is to critique and reconfigure what plasticity might mean in architecture—and in terms of the political—when it is no longer possible to define architecture as the "skillful, accurate, and magnificent play of masses seen in light."[23] Paul Rudolph's Crawford Manor, located in New Haven, and Venturi and Rauch's Guild House in Philadelphia—both built as housing for the elderly—are deployed as the contemporary examples of the sculptural Duck and the heraldic Decorated Shed (figure 3.3).[24]

Although the structure of Crawford Manor is really a "conventional" frame supporting masonry walls—consisting of poured-in-place concrete with concrete block faced with a striated pattern—it doesn't look it. It appears as if the supports are "made of a continuous plastic material reminiscent of *béton brut* with the striated marks of violently heroic construction process embossed in their form." Further, "interior light is 'modulated' by the voids between the structure and the 'floating' cantilevered balconies." In contrast, the system of construction and program in Guild House are ordinary and conventional and look it. It is constructed of poured-in-place concrete plate, with curtain walls "pierced" by windows. The facing material is common brick, darker than usual to match the aged brick buildings in the surrounding neighborhood.

The flatness of the cheap appliqué decoration on the Guild House facade contrasts with the plasticity of Rudolph's Crawford Manor. Its balcony railings recall patterns in stamped metal, and the double-hung conventional windows puncture the surface rather than articulate it; they are explicitly symbolic rather than serving to modulate exterior light. The comparison is crowned by the description of the "unconnected, symmetrical television antenna in gold anodized aluminum"—an imitation of an "abstract Lippold sculpture," or "almost sculpture" (their words)—that perches on the roof of Guild House and "ironically" refers to the sculptural qualities of Crawford Manor. As against the explicit, specific, and heraldic denotative sign that spells out "[I am] Guild House," Crawford Manor identifies itself through the "connotation implicit in the physiognomy of its pure architectural form, which is intended to express in

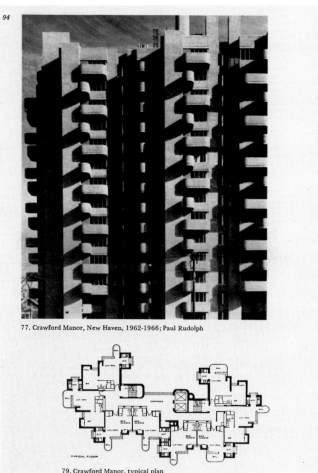

77. Crawford Manor, New Haven, 1962-1966; Paul Rudolph

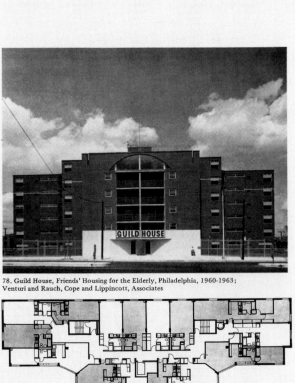

78. Guild House, Friends' Housing for the Elderly, Philadelphia, 1960-1963;
Venturi and Rauch, Cope and Lippincott, Associates

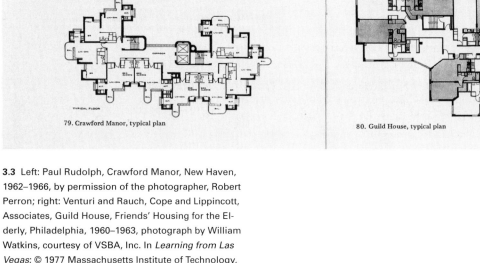

79. Crawford Manor, typical plan

80. Guild House, typical plan

3.3 Left: Paul Rudolph, Crawford Manor, New Haven, 1962–1966, by permission of the photographer, Robert Perron; right: Venturi and Rauch, Cope and Lippincott, Associates, Guild House, Friends' Housing for the Elderly, Philadelphia, 1960–1963, photograph by William Watkins, courtesy of VSBA, Inc. In *Learning from Las Vegas*; © 1977 Massachusetts Institute of Technology, by permission of the MIT Press.

some way housing for the elderly."[25] This contrast between the expressionism of Crawford Manor and the deliberate damming of expression in Guild House is "dramatized" by the strikingly different photographic perspectives of the two exteriors: a frog's-eye view of the undulating, striated, and chiaroscuro-lit balconies of the "soaring tower" is juxtaposed with a "deadpan" view of the tightly cropped, shadowless facade of Guild House (figure 3.4).[26] Like Ruscha's deadpan photographs in *Every Building on the Sunset Strip*, the photographs of Guild House appear to be taken as if at high noon, the time of the shortest shadow.[27]

This engaging and carefully staged comparison—we might call it a fantasy scene—enacts the differences between the Duck and Decorated Shed in the strongest possible terms. But at times the comparison seems to take on a life of its own, and suggests the symmetries as much as the asymmetries between the two positions. For example, what begins as a critique of Crawford Manor

3.4 Left: frog's-eye view of Crawford Manor, by permission of the photographer, Robert Perron; right: deadpan view of Guild House, photograph by William Watkins, courtesy of VSBA, Inc. In *Learning from Las Vegas*; © 1977 Massachusetts Institute of Technology, by permission of the MIT Press.

81. Crawford Manor (detail)

82. Guild House, windows

as a "sculptural duck" quickly transfigures into a statement about its "abstract expressionist" qualities, suggesting an analogy perhaps to the abstract expressionist painting of Jackson Pollock.[28] But Pollock's gesture of dispersing painterly expression over the surface of the canvas—so that the expression achieves a certain degree of explicitness (let us call it the painting's flatness, or better yet, its "candor")—might be a lot closer to the deadpan Decorated Shed, and to the issues raised by pop art in general, than Venturi and Scott Brown seem to acknowledge.

It seems fairly obvious that in their critique of the Duck, Venturi and Scott Brown are arguing for the irrelevance of any contemporary version of architecture based on the premises of an *architecture parlante*. As Detlef Mertens succinctly described this approach: "Eighteenth-century critiques of rhetoric, theatricality, and allegory sparked formal experiments in architecture that sought to eliminate the use of conventions or applied signs in favor of the direct expression of the inner nature of a building."[29] And as Karsten Harries has rightly pointed out, "Ledoux's *architecture parlante* is an architecture of ducks."[30] It doesn't take much extrapolation to conclude that Venturi and Scott Brown are engaging in a critique of what one might call the "logocentrism" of postwar modern architecture; that is, in de Man's definition, "the unmediated presence of the self to its own voice as opposed to the reflective distance that separates this self from the written word."[31] Although Venturi and Scott Brown's comparison of the Decorated Shed with the Duck is, in a sense, such a critique, it does not deny the fact that we are nevertheless still tethered to our words and, more specifically, to our *voice* in those words.[32] Thus, the issue of expression and inexpression and their relative "articulations" are at the heart of the comparison between the Duck and the Decorated Shed.

The Duck as Melodrama of Expression

If melodrama is characterized as the site of "excessive expression"—the point where, in the words of Venturi and Scott Brown, "expression has become expressionism"—then one might say that the Duck is the melodramatic figure in which a fantasy about absolute expressiveness is aired.[33] However, melodrama, as Cavell is quick to point out, is also the locus of the "emptiness of expression," a situation that resonates with *Learning from Las Vegas*'s critique of the "empty gestures" of postwar modernist architecture.[34] One might say that the excessive expression embodied in the Duck is meant to suggest a symptom of our inability to mean what we say or do, as if we were required to force an idea of architecture to fit a circumstance that is no longer viable—what Venturi and Scott Brown call, at various points, architecture's "strident," "overstated," and "irrelevant articulations."

The Duck stakes out the region of a modernist drive for transparency pushed to its breaking point—the condition in which the modernist quest for purity, totality, and its version of absolute expression would seem to suffocate us rather than express our needs, wants, and ideals. Wittgenstein explains the straits of this condition: "The ideal, as we think of it, is unshakeable. You can never get outside it; you must always turn back. There is no outside; outside you cannot breathe."[35] If this quest for purity and totality has created an absolute interior cut off from the world "out there," the "solution" is not simply to reach out to that world (where would you be reaching *to*?), but rather to reconsider how we came to occupy this condition in the first place. As Wittgenstein put it: "The *preconceived idea* of crystalline purity can only be removed by turning our whole examination round. (One might say: the axis of reference of our examination must be rotated, but about the fixed point of our real need.)"[36] Wittgenstein's sentiment is echoed by Venturi and Scott Brown in one of their key statements: "meeting the architectural implications and the critical social issues of our era will require that we drop our involuted, architectural expressionism and our mistaken claim to building outside a formal language and find formal languages suited to our times."[37] I take it that the quest to "find formal languages suited to our times" is somewhat analogous to Wittgenstein's "real need"; that is, both voice a desire to locate the criteria for our real needs in the ordinary, rather than in the ideal and its quest for purity and transparency (in Venturi and Scott Brown's sentence, the word "formal" does not mean, as it might suggest, an ideal or abstract language; it is closer to the simple word "form"). If we bring these thoughts to bear on the Duck, then its version of absolute expression would also seem to disclose a fear of absolute inexpression.

What was once the modernist optimism that we might be able to connect the material with the mental, behavior with its expression, architecture with that behavior, and those conjunctions with political and social change, now manifests itself as the suppression or suffocation of behavior, in which the modernist ideal has been twisted to such a degree that *what* was to be expressed is no longer even clear. Venturi and Scott Brown's critique of the Duck is not based on its "dishonesty," but rather on its irrelevance.[38] In other words, the Duck is not meaningless but pointless. The Duck marks the region in which the drive for expressive transparency begins to confront its unacknowledged aporia: a certain kind of opacity that is the condition of any communicability whatsoever. It is as if to say that that suppressed need had resulted in the twisting of architecture's "public face" into a thickened grimace or mask, in which "a certain theatricality [becomes] the sign of an inability to mean, to get our meaning across."[39]

The stakes of VSBI's critique are thus pitched at a very high level here, although that level might seem hard to register from our vantage point forty years later, in an age of media saturation, entailing endless diatribes against the "society of the spectacle" (I return to these issues in more depth in the following chapter). They are asking some crucial questions about architecture *as such* that I want to thematize at this juncture: Will architecture have *any* voice at all at this point in history and in our changing urban environment? What would it mean for architecture not to matter at all in our staking a claim to the world we live in now? How much is too much architecture and design? How little is too little? How can we prevent the *meaning* of architecture from suffocating at the hands of its own ideals (from being locked in)? Or, conversely, how can we prevent its disappearance in the face of and in competition with our media-saturated environment (being locked out)?

If VSBI struggle with the fact that architecture might disappear—as they obviously do in the images of night and day on the Las Vegas Strip, the false-facade architecture and billboards of the generic commercial strip, and their fascination with the "recessive" qualities of their own buildings (their reconstruction of the "ghostly" Ben Franklin House, or their "invisible" Fire House No. 4 come to mind)—it is in order to deal with the fact that architecture might no longer *count* in the conditions of our "overexposed" and "saturated" cities of information and image overload (figures 3.5, 3.6). At that juncture, architecture might be left with nothing relevant to say or do, reduced to making strident and empty gestures. If the disappearance of architecture in America is simply embraced as already accomplished in the writings of Jean Baudrillard, in *Learning from Las Vegas* that possibility is one that must be responded to with all the rigor, imagination, sensitivity, and humor one can muster.

In true modernist fashion, the authors explore how architecture might lose itself as it becomes decoration—what they call "articulation as ornament": the distortion of the whole building into "one big ornament," as in the case of the sculptural Duck. Or simply, how it might become irrelevant in the face of entertainment. (Let us call the latter desire completely separated from need, and no longer "propped" on it.)[40] This modernist affiliation is strikingly brought forth in the image of the "gilded rocaille" stucco decoration in the Amalienburg Pavilion, which is immediately followed by a photograph of the Las Vegas Strip at night (figures 3.7, 3.8). Both images demonstrate how an all-over bas-relief decoration, reflected by mirrors and crystals, like the neon lighting of Las Vegas, "disintegrates space into an amorphous glitter."[41] VSBI are trying to see how far the medium of architecture might absorb those conditions and, in the process, reconfigure the criteria for what architecture is *now*. What is architecture when space is no longer dominant, and no longer enclosed and directed on an urban scale? When issues of program must be more flexible than ever to accommodate the contingencies of the fast-paced information age (thus requiring a reworking of the relationship between form

and function, interior and exterior)? When issues of graphicness, electronics, and signage dominate our urban landscapes and require us to rethink the traditional qualities of form and space in architecture—*and still remain recognizable as architecture?*

If modern architecture had "sunk" the fragility and contingency of its conventions into the depths of a biological or technological determinism, *Learning from Las Vegas* seems determined to *expose* and reconfigure those contingencies. One might say that *Learning from Las Vegas* explores how we permit certain objects to count for us as architecture; it recounts the criteria used to regulate the application of the concept of "architecture."[42] The Duck would seem to mark the point where the drive for expressive "depth" and transparency has pushed so far that it begins to brush up against its own unacknowledged need for resistance and opacity. Precisely because it hasn't been acknowledged, that need has seemingly converted architecture's "public face" into a thickened grimace or mask in response to a constant overexposure and publicity. Gianni Vattimo notes that the utopian dream at the heart of modernism's quest for absolute self-transparency and open communication was "wrecked" by success; that is, it was undermined by the very expansion and proliferation of information and communication.[43] *Learning from Las Vegas* registers disappointment with this very success.[44]

3.8 Fremont Street at night, Learning
from Las Vegas studio, in *Learning
from Las Vegas*; © 1977 Massachusetts
Institute of Technology, by permission
of the MIT Press.

The Duck is a fantasy of the self-qua-architecture caught between an over-exposure that is the distorted counterpart to Benjamin's glass house with its "moral exhibitionism" and a concomitant suffocating privacy. The Duck reaches a pitch of expression that is somehow at an inappropriate level for its environment. Like "a minuet in a discotheque," or a mosh pit in a ballroom, it is either too subtle or too bombastic.[45] Postwar modernism's drive for a certain *kind* of explicitness had, according to Venturi and Scott Brown, resulted in the production of Ducks.[46] But their optimism lies in the possibility that this pitch could be recalibrated. What this condition calls for is not less exposure, in response to that overexposure, but rather more, and of a different kind. The dilemma might be to find the "perfect exteriority that communicates only itself," against an advertising that "is a system of signals that signals itself."[47] This would be a quest for a certain kind of expressiveness that no longer expresses an inner depth or core, but rather that exposes its conditions of mediation in the act of manifesting itself (I pursue this train of thought in depth in the following chapter); that is, an architecture reconfiguring its mode of mediation and encounter as a presentation of what community might mean for us now.

Dead Ducks and the Imagination of Stone

A certain strand of postwar modern architecture had been designing what *Learning from Las Vegas* specifically calls "dead ducks"—a phrase that is repeated in many variations throughout the book.[48] The word "dead" suggests a coldness that recalls a certain kind of response—or, more accurately, a lack of responsiveness—that brings architecture to such a "frozen" region. If we keep to the spirit of the skeptical account I am pursuing here, the designing of dead ducks suggests that "there is a life and death of the world, dependent on what we make of it."[49] In Cavell's analysis of Shakespeare's plays *The Winter's Tale* and *Othello*, he recounts a "tragedy" of skepticism (or better, skepticism *as* tragedy) involved in the avoidance of the other, an inability to acknowledge the other, that is allegorized by the male protagonists in those plays, Leontes and Othello, when they "turn" their female partners, Hermione and Desdemona, into stone (the latter figuratively before literally killing her).

It is the men's coldness that turns the women to stone, and Hermione is figured specifically as a stone *sculpture*.[50] This draining of life is a mark of Leontes's and Othello's inability—or is it rather their unwillingness?—to acknowledge the limitations of knowledge, their respective partners' separateness from them, and thus the seam of their connection to them. What was closer than they could "know" is placed beyond the warmth of human life, love, and liberty. One might call it Leontes's and Othello's interpretation of "metaphysical finitude as an intellectual lack."[51] They avoided the fact that the situation called for acknowledgment on their part.

The coldness that figures the woman as a stone sculpture in these accounts sounds remarkably like the "building-becoming-sculpture" that characterizes the Duck for Venturi and Scott Brown. To repeat, it is our mode of acknowledgment or avoidance of that acknowledgment—a certain category of response—that inflicts the status of duckdom on *any* building whatsoever. The explicitly gendered nature of Cavell's account of the tragedy of skepticism is even more poignant considering Scott Brown's early struggle with the architectural community's disavowal of her, and her contribution in the shared enterprise with Robert Venturi, her partner and husband.[52] It was in fact Denise Scott Brown's modification of her earlier work on the "physiognomic" and "heraldic dimensions" of architecture that resulted in the idea of the Duck and the Decorated Shed, and that came to exemplify their approach to architecture in *Learning from Las Vegas*. I would claim that the Duck and the Decorated Shed figure her critique of the discipline's inability to acknowledge issues of separateness and limitation that are at the heart of any shared enterprise, be it public or private.

It is striking to note that Scott Brown makes an analysis similar to Cavell's in her influential essay "Room at the Top? Sexism and the Star System in Architecture." At one point she uses the metaphor of a "lady . . . carved on the helm of the ship to help sailors cross the ocean" as a figure for the desire for guidance when faced with "unmeasurables."[53] This is clearly meant as an analogy to the "guru" system in architecture, as if to say that taking the "lead" and following the "star(s)" involved turning a woman to sculpture instead of acknowledging the unmeasurability of the difficulties and pleasures of shared life, labor, and "star power." This line in Scott Brown's essay also resonates with a sentence in *The Claim of Reason*: "What I have wished to bring out (in the discussion of Othello and Desdemona) is . . . the way human sexuality is the field in which the fantasy of finitude, of its acceptance and its repetitious overcoming, is worked out."[54] Perhaps we could see the discipline of architecture that Scott Brown was critiquing as avoiding that "finitude." If architecture is involved in issues of acknowledgment of the other, then an *ignoring* of Scott Brown, a response which is not simply an *ignorance* but, more precisely, an avoidance, thrusts aside both her public and private life, one through the other.[55] It denies Venturi and Scott Brown's shared life and work in and as "an exposure of finite singularities."[56] The Duck emblematizes the frozen denial of the state of the other, but together the Duck and the Decorated Shed are entwined as a figure of attempting to overcome other minds skepticism.

Writ large, the Duck enacts a "melodrama of modernism"—at one point in *Learning from Las Vegas*, it is called "an architectural soap opera"—in which the entire building becomes a (sculptural) "ornament" to its own communicative impasse.[57] Venturi and Scott Brown's understanding of the disavowal of ornament and its return as "one big ornament" perhaps finds more of an echo in Gianni Vattimo's understanding of ornament and kitsch than in Clement Greenberg's. To Vattimo, "*Kitsch*, if it exists at all, is not what falls short of rigorous formal criteria and whose inauthentic presentation lacks a strong style. Rather, *Kitsch* is simply that which, in the age of plural ornamentation, still wishes to stand like a monument more lasting than bronze and still lays claim to the stability, definitive character and perfection of 'classic' art."[58] The condition of transparency and its ideals caught up in its own communicative impasse is captured in an image from *Learning from Las Vegas* that equates the Duck with a "minimegastructure," rendered in much the same shape as the duck but drawn with jagged, expressionistic lines (figure 3.9). The equation is meant to imply that the totalizing, self-enclosed, overdesigned 1970s megastructure is the Duck's tautegorical double. The issue of the megastructure and "total design" allegorizes the inability to acknowledge "limitations" and issues of "separateness"—the fact that, in a particular light, (total) design might look like the point where reason has turned its attention to each social detail and personal relation, what Venturi and Scott Brown see as verging on "total control." (See chapter 5 for a further discussion of "total control" in relation to the design of the first edition of *Learning from Las Vegas*.)[59] Is the Decorated Shed, with its "explicit" symbolism and "deadpan" facade, indeed the therapy for "our involuted, architectural expressionism and our mistaken claim to be building outside a formal language"?[60]

3.9 "Equation of the minimegastructure with the Duck," in *Learning from Las Vegas*; © 1977 Massachusetts Institute of Technology, by permission of the MIT Press.

The Decorated Shed and the Melodrama of Inexpression

In contrast to the Duck, the Decorated Shed would seem to enact a certain hyperbolic inexpressiveness—what Cavell terms a "screened unknowingness." He characterizes this "melodrama of unknowingness" as "one of splitting the other, as between outside and inside."[61] Sometimes such divisions are necessary in the straits of what Venturi, drawing on Aldo van Eyck's terminology, calls the "sickness" of spatial continuity.[62] And sometimes the therapy for such ills is drastic. In a different scenario, but drawing on the same logic, Rem Koolhaas suggests the architectural equivalent of a lobotomy, in the form of a radical separation between exterior and interior in the Manhattan skyscraper.[63] This solution indicates not just an attempt to abolish "the dialectic of inside and outside," to use Jameson's phrase, but the acknowledgment and acceptance of distinctions, limits, and separateness that the Duck would disavow. It is as if we needed a good dose of *seduction*—to be separated from ourselves, led outside ourselves—in order to encounter new dimensions of what a "self" as a relation to others might mean.[64] In order to do so, it would seem that distinctions and limitations have to be acknowledged over and over again on a daily basis (which does not necessarily mean endlessly). One might say that the Decorated Shed articulates an architecture of the "secret," a word whose etymology and sense point toward a separation—a condition of "apartness," a necessary opacity—as a way of articulating our "shared" concerns,[65] or, as Deleuze and Guattari define it, "a content that has hidden its form in favor of a simple container."[66] *Learning from Las Vegas*'s "solution" is a simple "shed" for a secret. But it is a shed with no secret literally hidden within it. After all, if the Decorated Shed is exemplary of a *screened* unknowingness, its mode of illuminating that condition is surely through surface and exposure, not depth and interiority.

If we take visibility in Lyotard's sense to mean "an exteriority that discourse can't *interiorize* in signification,"[67] then the food for thought that the "Eat" sign in the Decorated Shed diagrams raise is indigestible. I take it that the speech balloon/large sign in the Decorated Shed diagrams—the sign reading "Eat" that separates the car from the building—is crucial to working out the stakes involved in the issues of separateness, limitation, and distinction that are at the heart of skepticism about other minds (figure 3.10). Although one has to wait until the end of the second part of *Learning from Las Vegas* to encounter speech balloons in their strict cartoon form—in an image from the Learning from Levittown studio (figure 3.11)—they are strikingly evident as literal balloons in the image of the Decorated Shed.[68] In fact, in most versions of the Decorated Shed, the quivering line of the pole carrying the "Eat" sign looks more like a string attached to a balloon than a solid columnar structure supporting an elevated sign (figure 3.2). In a recent book on cartoons, David Carrier has suggested that

3.10 Decorated Shed, in *Learning from Las Vegas*; © 1977 Massachusetts Institute of Technology, by permission of the MIT Press.

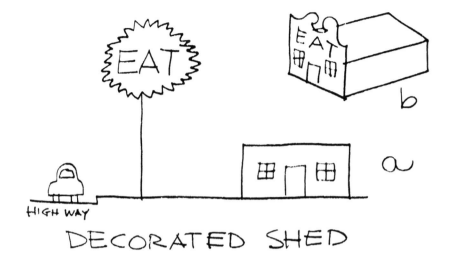

comic book speech balloons attempt to overcome the skepticism of other minds by revealing another (fictional) person's thoughts displayed transparently to the reader "as if" we could literally read (look into) their minds.[69] But one could just as easily argue that sophisticated uses of speech balloons are another manifestation of the skeptical dilemma of other minds, rather than a mere convention for its overcoming.

It is significant that in all the Decorated Shed diagrams, either the speech balloons are literally *untethered* from their "source," the architecture itself, or the sign is conspicuously "applied" to the false facade of the shed; they are placed either slightly in front of or farther away from the shedlike structures. Carrier notes that it is paramount that the "things" or characters in the fictional cartoon scenes never acknowledge the speech balloons *as* speech balloons because that would call attention to the opacity that supposedly makes it difficult to register other minds.[70] But if I am not mistaken, the little pools of ink in the eyelike building windows of an earlier rendition of the Duck and the Decorated Shed look remarkably like tiny pupils looking up at the separation of language from its physical body (figure 3.2).[71] In fact, owing to the dual register of the image above, it actually appears as if the Duck is looking up at the "Eat" sign that the Decorated Shed is also "looking" at.

How far is architecture separated from the words used to articulate itself or, more precisely, from its own voice in those words? Manfredo Tafuri's well-known response to this dilemma in regard to the increasing closure of capital and the capitalist city was to demonstrate a condition of architectural "muteness" on the part of some architects that potentially gave them a critical distance from those capitalist structures, but ultimately resulted in a condition of absolute alienation from the city as such. Fredric Jameson notes that Venturi and Scott Brown's Duck is perhaps a late capitalist version of Tafuri's account of the building's separation and isolation from its environment, now "celebrating its own disconnection as a message in its own right." In the language I am using, it is a monument unable to give voice to its expressions.[72] Venturi and Scott Brown forge another response to this dilemma. In an act of architectural ventriloquism, the "voice" of architecture is separated from its body in the Decorated Shed.[73] But the analogy to ventriloquism is not quite accurate; it is, in fact, a disanalogy. The Decorated Shed is a ventriloquism gone awry, and thus the situation is more akin to a badly synchronized film, as Maurice Merleau-Ponty describes it in *Phenomenology of Perception:* "When a breakdown of sound all at once cuts off the voice from a character who nevertheless goes on gesticulating on the screen, not only does the meaning of his speech suddenly escape me: the spectacle itself is changed. The face which was so recently alive thickens and freezes, and looks nonplussed, while the interruption of the sound invades the screen as a quasi-stupor."[74] In the speech balloons of the Decorated Shed, we get a real sense of how our words, and our voice in them, are achieved through fragile acts of barely achieved *composure.* The Decorated Shed calls attention to this fragility.

In doing so, they imply that the ways we converse and exchange words and ideas about architecture—about anything—might not express or reveal the attitudes and connections that we are willing to give voice to. This is all to say that the speech balloon in the Decorated Shed allegorizes the temptation of language to drive a wedge between us and other minds. But this is not a perspicuous way of putting things. After all, if our words drive a wedge between us, are we, in effect, saying that architecture has been "driven" to that same point, as if we were somehow in the thrall of a natural force that has pushed us outside our common "language games," and thus outside the social? It would be more accurate to say that if our words (on architecture) force a wedge between us, we are responsible for that condition, either because we have done the driving or because we don't have the will to undo it.[75] As Foucault put it, "Man" may be a "vehicle for words which exist before him," but those words "are called back to life by the insistence of his words."[76] Calling architecture back to life might involve seeing how it can remotivate itself within a range of communicative possibilities that are never strictly idiomatic (private and opaque) nor entirely conventional (public, shared, and transparent).[77]

What then does the "Eat" sign signify about our appetite for architecture? Is that appetite mostly for "images," as Fredric Jameson argues in *Postmodernism, or, The Cultural Logic of Late Capitalism*?[78] Or is it our appetite for "signs," "texts," or "theory," as many would argue of *Learning from Las Vegas*?[79] Considering the close connection between our appetite for books and for architecture, we can't help but wonder what kind of reader *Learning from Las Vegas* is trying to attract. Do VSBI want a reader of primitive judgment, either swallowing (good) or spitting out (bad), as Freud would have it? Or would they prefer a bovine reader, a "ruminator," as Nietzsche would say? I take it that they want the latter, considering their critiques of the relationship between interior and exterior, and their consistent demands for "delays in judgment." One thing is certain: the word "eat" is not *merely* a "sign." As Gertrude Stein once remarked: "Americans can and do express everything . . . in words of one syllable made up of two letters or three and at most four."[80] It is hardly surprising, then, that one of the inspirations for *Learning from Las Vegas* was the Los Angeles-based artist Ed Ruscha. His use of monosyllabic words such as "no," "ok," "smash," and "oof" suggests that Americans are somewhat comic, and definitely *primitive*.

I take the coupling of the schematic shed with the "Eat" sign less as an indication of *Learning from Las Vegas* initiating a linguistic turn in architectural theory than as an attempt to explore our primal needs and satisfactions: a taking stock of what we need from architecture, from life, in terms of what we are getting or not getting from it. To make a loose analogy, we might think of the Decorated Shed with its "Eat" sign as an updated version of Thoreau's declaration in *Walden* that "None of the brute creation requires more than Food and Shelter."[81] The first chapter of that book, "Economy," is taken up with a minute rendering of the monetary costs of materials and foodstuffs to provide for the author's nourishment and shelter for eight months. Thoreau's obsession with economics is his way of coming to terms with how "dear" things are to him, his attempt to account for how those sundry things might *count*.

Are we so needy that we can only utter our needs, or register "signs of life," in monosyllabic words? One doesn't have to imagine what Adorno's reply would be: "the bread on which the culture industry feeds humanity, remains the stone of stereotype."[82] But we often mistake stones for bread, and we are liable to break both too soon.

Clearly the word "eat" in the Decorated Shed image is not merely a word. Here we might fruitfully recall the opening passage of Wittgenstein's *Philosophical Investigations*, in which he asks us to conceive of four spoken words—"block," "pillar," "slab," and "beam"—as a complete primitive language. He then queries: "is the call 'Slab!' . . . a sentence or a word?"[83] And if it is a sentence, is it complete, or merely degenerate, elliptical, or truncated? As John Austin points out in *How to Do Things with Words*: "in primitive languages it would not yet be clear, it would not yet be possible to distinguish, which of various things that . . . we might be doing we were in fact doing. For example 'Bull' or 'Thunder' in a primitive language of one-word utterances could be a warning, information, a prediction, etc."[84] Primitive language games are constitutively indeterminate, as Wittgenstein, Austin, and Cavell have shown us.

When confronted with such extreme erasures of context, we must consider some different (primal) scenes for these calls.[85] We might surmise that the people speaking this language are incapable of speaking in sentences, "as though their words, hence their lives, were forever somehow truncated, stunted, confined, contracted"; or we might imagine that these words are spoken calmly in a "deserted landscape," or perhaps in the context of a "noisy environment"—let's say a construction site, or in the "cacophonic context" of Las Vegas, or any media-saturated environment—in which they are uttered not "sluggishly and vacantly, but vigorously, in shouts."[86] In such situations we must, out of necessity, pay close attention to the illocutionary force of the word.[87] As John Austin put it: "Language as such and in its primitive stages is not precise, and it is also not, in our sense, explicit . . . explicitness, in our sense, makes clearer the *force* of the utterances or 'how . . . it is to be taken.'"[88] The deliberate lack of *context* (or explicitness, to use Austin's wording) in which the word "eat" is exposed in the Decorated Shed is a provocation for the reader to acknowledge that it is up to us to locate the shared criteria, our attunement in ordinary words, and thus how the "Eat" sign is to be taken.

Is the word "eat" an imperative: "Eat, damn it!"? Imagine the harsh paternal voice of the culture industry ramming something down our throats. Do we take it willingly? Or is that voice the soft and loving one of a parent figure serving up what Adorno calls "pre-digested pablum" for our childish consumption (two sides of the same coin)? Or is it the muttering of a starving man, woman, or child, who can muster only a single word to express an urgent life-and-death need? Is it the pulsating, loud, shrill, and repetitive voice, "eat, eat, eat" that must scream to be heard in the din of Las Vegas (think of the title of Tom Wolfe's famous essay on Las Vegas, or imagine the chanting accompanying an eating competition)? Or is it the staging of a scene of reorigination in which we are again "in-fans," literally on the verge of language without yet being "in" it?[89] How are we to tell? It is as if we are afflicted with a case of tonal agnosia, in which "the expressive qualities of voices disappear—their tone, their timbre, their feeling, their entire character—while words . . . are perfectly understood."[90] This might be the appropriate time to return to the role of the deadpan in relation to the fantasy of expression and inexpression that takes place through the Duck and the Decorated Shed.

Deadpan and the Absorption of Skepticism

In a brief aside toward the end of the previous chapter, I touched upon Venturi and Scott Brown's interest in the "deadpan" as a technique and disposition to cultivate a responsiveness toward the imminent world that we live in now. I raised this issue in terms of Scott Brown's interest in Freudian models of nonjudgmental attitudes toward the world and other minds in it, such as the analytic technique of "evenly distributed attention."[91] I want to further pursue the concept of the deadpan as it elaborates the fantasy of expression and inexpression aired in the Duck and the Decorated Shed.[92]

Freud's even-handed, nonjudgmental attitude to psychic phenomena, which so inspired Scott Brown, can also be seen in Ed Ruscha's approach to the ordinary environment we live in. In fact, it was this approach that most attracted Scott Brown to Ruscha's work. Ruscha's art books began to appear in 1962, and no doubt inspired Scott Brown's own photographic record of vernacular architecture in Los Angeles while she was a professor at UCLA in the mid-1960s.[93] It is hardly surprising, then, that Ruscha was subsequently invited to VSBI's Learning from Las Vegas studio at Yale (he never came); that the Yale studio group visited Ruscha's studio during their four days in Los Angeles before proceeding to Las Vegas; that two of the photographs of the Las Vegas Strip in *Learning from Las Vegas* are directly inspired by Ruscha's book *Every Building on the Sunset Strip* (1966) (figures 3.12, 3.13); that they hired a helicopter in Las Vegas as Ruscha did to have photographs taken for *Thirtyfour Parking Lots;* that they produced a film called *Deadpan Las Vegas* (or *Three Projector Deadpan*); or that Scott Brown's article "Pop Art, Permissiveness, and Planning" is illustrated with three of Ruscha's photographs: one from *Thirtyfour Parking Lots* (1967), one from *Twentysix Gasoline Stations* (1962), and another from *Some Los Angeles Apartments* (1965) (figure 3.14).[94] For Scott Brown, Ed Ruscha's art books were the primary exemplification of a "deadpan," nonjudgmental approach to the environment.

She remarks: "His *Sunset Strip*, a long accordion fold-out, shows every building on each side of the strip, each carefully numbered but without comment. Deadpan, a scholarly monograph with a silver cover and slip-on box jacket, it could be on the piazzas of Florence, but it suggests a new vision of the very imminent world around us."[95] And in her notes for the Levittown studio at Yale (winter 1970), Scott Brown queries: "What new techniques are required to document new forms? We should aim to dead-pan the material so that it speaks for itself. Ruscha has pioneered this treatment in his monographs (*The Sunset Strip, Some Los Angeles Apartments*). It is a way to avoid being upstaged by our own subject matter."[96] In another reference to Ruscha, she notes, "His *Twentysix Gasoline Stations* are photographed straight: no art except the art that

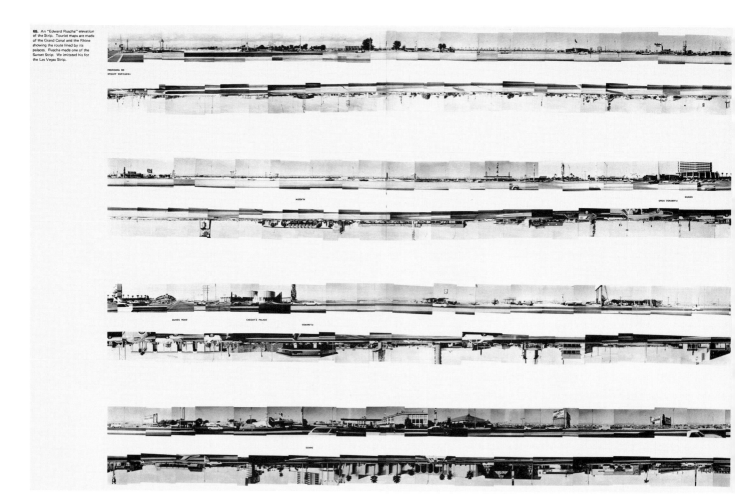

3.12 "An 'Edward Ruscha' elevation of the Strip," by Douglas Southworth, in *Learning from Las Vegas*; © 1972 Massachusetts Institute of Technology, by permission of the MIT Press.

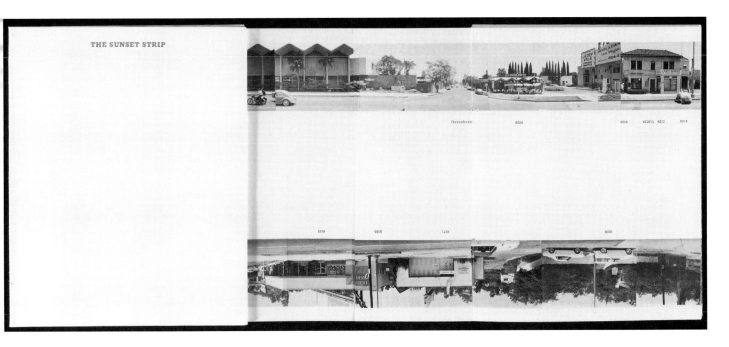

3.13 Ed Ruscha, *Every Building on the Sunset Strip*, 1966, offset lithograph on paper. Collection Walker Art Center, Minneapolis, 1997.

3.14 "Good Year Tires, 6610 Laurel Canyon, North Hollywood," in Ed Ruscha, *Thirtyfour Parking Lots*, 1967, offset lithograph on paper, photograph by Art Alanis. Collection Walker Art Center, Minneapolis, Walker Art Center Library Collection.

hides art."[97] This passage, from her essay "On Pop Art, Permissiveness, and Planning," echoes Ruscha's own claim that what he was after "was no-style or a non-statement with a no-style" that would result in a "collection of 'facts.'"[98] The point is further echoed when Scott Brown contrasts Ruscha's approach with the premature systematizing of some aspects of humanism and high modernism: "Where the facts and intangibles are many, a mystique or system—a philosophy of Man and the Universe or a CIAM grid—may substitute for the collection of facts or hard thought."[99] Later in the essay, she calls architects and urban designers "Johnnies-come-lately" on the scene who "can learn from others," such as Ed Ruscha.[100] Although this passage refers to a specific instance of "learning from" Ruscha, its lesson is better seen as a transcendental one: the first task of the architect and urban planner, she suggests, is a responsiveness that delays judgment in order to heighten sensitivity.[101] As Scott Brown puts it: "we are still outraged if an architect comes out for billboards or if a planner removes the *emotion* from his voice when talking of urban sprawl."[102]

Removing emotion from the voice should recall the issue of tonal agnosia in relation to the "Eat" sign, and alert us to the importance of the deadpan technique for Scott Brown and, ultimately, for the visual and rhetorical strategies in *Learning from Las Vegas*. There is no doubt that Venturi and Scott Brown's "aim to dead-pan the material so that it speaks for itself" contributed to their dissatisfaction with the "interesting Modern styling" of the first edition of *Learning from Las Vegas*—their feeling that the design and designer had upstaged their own subject matter—and their embrace of the newly "stripped" and "clothed" revised edition. (For a detailed account of the design of both the first and second editions, see chapter 5.)

Not surprisingly, it is the issue of "superficiality" that has exposed *Learning from Las Vegas* to the most criticism. Venturi and Scott Brown's interest in issues of image, surface, and flatness has been read reductively, with accusations of an "aesthetics of disappearance" à la Paul Virilio, Baudrillardian accounts of the simulacral condition of the American city, and critiques of postmodern "stage-set architecture" and its collusion with the culture industry.[103] I hope, instead, to try to come to grips with their acknowledgment of what the technique of deadpan flatness might mean in terms of their work.

Deadpan is "literally" defined as a flat or emotionless face, the word "pan" being slang for "face" in nineteenth-century America. It is a mode of rhetorical delivery, used in speeches, public lecturing, and comedy, that is primarily associated with Anglo-American society. As a sociohistorical phenomenon, deadpan has been linked to nineteenth-century American literature, oratory, and popular forms of theater; and it has played a role in facilitating the movement between high and low culture, and in negotiating issues of revelation and concealment within the shifting boundaries of the public and private in frontier

America.[104] If deadpan originated in the work of writers, humorists, and story-tellers, such as Mark Twain, it flourished in popular theater and subsequently in silent film. Its presence continues to resonate in the dry comedy of Bob Newhart, Bill Murray, and Rick Mercer, and in the farce of deadpan: the droning voices and placid faces ubiquitous in television and radio advertising.

The great silent-film actor and comedian Buster Keaton—popularly known as "Old Stone Face"—is probably the most famous and striking example of deadpan humor in action (figure 3.15). All of Keaton's movies feature his trademark deadpan visage that never flinches, no matter what mishap befalls him (figure 3.16). In three different stretches of writing, Cavell directly refers to the logic of Buster Keaton's comedy as one that "absorbs skepticism." As Cavell has posited, "[Keaton's] refinement is to know everything skepticism can think of."[105] He suggests that Keaton's deadpan humor is an ideal attitude in the face of skepticism: a stance toward the world and others in it that is an exemplary tarrying with skepticism that neither succumbs to it nor definitively overcomes it.[106] One might call it a "comic acknowledgment" of the world.[107]

Cavell's account of Keaton centers on his particular countenance and the "Olympian resourcefulness of his body."[108] The lack of emotion in his face and his eternal agility are signs of Keaton's peculiar receptiveness to the world. His gaze allows an evenness or readiness, in which any object might be as good or bad as any other.[109] Keaton, in other words, is ready for the best and worst that the world has to offer. Perhaps we might characterize his receptiveness as Keaton's acknowledgment "that it is not a matter of knowing but accepting the world."[110] This should recall Scott Brown's suggestion, using Ruscha as the primary example, that we might cultivate a sensitivity to the world—heighten our responsiveness to it—by delaying judgment. She reminds us that it is a matter of our attunement or mood toward objects in the world—in her words, "an open-minded and nonjudgmental investigation" of it—that would enable us to do so.[111] We should hardly be surprised, then, to find that Cavell also talks about Keaton in terms of the "philosophical mood of his countenance" and his "human capacity for sight, or for sensuous awareness generally."[112] In other words, mood brings a world—a totality of sense, a totality of facts—into existence.

This brings us back to Heidegger and the issue of mood that I began to discuss in chapter 1. The "mood" of deadpan that Cavell describes suggests that it is precisely the opposite—perhaps separated by a hair's breadth—of what Heidegger calls "The pallid lack of mood of indifference to everything."[113] In *Being and Time*, the mood of indifference is, at various points, described as a "muffling fog," "smooth," and the "gray everyday." These images conjure up an atmosphere in which everything is reduced to the same color, texture, and tone, and in which we are "in" the world, but in it in a literally oppressive way, with no way of voicing that condition. That is to say, we have no way of acknowledging

3.15 Buster Keaton as "Old Stone Face," publicity still.

3.16 Buster Keaton, *The Cameraman*, 1928, publicity still.

how or why we are "engulfed" by the world, yet we seem to withdraw from it, or it from us, such that it looses its hold. One might call it, for lack of a better word, a condition of apathy.

Heidegger specifies, "Indifference, which can go along with busying one-self head over heels, is to be sharply distinguished from equanimity."[114] In another passage in *Being and Time*, Heidegger calls it "undisturbed equanimity."[115] Equanimity is thus characterized by a calm and even-tempered "resoluteness" that has a vision of "the possible situations of the potentiality-of-being-as-a-whole."[116] Much like Cavell's understanding of the deadpan, equanimity is not the opposite of indifference, but rather its modification. Thus indifference is not merely "fallen" or "inauthentic"; it is also the (pre)condition that allows for the possible opening up of being-as-a-whole.

The sense of "resoluteness" and "sober readiness" at the heart of equanimity is intimately related to Heidegger's understanding of what he calls the "*equiprimordial disclosedness* of world."[117] And for Heidegger, disclosure and attunement are closely linked: "*In attunement lies existentially a disclosive submission to world out of which things that matter to us can be encountered.*"[118] What is striking in this sentence is that Heidegger italicizes *every* word, as if each one might matter to us; all bear equal weight of priority and expressiveness. This is, perhaps, the crucial difference between indifference and equanimity: indifference is a matter of not caring enough about anything, and equanimity is the openness to caring about possibly everything in the right mood. Venturi and Scott Brown put it this way: "*Learning from Las Vegas*—and learning from Everything."[119]

In the first chapter I claimed that wonder, unlike the mood of the "gray everyday," is characterized not by "indifference" but rather by the fact that the object does matter, without one's knowing precisely the mode of this mattering. I want to make the claim that the mood of awareness, readiness, and openness to the world exemplified in the deadpan attitude might be the "expression" of that wonder. This claim might strike us as counterintuitive, as we are so used to thinking about wonder in terms of the extremes of expression—perhaps as open-mouthed and wide-eyed awe or shock—that we are less alert to the fact that an expression of wonder might at times register as inexpression. Or to be more accurate, register as an evenly distributed expression—or, in Heidegge-rian terms, as "equanimity."

Wonder would then be continuous with what Heidegger characterizes as allowing things to be "encountered in a circumspect heedful way," which, he continues, "has . . . the character of being affected or moved."[120] Wonder might very well look like a deadpan expression, just as a state of calm and cheerfulness might pervade "authentic anxiety," as indeed it does for Heidegger.[121] Heidegger has a wonderful phrase that seems to capture the idea of wonder as deadpan expression: "resolute raptness."[122] Ruscha makes a similar claim in an interview when he notes that his first book, *Twentysix Gasoline Stations*, had "an inexplicable thing I was looking for, and that was a kind of a 'Huh?'" A few lines later, he notes: "One of them [his books] will kind of almost knock you on your ass."[123] That response seems to be what Scott Brown was looking for in the design of *Learning from Las Vegas*. Jean-Luc Nancy has posed the question: "Can we think of a triviality of sense—a quotidianness, a banality, *not* as the dull opposite of a scintillation, but as the grandeur of the simplicity in which sense exceeds itself?"[124] Perhaps we can.

It is as if the deadpan attitude exemplified by Keaton, Ruscha, and the Decorated Shed refuses to give us the "out" of being too quickly normative in our categorization of good, bad, best, or worst objects or people in the world. This is dramatized by Cavell's point that Keaton appears in his films to be *of a piece* with objects in the world. (Heidegger might say "together with." To be of a piece with objects in the world does not necessarily mean to be at peace with them.) Keaton's "pursuit of happiness" registers as an "ontological equality" between objects and human subjects.[125] In "Pop Art, Permissiveness, and Planning," Scott Brown also notes, in relation to her ideas about delaying judgment in order to heighten sensitivity, that "[a]rchitects and urban designers have been too quickly normative." Here a sentence from Freud's essay "Negation" comes to mind: "Judging is the intellectual action which decides the choice of motor action, which puts an end to the postponement due to thought and which leads over from thinking to acting."[126] In fact, Scott Brown has entitled one section of her and Venturi's most recent book, *Architecture as Signs and Systems in a Mannerist World*, "Think before You Judge."[127]

Although I won't pursue it here, Scott Brown's discussion about delaying judgment, or as she so wonderfully puts it, "judgment with a sigh,"[128] exemplifies what is arguably the most important approach to architectural theory and practice in the last forty years: taking architectural production as a form of research. Take as examples Rem Koolhaas's *Delirious New York*, which he characterizes as a "manifesto with research," or his research-intensive design studios at Harvard, or the Dutch architectural firm MVRDV's projects, such as "Data City," that explore the relationship between the accumulation of information and issues of form. As Stan Allen has described the latter: "MVRDV work to keep the schema open as long as possible, so that it can absorb as much information as possible."[129] If this delay in judgment might heighten our sensitivity to the world, then, as Cavell, Heidegger, Ruscha, and Scott Brown emphasize, that would seem to involve a sense of openness, readiness, equanimity, and, at times, inexpression. How might we relate this to the (re)presentational strategies in *Learning from Las Vegas*?

Of course the issue of flatness is operative throughout the text, with its emphasis on the false-front, billboard-like architecture of Las Vegas, exemplified by the Decorated Shed with the big sign dominating the generic building behind. The signs that read or speak, "I Am a Monument," "Fire Station No. 4," or "Guild House" are the primary instantiation of a deadpan approach—a flat denotation—that would allow the architecture to "speak" in order to avoid upstaging itself. Although I will return to Venturi and Scott Brown's proposal entitled "I Am a Monument" in detail in the next chapter, I would like to make the claim here that the desire not to be upstaged that the deadpan epitomizes is a way of acknowledging that our expressions, our needs, our satisfactions should not be overwhelmed or denied by vehicles of expression that do not satisfy us. It voices a desire to avoid a mode of *theatricality* that might prevent us from getting our meaning across, or to be receptive enough to enable "a submission to the world out of which things that matter to us can be encountered."[130] Deadpan takes the issue of voice, expression, and encounter down a notch, in order to reimagine how and where they might *seam* together differently.

In terms of flatness, we also need to examine Venturi and Scott Brown's built work. One obvious example would be one of Venturi's early buildings, the Vanna Venturi house, built for his mother in 1962 (figure 3.17). The clapboard front and back denoting "home" is merely a flat appliqué that provides a "sandwich" for the middle ground of the interior "lived" space. Or consider the facade of Guild House, which extends beyond the bulk of the shed at the front (figure 3.3).[131] In *Learning from Las Vegas*, not only is Guild House photographed in an extreme close-up that serves to stupefy it beyond all expression, but the flatness is accentuated by the fact that the windows in the second recessed plane are slightly larger than the ones on the front facade, thus counteracting any sense of recession in perspectival depth.[132] What is never noted is that we somehow needed Venturi and Scott Brown to point out these urban phenomena. After all, this kind of decorated shed has been ubiquitous in American culture for decades, in fantasy and reality, not to mention *Learning from Las Vegas*'s tracking of that genealogy back to Egyptian architecture. And the Duck, for that matter, is a phenomenon that was conceptualized, if not theorized, years earlier by Norman Bel Geddes as "Coney Island Architecture."[133]

Venturi and Scott Brown's insistence on the disruption of the smooth workings of the dialectic between interior and exterior in architecture calls attention to the world *as* obtrusive, opaque, and disrupted.[134] If media seems to saturate our environment in a "seamless" way, as we hear endlessly repeated, then Venturi and Scott Brown's operations find the seams, not exactly by seaming it actively, but as if they were allowing the world to reveal its seams to them. They seem to suggest that, with enough patience and resolve on our part, the seams might be rendered visible to us, and thus the world and our desires for the seams that we want might coincide. I see this attitude as informing an intriguing passage in *Walden:* "Look at a meeting-house, or a court-house, or a jail, or a shop, or

a dwelling-house, and say what that thing really is before a true gaze, and they would all go to pieces in your account of them."[135] This passage could easily be read as perpetuating the division between appearance and reality—the desperate "wish to read the reality behind the architectural mask," in the words of Bernard Tschumi[136]—but I would rather see it as something akin to Cavell's claim, in relation to Buster Keaton and Charlie Chaplin, that "No possibility, of fakery, simulation, or hallucination, goes beyond the actualities of their existence," or Ruscha's observation that Los Angeles makes one aware that everything is ephemeral from the right angle.[137] After all, who hasn't had their world unseam itself along the lines out of which they have constructed it?

Although Venturi and Scott Brown do state at times that if we removed those facades there might be nothing left behind them, there *is* something behind them—it may be the wasteland of a beer-can-strewn desert at the limits of

3.18 "The Strip from the desert," Learning from Las Vegas studio, in *Learning from Las Vegas*; © 1977 Massachusetts Institute of Technology, by permission of the MIT Press.

the city, or the comfy interior of Vanna Venturi's house (figure 3.18). As Ruscha writes, sounding a lot like Venturi and Scott Brown, "there's *almost* . . . nothing behind the façades."[138] It is not as if the false facades are "hiding" anything or acting as a screen to prevent us from seeing that there is nothing behind them. We *know* that the inside is different from the outside; it announces that fact in a very straightforward manner. And what would it be like to know all those possibilities and more? It would be, to repeat Cavell's characterization of Buster Keaton, "to know everything that skepticism can think of." Is that refinement somehow beyond the actualities of our existence? Is that possibility only available to us in film? If it is only available in film, why does it always seem that architecture bears the burden of exemplifying living in the face of such a world? I am thinking of the well-known sequence in *Steamboat Bill Jr.*, in which the facade of a house collapses around Buster Keaton, yet he emerges unscathed owing to a well-placed open window (figure 3.19). Or is that a well-placed Keaton? Timing is everything.[139] Only someone with the right attitude, with a knack for the openness, receptivity, and awareness of a Keaton, can prepare you for whatever fate befalls you. If Keaton is dashing, perhaps more importantly he is also undashable.[140]

3.19 Buster Keaton's impeccable timing and undashable attitude, *Steamboat Bill Jr.*, 1924.

The British artist Steve McQueen's short black-and-white video *Deadpan* (1997) draws many of these issues forward (figure 3.20). It is a restaging of that famous scene in *Steamboat Bill Jr.* in which McQueen himself plays the role of Keaton.[141] In the video, in contrast to the film, the facade does not fall once but perpetually, captured from different angles by the camera, as if to say that an acceptance of distinctions and limits is, if not exactly endless, at least an event that we must perpetually risk. To quote Ruscha: "It [the Hollywood sign] might as well fall down. That's more Hollywood—to have it fall down or be removed. But in the end, it's more Hollywood to put it back up, see? [Laughter.]."[142] Or perhaps, it is more (Learning from) Las Vegas?

At this point the "dialectic" between inside and outside is *beside* the point. Mood, after all, comes neither from the "outside" nor from the "inside" but rather from the fact that "knowing is grounded beforehand in a Being already-alongside-the-world."[143] What "befalls" us in such a mood is that architecture would no longer seem to be "grounded" in the traditional metaphorics of building as such, but rather would seem more concerned with our imaginative confrontation with the fragility and depths of surfaces, and the way they are posed, exposed, and deposed.[144]

3.20 Steve McQueen, *Dead-pan*, 16mm black-and-white film, video transfer, silent, 4 min. 30 sec., 1997; © Steve McQueen, by permission of the Marian Goodman Gallery.

Fallen Words Flat Out

In 1972, the year of the first edition of *Learning from Las Vegas*, art historian Leo Steinberg published his book of essays *Other Criteria*. In his section on "The Flatbed Picture Plane," Steinberg argued for a "reorientation" of the picture plane from the vertical to the horizontal, thus marking an epochal shift from a primary reference to "visual experience"—oriented to an upright posture—to that of an "operational process."[145] As Steinberg's title suggests, the postwar picture plane—with Robert Rauschenberg's paintings and combines as the primary examples—now refers to any "[hard] receptor surface on which information may be received, printed, impressed—whether coherently or in confusion."[146] The analogy might be made to any "flat documentary surface that tabulates information": tabletops, architectural plans, studio floors, charts, maps, aerial views, newspapers, or bulletin boards. This might remind us of the charts, maps, plans, schedules, aerial views, postcards, and brochures that were operative in Venturi and Scott Brown's Yale studio, and that appear in *Learning from Las Vegas* as an attempt to capture the sense and sensibility of Las Vegas through a plethora of graphic techniques. Steinberg's claim for Rauschenberg could easily apply to the first edition of *Learning from Las Vegas* with only a slight shift in wording: "Rauschenberg's picture-plane is for the consciousness immersed in the brains of the city."[147] The crucial point of "The Flatbed Picture Plane" is that it is not the actual physical placement of the image that counts, but rather its "psychic address" and its mode of "imaginative confrontation."[148]

These ideas are strikingly pertinent to the astonishing map in *Learning from Las Vegas* labeled "Map of Las Vegas Strip showing every written word seen from the road" (figure 3.21). In this map, all the "tethered" balloon signs from the Strip have become untethered (or have we let them go?) and eventually crash-land, after a heady ascent, across pages 20 and 21 of the first edition.[149] These signs are no longer in their vertical position, facing us "from" the road, as if standing for something; instead, all the words on the Strip seem to have fallen to the ground, too weak to stand on their own or to compete with each other for our attention; or as if the words were straining under their burden to bear meaning, as if they had escaped their upright constraints. Thrown out onto the "public" street.

The question is: Are we looking at a further scrambling of those words or at an attempt to make *sense* of them? How are we supposed to read them? Perhaps the map is a literal enactment of those words returning to the horizontal "refuge" of "our city of words"—the book we are reading—from their vertical exile in what John Dos Passos called the "city of scrambled alphabets."[150] We might stumble or trip over these scattered words. Who knows, maybe Venturi and Scott Brown might want the words there—consciously or unconsciously—

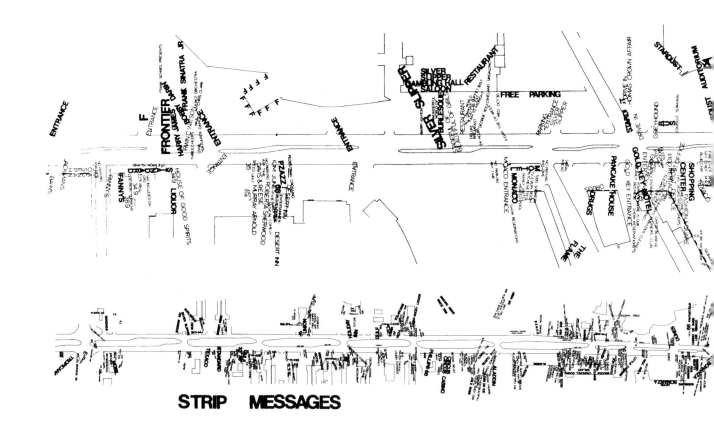

STRIP MESSAGES

3.21 "Map of Las Vegas Strip showing every written word seen from the road," by Ron Filson and Martha Wagner, in *Learning from Las Vegas;* © 1972 Massachusetts Institute of Technology, by permission of the MIT Press.

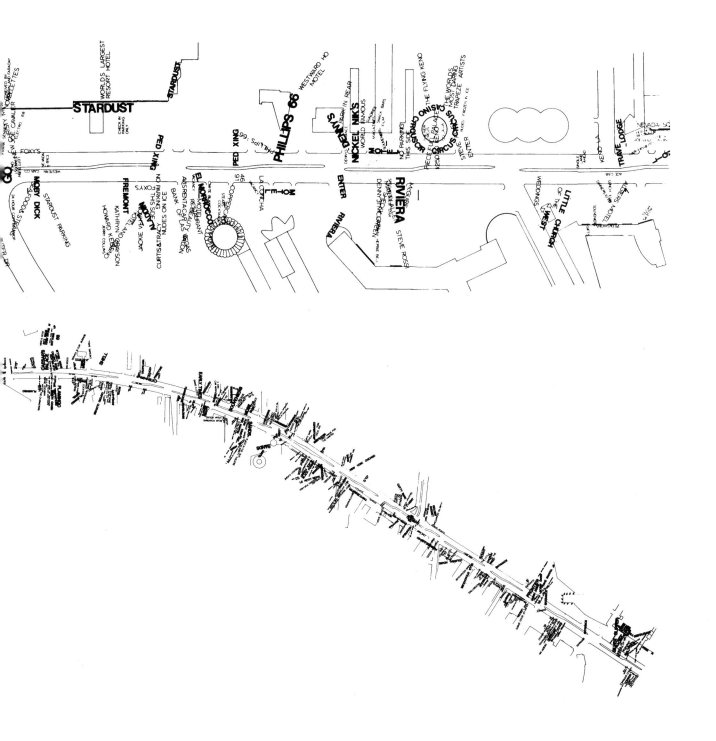

92, 93. Fremont Street Casinos

precisely because we might trip over them. I like to think of Venturi and Scott Brown's "ambivalence" toward them in terms of a particularly revealing "symbolic and compulsive act" from Freud's analysis of the Rat Man: "One day, when his lady was due to go to the country, he [the Rat Man] took a walk, in the course of which his foot knocked against a stone. He kicked the stone out of the way, because, he reflected, his lady might shortly pass along this road, she might come to grief. Twenty minutes or so later, the Rat Man thought what he had done absurd, and he walked over to the stone, picked it up, and replaced it in the middle of the road."[151] Freud speaks here to the condition of these words that are both "fixated" and yet mobile—"on the road."

A more literal example of this stumbling might be Venturi and Scott Brown's Franklin Court restoration on the excavated site of Benjamin Franklin's home in Philadelphia. Excerpts from Franklin's letters and household records describing the house were inscribed in the rough paving stones underneath the bare structural frame of the house, which Venturi and Scott Brown referred to as a "ghost architecture." A fragment from Baudelaire seems to strike the right tone: "Stumbling over words as over cobblestones, colliding now and then with long-dreamed-of verses."[152] It is as if wording the world is also our stumbling block, our collision with "long-dreamed-of verses."[153] Descartes's dream of a philosophical "bedrock" is also uneven when it comes to words—even when just thinking about them: "But it is surprising how prone my mind is to errors. Although I am considering these points within myself silently and without speaking, yet I stumble over words and am almost deceived by ordinary language."[154] After all, as Cavell points out, "the capacities for walking and talking are the same as the capacities for stumbling and stammering."[155]

The language and imagery of stumbling suggest the act of walking rather than the more obvious situation that *Learning from Las Vegas* is predicated on: the city experienced through the mediation of the automobile. I don't deny this for a minute. Within the car we do not have the same point of view on the city, nor do we have the same city as seen on foot. The oscillation between the horizontal and vertical planes enacted through the movement of the car enables the imaginative confrontation between the driver/viewer and the city to occur. For example, think of the strange effects of the car hood, rearview mirror, side mirrors, and the "play" between them, in many of the photographs and films made by the Yale studio participants in Las Vegas (figure 3.22). The condition in the car marks what Deleuze has identified as an overtaking of the "monad" by a "nomadology"; a *shift* from a world closed within a room with imperceptible openings to a "sealed car" on the highway.[156] Significantly, the shift from monad to nomadology is specifically raised in relationship to Tony Smith's famous account of driving on the unfinished New Jersey Turnpike at night. Needless to say, the conditions in Las Vegas are different, and I realize that the visual markers for orientation on

3.22 "Movie sequence traveling north on the Strip from Tropicana Avenue to Sahara Avenue," Learning from Las Vegas studio, in *Learning from Las Vegas*; © 1972 Massachusetts Institute of Technology, by permission of the MIT Press.

the Strip are more prominent than in the situation described by Smith. But contrary to their explicit statements, within the car the underlying harmonic "order" Venturi and Scott Brown want to recover from Las Vegas—all the "grids," "rows," and "points of identity" in what they call the "expansive texture" of the Strip—begins to free itself from such containment. Seated in the car, figure and ground are in movement within this desert city.[157] The tumbling of the words onto the horizontal plane of the map is an acknowledgment that point of view and encounter are unhinged from their strict x,y coordinates. Again, how do we read these signs now?

What is really at stake in these examples is how such "signs" relate to the ground in a groundless world and how that reconfigures our mode of encounter with them. That is to say, it is the ground of the image that is at stake; the point where the sign manifests, and acknowledges, its own exteriority and conditions of sense. Art historian Meyer Schapiro characterizes this situation in terms of the "vehicle and field" in the constitution of image-signs.[158] The "vehicle and field" are the nonsemiotic and material conditions that enable us to make any sense whatsoever—aesthetic, ethical, or political—and that enable an encounter with them to take place. Perhaps this suggests a way to think about signs whose meanings are never given, and certainly never given to a preexisting "us." The "I Am a Monument" proposal in *Learning from Las Vegas* explores these issues with incredible imagination and logic, and we need to consider now what that "blinking sign" might indicate.

4 A MONUMENT FOR EVERYONE AND NO ONE

We don't see the human eye as a receiver. . . . When you see the eye, you see something go out

from it. You see the blink of an eye.

—Wittgenstein, *Remarks on the Philosophy of Psychology*

"I Am a Monument"

One can't avoid the blinking, flashing lights of Las Vegas. They are everywhere: in the streets, in the casinos, in the airports. As one author has described it: "they're all moving—flickering, twitching, blinking; turning on and off; running up and down and across; shooting across space and back again; starting at the bottom, speeding to the top, and exploding."[1] It is within such an environment that Venturi and Scott Brown made their "recommendation for a monument": a blinking sign that exclaims "I Am a Monument" (figure 4.1). This is one of the most striking images in the book, and it is the other major exemplification of the denotative, heraldic, and ordinary Decorated Shed as opposed to the overly expressive, physiognomic, and heroic Duck (figure 3.1). It is referred to twice in Part II of *Learning from Las Vegas*. First, the authors suggest that if Rudolph's Crawford Manor had to be a monument, it would have been preferable to have a "conventional apartment building, lost by the side of the expressway, with a big sign on top blinking, I AM A MONUMENT."[2] They

4.1 "Recommendation for a monument," in *Learning from Las Vegas*; © 1977 Massachusetts Institute of Technology, by permission of the MIT Press.

next recommend that Kallmann, McKinnell, and Knowles's Boston City Hall (1963) might be more apropriate if it were a "conventional loft [that] would accommodate a bureaucracy better, perhaps, with a blinking sign on top saying 'I AM A MONUMENT'" (figure 4.1).[3] There is little doubt that Tom Wolfe had the "recommendation for a monument" in mind when he called VSBI's entire enterprise "Venturi's Big Wink" in *From Bauhaus to Our House*.[4]

Wolfe's characterization reiterates a long intellectual tradition that claims that our thinking is tethered to a moral and cosmotheological compass linking us to the firmament and the starry heavens at the outer reaches of our worldview. Such critiques have their modern *fons et origo* in Kant's famous sentence from the *Critique of Pure Reason*: "Two things fill the mind with ever new and increasing admiration and awe, the more often and steadily we reflect upon them: *the starry heavens above me and the moral law within me*."[5] The transformation of the cosmos into a network of stupid and incessant blinking lights in the modern city is thus symptomatic, for many critics, of the untethering of this cosmotheological order. Venturi's "Big Wink" would be an instantiation and further exemplification of the "stars coming down to earth"—with all its apocalyptic connotations stretching back to the book of Revelation—and our blinking response to this condition seen as a further extension of a reign of stupefaction, facile irony, and the workings of the culture industry. We are most familiar with this critique from Adorno's essay "The Schema of Mass Culture": "The neon sentences which hang over our cities and outshine the natural light of the night with their own are comets presaging the natural disaster of society, its frozen death. Yet they do not come from the sky." He continues, "The information communicated by mass culture constantly winks at us."[6] I am not sure whether the architectural critic Joseph Rykwert was aware of Adorno's words, but his description of how such a "comet" might appear is striking: "*Learning from Las Vegas* was, you might say, the architectural tail of the comet which had Tom Wolfe as its flashing head."[7]

Needless to say, the major example that links blinking eyes, stars, and the demise of moral order into stupefaction is Nietzsche's Last Man, who makes his dramatic appearance in the prologue to *Thus Spoke Zarathustra*: "Alas! The time is coming when man will give birth to no more stars. Alas! The time of the most contemptible man is coming, the man who can no longer despise himself. Behold! I shall show you the *last man*. What is Love? What is Creation? What is Longing? What is a Star? thus asks the last man and blinks. . . . 'We have discovered happiness,' say the Last Men and blink."[8] These passages might lead us to ask: Is Venturi and Scott Brown's ugly, ordinary, and "dumb" (they call it "think little") conventional building with a blinking sign on top reading "I Am a Monument" the architectural equivalent of Nietzsche's Last Man? My claim is that the "recommendation for a monument" provokes such interpretations, but is not to be equated with them. On the contrary, it makes a claim for us to embrace the ethical possibilities of those stars come down to earth, with new constellations of meaning and sense, spacing and displacements to be explored, not yet named and not yet disengaged from the force and intensity of those singular stars.[9] It is an exploration that would require a literal reconsideration of the contemporary city and its luminous, pulsating points of light as the material figure for its multiplicity, in which our condition is, as Venturi and Scott Brown note, "being together and yet separate."[10] George Santayana has captured this thought beautifully: "things which have enough *multiplicity*, as the lights of a city seen across water, have an effect similar to that of the stars."[11] The "I Am a Monument" proposal is an exploration of that thought as simultaneously an aesthetic, social, and political question.

In other words, *Learning from Las Vegas*'s "recommendation for a monument" puts into relief many of the characterizations and critiques of the book, and what it supposedly initiated in historical and theoretical terms. To summarize briefly, the "I Am a Monument" proposal is often seen as the exemplification of *Learning from Las Vegas*'s postmodern irony; its fundamental concern with architecture as representation bordering on spectacle; its initiation of a linguistic turn in architecture, toward theory and the textualization of architecture at the expense of materiality and embodied meaning; and the reduction of architectural meaning to issues of communication and its message-bearing function. In this chapter, I want to engage in a reading that shifts us away from such interpretations, and suggest that it is not so easily categorized, that in fact it puts such interpretations under pressure. The "I Am a Monument" proposal suggests how we might shift our attention and sensibility through its unthought dimensions, which are never simply a lack, but are present in the book *as* unthought.

Architecture Presents Itself

One of Venturi and Scott Brown's major critiques of the Duck was its emphasis on expression over representation, ultimately leading to a distorted "expressionism" in architecture. This seems to suggest that Venturi and Scott Brown embrace representation in architecture (ultimately I will disagree with this suggestion). For example, in talking about the windows of Guild House, they demonstrate that one starts not with a window's "abstract function" of modulating light rays and breezes to serve interior space but with the *image* of a window, "adapted from existing vocabularies that evoke associations from past experience."[12] According to VSBI, this emphasis on convention and acknowledged symbolism promotes an architecture less dramatic, but broader and richer in meaning, than an architecture of dramatic expression. This approach to connotation is contrasted with the Duck, which achieves dramatic expression from the connotative meanings of its original structural elements, derived from their abstract function, which is, in turn, expressed through the physiognomic character of those elements (also see chapter 3). The authors argue that the Duck's "total image" is primarily derived from an implicit symbolism associated with the undecorated physiognomy of the building.

In contrast, the Decorated Shed's image derives from elements that they claim are used in explicitly symbolic ways. So for example, in Venturi and Rauch's Fire Station No. 4 (1965–1967), the "total image"—its specific use and its implied civic character—mobilizes ordinary, banal, and conventional elements such as a standard aluminum sash, roll-up doors, a flagpole in front, and a denotative sign spelling out "Fire Station No. 4," that act as explicit symbols as well as architectural abstractions. Fire Station No. 4 is not "merely ordinary," as they put it, but rather "represent[s] ordinariness symbolically and stylistically."[13] VSBI acknowledge that the modern movement also embraced representation and symbolic content—for example, its love for the "industrial vernacular" of grain elevators, factories, steamships, and locomotives, all of which had an "iconic power" for architects of the modern movement—but modernists tended to disavow these associations in favor of pure, simple forms. VSBI characterize this as "symbolism unadmitted."[14]

In thinking about these issues, Venturi and Scott Brown acknowledge their debt to Colquhoun's essay "Typology and Design Method" (see chapter 3). By extension, they are indebted to the theories Colquhoun draws on in his essay: Gombrich's critique of modern expressionist theory and the physiognomic fallacy, and Claude Lévi-Strauss's writings on primitive kinship systems, which, as he famously noted, have their basis in "arbitrary systems of representation, not the spontaneous development of a *situation of fact*."[15] Based on Lévi-Strauss's work, Colquhoun's essay claims the "need to represent the phenomenal world in such a way that it becomes a coherent and logical system."[16] He then couples this with Gombrich's argument for the "perceptual-psychological necessity for representation in art" due to the fact that there is no expressive content that communicates to us directly without recourse to a particular cultural milieu.[17]

But Venturi and Scott Brown also refer to Colquhoun's insistence that "systems of representation are not altogether independent of the facts of the objective world."[18] This citation suggests that issues of "fact" and "evidence," if taken in the right sense, are deeply relevant to the "I Am a Monument" proposal, and actually trouble the oft-claimed critique that *Learning from Las Vegas* is solely concerned with issues of image and representation. In fact, I am inclined to say that the "I Am a Monument" proposal shifts emphasis from issues of *representation* (or better, image as representation) and *symbol* to the evidence of image as force, or otherwise put, to the presentation of representation.[19]

Although this interpretation may seem contrary to the explicit "intentions" of *Learning from Las Vegas*, there are plenty of indications for such a position in their work. Indeed, Scott Brown's account of Ruscha's deadpan photographs seems to move in this direction. Her claim that Ruscha offers a new vision of the imminent world around us through the collection of facts suggests a fantasy of a *presymbolic* condition. That is to say, Ruscha's work acknowledges the conditions of possibility of breaking and making links within the world of fact, thus rethinking what world we might want here and now, rather than prematurely fulfilling a drive for a "mystique" or "system" that would foreclose an exploration of how those facts make a world.[20] Ruscha's photographs "delay judgment" in order to accumulate facts and thus show how we might find new "worlds" emerging from them. Likewise, Ruscha's dismemberment of the referential meaning of words in his paintings and prints, by boiling, melting, cutting, clamping, setting on fire, and smashing the words, is an exploration of the materiality of the letter as a physical fact. As Roland Barthes put it in his essay "That Old Thing, Art . . .": "What pop art wants is to desymbolize the object, to give it the obtuse and matte stubbornness of a fact. . . . It is no longer the fact which is transformed into an image (which is, strictly speaking, the movement of metaphor, out of which humanity has made poetry for centuries), it is the image which becomes a fact. Pop art thus features a philosophical quality of things, which we may call *facticity*."[21] But we don't have to conclude, as Barthes goes on to do, that this facticity is, in the end, "the Signifier," which pop art reproduces and replicates.

It is perhaps most helpful to consider facticity as Heidegger does. In *Being and Time* and *Ontology—The Hermeneutics of Facticity*, facticity is the "how" of *Dasein*'s being-there; the how opens up the "thereness" of the there in *Dasein*, its condition of self-encounter and self-situating.[22] Facticity differs from factuality in that it is a way of being-in-the-world and not simply an entity in the world (of course factuality is the condition of possibility for any facticity). In this light, the "I Am a Monument" proposal is not simply a "fact" or "evidence" in our everyday understanding of that word; it is not something pregiven, or subsumed into meaning. A fact is not merely an event in the world, but rather the assertion of an event. It is a way of bringing to the fore what has been gathered and making that *evident*.[23] I have always thought that Roland Barthes's characterization of the flat, platitudinous photograph as "at once evidential and exclamative" captures what is at play in the "I Am a Monument" proposal."[24] Thus we might say that, in the right light, the proposal is indeed a "situation of fact"—or perhaps a fact of situating—as it posits, positions, and presents itself, not to situate itself in a *given* environment, nor to represent any predetermined context, but rather to create new architectural situations. "Evidence," Jean-Luc Nancy writes, "refers to what is obvious, what makes sense, and what is striking and, by the same token, opens and gives a chance and an opportunity to meaning. Its truth is something that grips and does not have to correspond to any given criteria."[25] In other words, the "I Am a Monument" proposal is an "evidencing," but there are no *kriteria*—no clear "signs," no distinguishing marks or traits—that would secure its identity for us.[26] As Cavell has written, "The other can present me with no mark or feature on the basis of which I can *settle* my attitude."[27] The "I am a Monument" proposal is arresting precisely because it is never settled; it is always concerned with new evidence, new values, and potentially new responses.

The "recommendation for a monument" explores the work of the image, and thus, how representation works. In many ways, that is dependent on *evidencing* the becoming of an image: how it pulls and cuts itself out from the ground of architecture and then frames itself as image.[29] The rectangular sign saying "I Am a Monument" does not just send out explicit messages; rather, it indicates how it emerges from its own ground, and the fragile lines in the building below gather together to "image" itself. It is as if one side of the shed—with its rough, overlapping corners, and the multiple black marks on its surface planes—had literally "expressed" itself into the more regularized sign above, with its lines meeting at tighter, cleaner corners and the black graphic marks now emerging into a legible graphology. But this is not to argue that the shed below is *not* an image, and purely ground, but rather that the "recommendation for a monument" shows the "doubling operation" in which an image is cut out from the ground of architecture and in framing itself as an image makes the ground disappear as ground.[29]

But how does this claim square with Venturi and Scott Brown's insistence that their Decorated Sheds are "recessive" almost to the point of disappearing into total background? I believe we need to think of the "recommendation for a monument" as a kind of "positive image" of that claim "developing" before our eyes; a situation in which the background becomes foreground. But these kinds of reversals are also in micro-operation throughout the image, and call attention to the *oscillating* relationship between ground and image. For example, notice how the ground or horizon line rendered on either side of the shed extends into it on one side, and on the other is free-floating on the white page. This seems to suggest on the one hand that the building is situated on a firm ground, and simultaneously that there is no fixed delimitation of ground and image, but that that condition is precisely what is being negotiated. This condition is further enhanced by the fact that the free-floating horizon line to the left can be seen as another "force" line that reverberates out from the shed, like the black lines flashing out from the "image-sign" above.

We might say, then, that the "I Am a Monument" proposal explores how a "face" is extruded from "surface"; how a face literally surfaces to the top, and is brought to the fore.[30] The rectangular sign is not only extruded from its tenuous ground; it also cuts itself out and faces us with its (relatively) clear edges and corners framed by the white page. The sign is placed so that it confronts us more directly, rather than raked at the same left angle as the shed. But this is not to say that the face ever disengages totally from the surface, or figure from ground. The traces of ground and surface appear as the energy and force expended in that act of facing or imaging. These traces are registered in the upward thrust of the sign from left to right, the visible undulations of the lines of the sign that never really become a "true" rectangle, and the singularity of the black marks that radiate out from the "sign" and the shed below (notice the two isolated marks below the shed) onto the white page, each with their own particular graphic intensity.

The inspiration for the "recommendation for a monument" might have come from the generalized idea of "roadside commercial architecture," but perhaps it arose more specifically from a small, banal image in an advertising brochure preserved in the VSBA archives at the University of Pennsylvania that reads, "I AM AN ELECTRIC SIGN."[31] This seems to be a way of articulating that what counts is the point where denotation and connotation seem to conflate, or better yet, conflagrate, so that their opposite pulls—one outward and the other inward, one particular and the other general—become the pulsating, blinking sign that is the *force* of the image. The Decorated Shed presents a condition where materiality, language, and image touch upon each other without one grounding the other. This interweaving of the conditions of image making, including its non-mimetic aspects, is crucial to the authors' exploration of the Decorated Shed.

The "I Am a Monument" proposal is, to use Meyer Schapiro's terminology, intimately caught up with the "non-mimetic elements of the image-sign and their role in constituting the sign," and with what Roland Barthes calls the "grain of the voice."[32] These nonmimetic elements are never merely support or background for the "image-sign," nor is the grain simply the tenor of the voice; instead, they permeate the "image-sign" and "voice" through and through. Although the multiple black marks on the surface of the two planes of the shed are supposed to "represent" schematic windows, they are also the indexical marks of mark-making itself. They inflect the building with the same pulsating force as the marks radiating out from the sign. The Sharpie marks *cum* windows also recall a rudimentary notational system that suggests a kind of rhythm of readability that extrudes itself into "legibility" in the words on the sign above. One might say the whole "I Am a Monument" image is "inflected" from the ground up, or all the way down, and not merely in terms of the advertising sign being "directed" toward the street, as the authors argue in *Learning from Las Vegas*. The image ranges from the connotations of inflection that emphasize expressive patterns of stress, intonation, and modulation, to its sense of marking a word to reveal particular grammatical information.

What is important is that the "recommendation for a monument" is continuously ranging across all aspects of this inflection without ever completely occupying one pole or the other. For example, the words "I Am a Monument" are never entirely cleaved apart from their status as graphic marks: one might see the reverberating black marks around the sign as an indication of those words returning to their status as illegible markings, as if the force and sense of matter are always in excess of signification. Billboard signs are, in many ways, exemplary of this condition, and we might say they are an amalgam of the facticity of pop art coupled with op art's emphasis on sensorial intensity and impact (as we well know, advertising is meant to maximize appeal and minimize information).[33] The two small, seemingly useless and irrelevant black marks below each side of the shed in the "I Am a Monument" image are the most striking "indications" of this excess. They recall Benjamin's comment that advertisements' power lies not in what the neon sign says, but in the "fiery pool reflecting it in the asphalt."[34] The "recommendation for a monument" is not just a schematic reduction or representation of some fuller, more sensory example out "there," but rather a fully sensuous entity in its own right.

VSBI also derived other important lessons from billboard advertising. The Tanya billboard image is a powerful critique of widespread claims about the "seamlessness of the media" in our contemporary society, that is, the criticism that we are saturated with media and advertising, from which there is no outside perspective. *Learning from Las Vegas* leads us back to our ordinary lives, in which such a condition hardly ever holds. The authors often call attention to the scaffolding, seams, and framing conditions that are within the image yet call out the necessity for us to seam them together differently. For example, in the Tanya billboard we can see the crisscrossed scaffolding that extends up from tufts of vegetation and sand in the desert to "support" the billboard sign above (figure 2.9). This scaffolding, however, does not extend directly up to support the billboard sign, but connects to an intermediary zone of an entablature-like support, consisting of thin horizontal boards, also seamed vertically, with the name of the billboard company, Donley, prominently located in the center.

The scaffolding does not primarily emphasize that architecture is now the mere support for the dominant sign above. The billboard sign calls attention to the fact that the work of the image is always under construction, and that its framing conditions are within the scene of representation. The vertical seams of the billboard sign are visible in all photographs in the book, and their orientation and rhythm work both with and against the horizontal flow of the reclining Tanya and the exaggerated horizontality of the text. Further, the left-hand side of the sign literally cuts off part of the forearms and part of the face of the Tanya figure, so that only *one eye* looks out at us, thus calling attention to the act of framing and cutting out as such.[35] If the Tanya image demonstrates that seaming is always at play in so-called seamless images, then the question becomes, What is the rhythm and nature of that seaming? In the "I Am a Monument" image, that seaming is intimately related to the particular rhythm of its "blinking" eye.

Visibility, Legibility, Exscription, and the Eye of Architecture

It is worth repeating that the sign saying, "I Am a Monument" resembles both a flashing neon sign *and* a blinking eye. The radiating black marks around the "high reader" suggest both flashing neon lights and the cartoon-like indication of the force lines/lashes of a blinking eye. The "recommendation for a monument" thus further explores the issues of skepticism about other minds raised in the Duck and the Decorated Shed, which similarly addressed the topic of architecture facing itself through an emphasis on the "eyes."

However, in the "I Am a Monument" proposal the stakes have been ratcheted up a notch, so that it seems even more appropriate to say of it that it is a "mood of nothing but eyes" or that it is a "thing with senses, mostly eyes."[36]

This is simply to reiterate that architecture is one of the privileged sites that reveal the two overlapping yet asymmetrical aspects of the threat of skepticism: external-world skepticism (material) and skepticism about other minds (mental). Accordingly, the "recommendation for a monument" both presents itself as a monument that puts forth a particular world in a compressed way *and* introduces itself—one might say makes a gesture toward us—with the expectation of some kind of response. It seems to push the exemplarity of this overlapping to the breaking point, where it would be a case not just of a "thing with senses, mostly eyes," but rather one solipsistic, disembodied eye removed from materiality, life, or grounding in the world of sense, as if the "eye" of Tanya had been isolated, enlarged, and schematized. But the "recommendation for a monument" does not have to *look* that way.

The first thing we should notice is that the words "I Am a Monument" are not exactly written "in" the eye of the billboard but right *at* its outermost surface. The letter "T" in the word "Monument" extends toward, touches, and overlaps the vertical line of the rectangle as if it were level with it, or even slightly in front of it. The words do not come up from the depth of that "eye," nor does the eye give them any further depth than they might have at its surface. Legibility is not grounded in visibility, nor is visibility grounded in legibility. Rather, they traverse and mutually define each other on that surface. One might say that they meet "at" their very (de)limitation. The "I Am a Monument" proposal evidences the fact that vision and legibility are woven into each other, and into architecture, in a way that does not close off meaning or stabilize it, but rather opens up the possibility *for* meaning. The concept of "graphicness" so much at issue in *Learning from Las Vegas* is meant to suggest that point where writing is not merely looked at but "pulsated," as if vision were in it; it also suggests the point where visibility is punctuated, not primarily in grammatical terms, but as a scintillation of points. In the words of Venturi and Scott Brown, the Las Vegas Strip signs are not forms reflected "in" light; rather the signs themselves are often the source, and they glitter rather than glow.[37] In many ways, the "reciprocal supplementation" of legibility and visibility in the "recommendation for a monument" is the fragile counterpart to the "symbolic" CBS logo of an eye plastered over the Duck that figures so prominently in Part I of *Learning from Las Vegas*, in which text and image, visibility and legibility, are isomorphic rather than supplemental.[38]

But to say there is a point of contact between visibility and legibility is not to suggest the fixing of architectural meaning. Although the "I Am a Monument" sign boldly announces its status, and thus appears self-assured to its depths like a traditional monument, it is in fact quite vulnerable. The words are literally exposed on or at the surface of the "blinking" eye rather than being *inscribed* in it, as if set in stone. According to VSBI, the statements of today will come from media that are, as they say, "less static."[39] But we should read this in the skeptical sense as well: it is not just a change in physical "medium" that is required, a shift from heroic statements in pure architecture to the mixed media of the Strip, but also a change in the pitch of our response, so that we might rethink how our approach to architecture is involved in immobilizing its possibilities, and thus encouraging the production of "dead ducks," or alternatively how our attitude might unleash new possibilities. Here the emphasis on plasticity demands a suppleness of response. In other words, the "I Am a Monument" proposal fosters the conditions of a possible *encounter*, rather than just a bold declaration of self-identity. It is not fundamentally a "sign" that we are supposed to look at, nor a "screen" on which we might project our fantasies, but rather a rhythm of opening and closing—that is to say, a "blinking"—that we are meant to engage with and respond to.

Thus expression is not avoided in the deadpan "recommendation for a monument," it is simply reconfigured. Plasticity is now concerned with how issues of image, language, and architecture form themselves in relation to each other and the world, rather than directing us toward physiognomic depth, interiority, and signification.[40] The explicit and denotative sign spelling out "I Am a Monument" is, of course, "self-referential"—a traditionally modernist notion of the "sign"—but its essential thrust is a mode of self-referral that calls attention to how its mode of expression is concerned with the way the eye is in contact with the outside. The eye does not simply see, it looks; and we respond to that looking. As Wittgenstein has expressed this thought, "We don't see the eye as a receiver. . . . When you see the eye, you see something go out from it. You see the blink of an eye."[41] In this regard, and practically all others, the "I Am a Monument" proposal is exactly the opposite of Wolfe's characterization of it as a "Big Wink," which suggests a closing of the eye and, in its superficial understanding of irony, a stress on its indirect, all-knowing, and fundamentally privative status. When the eye blinks it encounters and opens up onto the world in a rhythmic patterning of connecting and disconnecting, opening and closing, surfacing and receding.[42]

The interweaving of visibility and legibility "draws" the eye outside itself, and this "drawing out" is literally accomplished through the rich, black lines that render the "I Am a Monument" as if it were an epiphany emerging from the white page. The "recommendation for a monument" is hand-drawn with Venturi's favorite instrument, the Sharpie. We get a literal sense of his touch, how the black lines are darker and fuller in some spots and more grainy, porous, and sketchy in others, depending on the rhythm of tactile pressure. There is nary a straight line to be seen throughout the image, nor do the lines of the shed ever meet at clean corners. It is a deliberately *sketchy* proposal that is meant to exist cheek by jowl with its bold claims for itself, as if to testify that the kinds of connections we want to make in architecture are held together only by our willingness to give "voice" to our expressions. And we should emphasize that the materiality of the "sign"—the high reader that says "I Am a Monument"—is formed from the same matter and medium as the supposedly meaning-bearing function of the "conventional shed" that "supports" the blinking sign on top.

But *Learning from Las Vegas*'s acknowledgment of the "graphic" nature of architecture in the mediated city is not just a way of talking about the relationship of text to image. It also brings other "senses" into the configuration of what architecture is and can be. For example, the first-person, declarative speech act that states "I Am a Monument" not only denotes a sense of "voice" through its words, it also connotes it through its expressive line. It suggests that we "image" those words not only by writing, but also by speaking them. Thus, the sign evokes a mouth opening and closing as it voices the words in a particular intonation and pitch. The Duck and the Decorated Shed had eyes and noses but no mouth, whereas in the "recommendation for a monument" there is a mouth that enunciates its vision, and an eye that gives vision to that voicing. The sign's blinking is precisely the oscillation between mouth and eye that surfaces a face for us to encounter.[43] And because we get a better sense of the "force" of this utterance as compared to the "Eat" sign in the Decorated Shed, it prompts us to respond to its call in a more direct way, but one that still involves *hearing* what it is voicing. This voice calls into play the sense of hearing in general and makes us aware—as part of its echo and reverberation—that we need to be more attentive to hearing our own voices in order to give voice to what we want to claim for architecture (more on this below). The Learning from Las Vegas studio was deeply interested in issues of sound and hearing, and tried to express their qualities through the media of writing, typography, graphic design, color, film, and scale.

My calling attention to issues of the five senses—seeing, hearing, touching, tasting, and smelling (the latter two in the previous chapter)—and their articulations through different media is meant to suggest that the "I Am a Monument" proposal literally draws out a new sense of what *making sense* entails in architecture. It demonstrates that each new definition of an art or practice necessitates coming to terms with how it touches on all the other arts and, in that touching, enacts a new redistribution and partition of sense *for* that particular practice.[44] That is, architecture always reconfigures what a medium is *within* architecture; how a new medium is discovered or invented *out* of itself.[45] If a new medium is to be found for architecture, this can happen only in a concomitant redefinition of what architecture is and what it has been, which is simply to say that issues of medium are both ontological and historical in nature. Questioning that history and ontology is what the "recommendation for a monument" does. And this depends, as I have attempted to show, on how aspects of language, matter, and medium negotiate new configurations and relations among themselves.

Jean-Luc Nancy's word "exscription" seems to strike the right tone for this reconfiguration.[46] The act of exscribing suggests the point of contact and disruption between impenetrable matter and bodily sense, and between bodily sense and linguistic signification.[47] That is, it demonstrates how matter and medium touch on one another and mark new contours of sense. The "I Am a Monument" proposal is a way of thinking about how exscription makes sense: where the tip of a Sharpie touches a flat piece of paper and, in the process, simultaneously separates and links body, instrument, vision, and writing; or the point of contact and disruption between eye and eyelids in "blinking"; or the electrical currents in neon signs that require a mode of connection and disconnection that enables it to "blink" on and off; or two lips coming together and separating as they say "I Am a Monument"; or even the moment when inscription exscribes itself in the very writing of "I Am a Monument," thus dislocating writing from itself (not to mention its "body") and from any "fixed" idea of the "monument." But the tendency has always been to take that evidencing of exscription in *Learning from Las Vegas* as an accomplishment, or a deliberate cleaving apart of body, matter, and language, rather than as an exploration of how one might make sense in architecture. This making sense— which is always a placing into relation—leads us to the question of what kind of community *Learning from Las Vegas* is proposing in the "recommendation for a monument."

The Arrogation of Voice, or Looking through Each Other's I/Eyes

The "recommendation for a monument" is deeply involved with changing attitudes toward the monument and monumentality that were in full force among theorists in the 1960s and 1970s. I am not interested in the generalities of this critique, which can be culled from other sources, but rather the particularities of how *Learning from Las Vegas* engages the relationship between the individual and society that the traditional monument is supposed to symbolically represent. What I want to flesh out in this section, carrying on from the work in the previous two, is the phatic rather than semantic dimensions of the "I Am a Monument" proposal: how it is primarily engaged in bringing about conditions of relationality, communicability, and community rather than communicating meaning through signs.

Simply put, the "recommendation for a monument" makes what Cavell has termed a "claim for community."[48] Claims are based on criteria that we either agree on or not, and on the basis of this judgment they determine our ordinary ability to say what anything is or could be. A claim is inherently fragile and is no stronger than our agreement to go on with the ordinary criteria we are willing to speak for in making those claims. In Cavell's words, "the search for our criteria on the basis of which we say what we say, are claims to community. And the claim to community is always a search for the basis upon which it can or has been established. I have nothing more to go on than my conviction, my sense that I make sense."[49] Community is as fragile or strong as the claims made for it, and therefore it does not presuppose any given basis for connection; rather, we enact the conditions of possibility for its formation and continuation. Skepticism is the denial of those ordinary criteria, the always-present temptation to *strip* us of our "attunement in criteria," rendering us unable to make sense to ourselves or each other (also see chapter 5).

Learning from Las Vegas makes a very strong case against the ethical and practical relevance of any kind of "unary" monument—one without disturbance, without singularity, without any trace of the supplemental—that would close it off and render it self-sufficient.[50] The book is interested in exploring a community that does not substantialize itself into a false cohesiveness or organic unity. As the authors state, "our money and skill do not go into the traditional monumentality that expressed cohesion of the community through big-scale, unified, symbolic, architectural elements."[51] The primary example of the unary monument in *Learning from Las Vegas* is the minimegastructure. The latter's emphasis on the "easy whole," the expressionism of its formal properties, and its emphasis on total design are contrasted with the difficult whole of the Decorated Shed and urban sprawl—the incremental spread of the city that "grows through the decisions of many"—in their concern for image and conventional symbolism.[52] Not surprisingly, the minimegastructure is equated with the Duck in *Learning from Las Vegas* (figure 3.9). VSBI's comparison of Moshe Safdie's Habitat, built for Expo '67 in Montréal, with a residential strip recalls their comparison between Crawford Manor and Guild House. As in those comparisons, the "total design" of the minimegastructure is equated with "total control," a condition in which issues of limitation, separateness, and singularity are avoided or disavowed.

In a revealing statement, *Learning from Las Vegas* suggests that now the "occasional communal space . . . is a space for crowds of anonymous individuals without explicit connections with each other," and these spaces—such as a Las Vegas casino or a big-city subway system—combine "being together and yet separate."[53] VSBI note that, because of lighting effects, the atmosphere of such places is akin to being in "the twinkling lights of the city at night" rather than in a "bounded piazza."[54] I want to claim here that this "being together and yet separate," like the "twinkling lights of the city," is a profound reconsideration of the multiplicity of the contemporary city, with an attention to how every*one* is "in-common" without subsuming the one into any given community. In his book *La ville au loin* (1999), Nancy talks about the exteriority of relations of singular individuals in the city who brush by each other in the Métro or on an escalator or pass each other in cars, and where the "in-common of the city has no identity other than the space in which the citizens cross each other's paths, and . . . has no unity other than the exteriority of their relations."[55] Like the starry skies come down to earth, the city is extended *partes extra partes* in a condition of pulsating and dispersed singularities.[56]

The "recommendation for a monument" is an attempt to proclaim such a community's conditions of possibility. Simply put, it articulates the need to "voice" our claim to community, and that proposal is its literal "proclamation." As I argued earlier, this claim has to be voiced by each and every *one* of us—by each and every one *as* an "us"—because the criteria for community are "ours"; they come from "us," and thus, as Cavell points out, the only source of confirmation is ourselves, and we are all individually answerable "not merely to it, but for it."[57] This claim to community requires what Cavell terms an "arrogation of voice."[58] It suggests that each of us as a singularity is "representative" of what being in common is, and a condition of that singularity is to speak for being in-common with no more boldness or fragility than the depths of our exposure to each other. The arrogation of voice recognizes the fact that "we live lives simultaneously of absolute separateness and endless commonness."[59] I would suggest that Cavell's understanding of the "arrogation of voice" might be brought into relation with what Nancy calls the "seizure of speech," which for him marks "the emergence or passage of some *one* and every *one* into the enchainment of sense effects."[60] This connection would help us to further link the aesthetic and bodily dimensions of sense in the "I Am a Monument" proposal, which I outlined in the previous section, to the political and social dimensions of sense that are attested to in Nancy's work and in Cavell's statement that a claim to community has nothing more to go on than "my sense that I make sense."[61]

This arrogation of the voice is precisely what the words "I Am a Monument" enact. Saying "I Am a Monument" is the arrogation of speaking for community as such, evoking the conditions of possibility for such a community. These words, which we might call a speech act, do not refer to something; instead, they bring something about. The "recommendation for a monument" is referring not to any monument "out there," but rather to its own invocation of that community that it literally "pro-claims." For the "I" in the "I Am a Monument" is not a fixed or stable "I," but rather a personal pronoun operating as a "shifter," which can be understood only by reference to the context in which it is uttered. It is the capacity of the pronoun "I" to substitute for everyone, so that what each "I" shares is his or her own unsubstitutable singularity.[62] That is, we are meant to participate in the arrogation of voice by saying "I Am a

Monument," thus voicing our claim to speak for being in-common. And likewise for the next some*one* who will say "I . . . ". Thus, the "recommendation for a monument" suggests a condition in which each and every *one,* all "I's," might have access to what Nancy has called a "concatenation of acts of speech" that is "infinitely interrupted and retied."[63] It is a chain of singularities that is only as strong as the willingness to participate in the seizure of speech that it proclaims. The "recommendation for a monument" calls for a response: "I am a monument too," or alternatively, "I am not a monument, and neither are you." We can enter into its claim, or disclaim it if we disagree, but in both cases we are still giving our voice in the matter. The "I Am a Monument" proposal evidences a "placing-into-relation," and doesn't simply provide a "space" or "representation" of that condition. It articulates the kind of plasticity that *Learning from Las Vegas* at its most ambitious moments argues for: a mode of response that exposes the fragility of our claims to what architecture is and can be without suggesting that those claims are "superficial" or "arbitrary"—instead, they are deeply binding, and yet always open to reconfiguration. *Learning from Las Vegas*'s emphasis on receptivity and response in conjunction with the boldness of its proclamations—its arrogation of voice and its willingness to withhold that voice at times—is the best indication of its engagement with the condition of skepticism, and the authors' desire to give voice to their claims for architecture.

One might even see the "recommendation for a monument" as claiming that an ideal society might entail the fantasy, as Thoreau proposed, of being able "to look through each other's eyes for an instant."[64] This fantasy entails looking out, not in, and requires our willingness to think further about the rhythm of blinking eyes, what they are signs for, and how we should respond to them.

Blinking Signs and the Last Man

If the eruption of blinking, flashing lights in Las Vegas is, for many, the counterpart of the Last Man's blinking eye, then how does *Learning from Las Vegas* acknowledge the world out there, and respond to the vacant bliss captured in the eyes of those men who have discovered happiness and who "love the world"? Descartes found a way to avoid all sensory deception: "I will now shut my eyes, stop my ears, withdraw all my senses."[65] This strategy did not work for the psychotic Daniel Schreber, who had quite a different understanding of what he, like Descartes, called "seeing with the mind's eye": "I see such events even with my eyes closed and where sound is concerned would hear them as in the case of the 'voices,' even if it were possible to seal my ears hermetically against all other sounds."[66] And remember that Descartes could still stumble over ordinary words by just thinking about them. We can always close our eyes and try to make our dissatisfaction and doubt go away, but in the process we are avoiding the world we actually live in. In the words of Denise Scott Brown: "if activities which appear to be 'dysfunctional' continue to exist, they must obviously be functional for someone, ergo closing one's eyes and ordering them to go away won't remove them."[67] And there is a further risk in doing so: in shutting our eyes, we close ourselves off from the dilemma of skepticism that marks our enchantment and disenchantment with the world.

Eyes shut. Eyes open. Both extremes are untenable. Think of the game children play of staring into each other's eyes until one "gives in" and blinks.[68] In this contest the blinking—the brief closing of the eye—is an acknowledgment of defeat. But do we really know who is the winner and who the loser in this game? After all, isn't the ability to keep one's eyes open at all times monstrous? Think of the opening of Stanley Kubrick's *A Clockwork Orange,* in which Alex de Large stares out at us with his unblinking eye, a fact accentuated by his false eyelash (figure 4.2). What can one make of the fact that the blinking sign "I Am a Monument" shares a striking family resemblance with Alex's exaggerated open eye?

Blinking is not an *open* or *shut* case. It is the tone or rhythm of the "blinking" that counts. I take this rhythm to be encapsulated in the many alternations of night and day images that are ubiquitous in *Learning from Las Vegas* (figures 3.5, 3.6). It is the sequence of night and day, the extraordinary possibilities latent in our "daily" lives, that marks out the contours of our commitment to engage with these possibilities. One might say that this diurnality, the everyday world we live in, is something to be achieved over and over again. Its literary correlate would sound something like T. S. Eliot's words from "Fragment of an Agon": "And the morning / And the evening / And noontide / And night / Morning / Evening / Noontime / Night."[69] That is all.

Venturi and Scott Brown seem to be arguing that we need to be responsive to our environment, which requires repeated acts of looking and acknowledging. Thus we should read the "I Am a Monument" proposal as blinking and not as an ironic winking. And at times we need to see this blinking, as Cavell wrote, "as a wince, and connect the wince with something in the world that there is to be winced at."[70] Or at times we might follow the lead of Ralph Waldo Emerson: "When I converse with a profound mind . . . or . . . have good thoughts, I do not at once arrive at satisfactions, as when, being thirsty, I drink water . . . ; no! but I am at first apprised of my vicinity to a new and excellent region of life. By persisting to read or to think, this region gives further sign of itself, as it were in flashes of light."[71] These flashes of light are not simply "signs" that convey information, but rather indications of possible ways, paths, invitations, even seductions. Venturi and Scott Brown do not sit on the fence: they take the pulse of the rhythm of the skeptical dilemma that does not call for easy solutions, despair, unadulterated ecstasy, or nihilistic pessimism. The rhythm is interesting

4.2 Malcolm McDowell as Alex de Large, *A Clockwork Orange*, dir. Stanley Kubrick, 1971.

enough. What I find *ethically* seductive in *Learning from Las Vegas* is the emphasis on how we acknowledge or refuse to acknowledge our responsiveness, and hence our responsibility, to the actual environment we live in now and to the eventual one that will emerge from it.

To paraphrase Vincent Scully's introduction to *Complexity and Contradiction*, which could be an even more appropriate introduction to *Learning from Las Vegas*: "This is not an easy book, and is not for those who, lest they offend them, pluck out their eyes."[72] This intriguing sentence suggests not only a reader plucking out his or her own eyes—an avoidance of the book's particular vision—but also how visibility—and for that matter a *theory*—can be "plucked" out of a text. This suggests, however, that whatever "vision" is expressed in *Learning from Las Vegas* is woven into the materiality of that book. Here we can't avoid the realization that the rhythm of blinking that the authors are after is inseparable from how the book *looks*, and thus the way it *blinks*. And that is inseparable from how a page of *Learning from Las Vegas* might look to us, and how our palpitation of its vision is enacted by the rhythm of our turning the pages as they lift, separate, and fold back down to contact one another . . . again.

5 REDUCKS, 1972, 1977

One text finds itself, is found . . . in the other. . . . Does that mean, then, that there is no difference between the two texts? Yes, of course, many and many a difference. But their coimplication is more contorted than one might believe.

—Derrida, *The Postcard*

"Stripped and Newly Clothed"

Most readers know *Learning from Las Vegas* only as a diminutive paperback book published by the MIT Press in 1977. The paperback edition's appearance—its pale blue cover as a background for the Tanya billboard image, its title in bold uppercase Baskerville with the much smaller words "Revised Edition" centered beneath it, and beneath that, the names of the three authors—is anything but monumental (figure 2.6). But the modesty of the cover belies the success of the paperback edition, which has sold over 80,000 copies, been reprinted many times, and been translated into some dozen languages. Indeed, there is every indication that this book will continue to be read by architectural students, architects, professors, and lay readers throughout the world for generations to come. The revised paperback edition did not merely replace the first edition of *Learning from Las Vegas,* published five years earlier by the same press; for all practical purposes, it erased the memory of it (figure 2.5). In this chapter, I want to revive the memory of the first edition, and in doing so, try to understand the relationship between it and the edition that replaced it.

At issue will be the conflict over Muriel Cooper's design of the first edition of the book, Denise Scott Brown's subsequent design of the revised edition, and the words and phrases mobilized by Venturi and Scott Brown to describe the relationship between the two editions.[1] That language, particularly the phrase "stripped and newly clothed," will be closely attended to, as it raises questions about the relationships between inner and outer, acknowledgment and avoidance, violence and the text, that intimately link issues of skepticism with the conflict over the design of *Learning from Las Vegas.* As we shall see in more "graphic" detail than in previous chapters, the tone of these writers and designers is inseparable from what a page of their book might look like.[2]

The first line of the preface to the revised edition begins innocently enough: "This new edition of *Learning from Las Vegas* arose from the displeasure expressed by students and others at the price of the original version."[3] If this new edition arose from displeasure, the authors immediately relate it to issues of audience, price, and distribution. In "response" to that displeasure, and the prohibitive cost of reprinting the first edition, Venturi and Scott Brown decided to "abridge the book to bring its ideas within reach of those who would like to read it."[4] According to Scott Brown, the "opportunity" to rework the book also enabled them to "focus our arguments more clearly and to add a little, so the new edition, although abridged, stands on its own and goes *beyond* its progenitor."[5] Thus, the revised edition of *Learning from Las Vegas* is not merely an "abridgment" but also, as she put it, an "augmentation." Of the significant changes that were made, some are acknowledged forthrightly in the preface and back cover of the revised edition, and some, more interestingly, are glossed over in Scott Brown's foregrounding of economic priorities. The changes in layout and design are worth noting in some detail, as they form the basis for much of what follows.

What is immediately noticeable is the radically different format of the revised edition, which reduced the large hardback first edition from an imposing 10½ x 14 inches to the much smaller, conventional paperback dimension of 6 x 9 inches.[6] Other changes include the following: the deletion of Part III of the book on the architectural work of the firm Venturi and Rauch since 1966; the addition of a bibliography;[7] the shifting of the studio notes from the margins parallel to the body of the text in Part I, to a separate section following it; the reduction of the number of images by two-thirds, from 452 to 151 in the revised edition, including the omission of all 182 color photographs in favor of halftones and line drawings;[8] the grouping of all the images in signatures, separate from the body of the text, rather than integrated, as they had been in the first edition; a change in font from sans serif Univers to serif Baskerville, with the formerly extreme leading—the generous spacing between lines of text, particularly in Parts I and II—reduced to more standard spacing, and the text block justified rather than ragged right;[9] the use of only one column of text in Parts I and II in the revised edition, instead of the progression in the first edition from single-column text in Part I to double-column text in Part II and triple-column text in Part III;[10] the shifting of the small, asymmetric titles in the first edition, from their location on the upper left registers of the front matter and chapter pages to an axial position mid-page in the title and chapter pages of the revised edition; and the removal of the two-page "Note on Author-ship and Attribution" written by Robert Venturi, which followed the preface to the first edition signed by Venturi and Scott Brown, now replaced by a "Preface to the Revised Edition" signed only by Scott Brown.

The significant changes in format and graphic design enabled Venturi and Scott Brown, in her words, "to shift the book's emphasis from illustrations to text, and to remove the conflict between our critique of Bauhaus design and the latter-day Bauhaus design of the book: the 'interesting' Modern styling of the first edition, we felt, belied our subject matter, and the triple spacing of the lines made the text hard to read."[11] The revised edition regularized what Venturi and Scott Brown considered the more idiosyncratic elements of Muriel Cooper's "latter-day Bauhaus design" into a more traditional textbook-like format (figures 5.1, 5.2, 5.3). The revised edition was, according to Scott Brown, more in keeping with what they intended it to be: a "treatise on sym-bolism in architecture." As she put it: "Las Vegas is not the subject of our book. The symbolism of architectural form is."[12] In order to emphasize this shift, the authors added a subtitle to the revised edition: "The Forgotten Symbolism of Architectural Form."[13] The new edition was also an opportunity, Scott Brown wrote, to "desex" the language of the first edition. As part of this "desexing," Parts I and II of the first edition were, as Scott Brown put it, "stripped and newly clothed."[14] (Since the revised edition omits Part III of the first edition, this means the whole book.)

Simply put, besides being completely reset, the revised edition of *Learning from Las Vegas* was also redesigned. And as the phraseology used to describe that process makes clear, what is at stake are issues of violence, truth, and owner-ship in relationship to *Learning from Las Vegas*'s status as a text.

Symbol in Space Before Form in Space: Las Vegas as a Communication System

The sign for the Motel Monticello, a silhouette of an enormous Chippendale highboy, is visible on the highway before the motel itself. This architecture of styles and signs is antispatial; it is an architecture of communication over space; communication dominates space as an element in the architecture and in the landscape. But it is for a new scale of landscape. The philosophical associations of the old eclecticism evoked subtle and complex meanings to be savored in the docile spaces of a traditional landscape. The commercial persuasion of roadside eclecticism provokes bold impact in the vast and complex setting of a new landscape of big spaces, high speeds, and complex programs. Styles and signs make connections among many elements, far apart and seen fast. The message is basely commercial; the context is basically new.

A driver 30 years ago could maintain a sense of orientation in space. At the simple crossroad a little sign with an arrow confirmed what he already knew. He knew where he was. Today the crossroad is a cloverleaf. To turn left he must turn right, a contradiction poignantly evoked in the print by Allan D'Arcangelo. But the driver has no time to ponder paradoxical subtleties within a dangerous, sinuous maze. He relies on signs to guide him — enormous signs in vast spaces at high speeds.

The dominance of signs over space at a pedestrian scale occurs in big airports. Circulation in a big railroad station required little more than a simple axial system from taxi to train, by ticket window, stores, waiting room, and platform — all virtually without signs. Architects object to signs in buildings. "If the plan is clear, you can see where to go." But complex programs and settings require complex combinations of media beyond the purer architectural triad of structure, form, and light at the service of space. They suggest an architecture of bold communication rather than one of subtle expression.

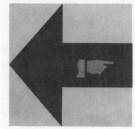

2. The trip. Allan D'Arcangelo

LAS VEGAS AS A COMMUNICATION SYSTEM

WELCOME TO FABULOUS LAS VEGAS, FREE ASPIRIN — ASK US ANYTHING, VACANCY, GAS.

All cities communicate messages — functional, symbolic, and persuasive — to people as they move about. Las Vegas signs hit you at the California border and before you land at the airport. On the Strip three message systems exist: the heraldic (the signs) dominates; the physiognomic, the messages given by the faces of the buildings (the continuous balconies and regularly spaced picture windows of the Dunes saying HOTEL and the suburban bungalows converted to chapels by the addition of a steeple); and the locational (service stations are found on corner lots, the casino is in front of the hotel, and the ceremonial valet parking is in front of the casino). All three message systems are closely interrelated on the Strip. Sometimes they are combined, as when the facade of a casino becomes one big sign or the shape of the building becomes its name, and the sign, in turn, reflects the shape. Is the sign the building or the building the sign? These relationships, and combinations between signs and buildings, between architecture and symbolism, between form and meaning, between driver and the roadside are deeply relevant to architecture today and have been discussed at length by several writers. But they have not been studied in detail or as an overall system. The students of urban perception and imageability have ignored them, and there is some evidence that the Strip would confound their theories. How is it that in spite of "noise" from competing signs we do in fact find what we want on the Strip? Also, we have no good graphic tools for depicting the Strip as message giver. How can the visual importance of the Stardust sign be mapped at 1 inch to 100 feet?

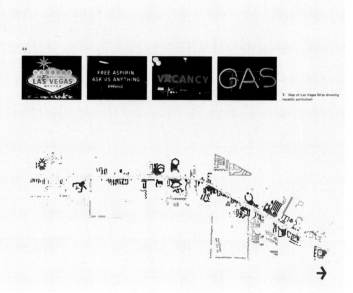

7. Map of Las Vegas Strip showing heraldic symbolism

5.1 Pages 4 and 5, *Learning from Las Vegas*; © 1972 Massachusetts Institute of Technology, by permission of the MIT Press.

communication. Just as an analysis of the structure of a Gothic cathedral need not include a debate on the morality of medieval religion, so Las Vegas's values are not questioned here. The morality of commercial advertising, gambling interests, and the competitive instinct is not at issue here, although, indeed, we believe it should be in the architect's broader, *synthetic* tasks of which an analysis such as this is but one aspect. The analysis of a drive-in church in this context would match that of a drive-in restaurant, because this is a study of method, not content. Analysis of one of the architectural variables in isolation from the others is a respectable scientific and humanistic activity, so long as all are resynthesized in design. Analysis of existing American urbanism is a socially desirable activity to the extent that it teaches us architects to be more understanding and less authoritarian in the plans we make for both inner-city renewal and new development. In addition, there is no reason why the methods of commercial persuasion and the skyline of signs analyzed here should not serve the purpose of civic and cultural enhancement. But this is not entirely up to the architect.

BILLBOARDS ARE ALMOST ALL RIGHT

Architects who can accept the lessons of primitive vernacular architecture, so easy to take in an exhibit like "Architecture without Architects," and of industrial, vernacular architecture, so easy to adapt to an electronic and space vernacular as elaborate neo-Brutalist or neo-Constructivist megastructures, do not easily acknowledge the validity of the commercial vernacular. For the artist, creating the new may mean choosing the old or the existing. Pop artists have relearned this. Our acknowledgment of existing, commercial architecture at the scale of the highway is within this tradition.

Modern architecture has not so much excluded the commercial vernacular as it has tried to take it over by inventing and enforcing a vernacular of its own, improved and universal. It has rejected the combination of fine art and crude art. The Italian landscape has always harmonized the vulgar and the Vitruvian: the *contorni* around the *duomo*, the *portiere's* laundry across the *padrone's portone, Supercortemaggiore* against the Romanesque apse. Naked children have never played in *our* fountains, and I. M. Pei will never be happy on Route 66.

ARCHITECTURE AS SPACE

Architects have been bewitched by a single element of the Italian landscape: the piazza. Its traditional, pedestrian-scaled, and intricately enclosed space is easier to like than the spatial sprawl of Route 66 and

Los Angeles. Architects have been brought up on Space, and enclosed space is the easiest to handle. During the last 40 years, theorists of Modern architecture (Wright and Le Corbusier sometimes excepted) have focused on space as the essential ingredient that separates architecture from painting, sculpture, and literature. Their definitions glory in the uniqueness of the medium; although sculpture and painting may sometimes be allowed spatial characteristics, sculptural or pictorial architecture is unacceptable—because Space is sacred.

Purist architecture was partly a reaction against nineteenth-century eclecticism. Gothic churches, Renaissance banks, and Jacobean manors were frankly picturesque. The mixing of styles meant the mixing of media. Dressed in historical styles, buildings evoked explicit associations and romantic allusions to the past to convey literary, ecclesiastical, national, or programmatic symbolism. Definitions of architecture as space and form at the service of program and structure were not enough. The overlapping of disciplines may have diluted the architecture, but it enriched the meaning.

Modern architects abandoned a tradition of iconology in which painting, sculpture, and graphics were combined with architecture. The delicate hieroglyphics on a bold pylon, the archetypal inscriptions of a Roman architrave, the mosaic processions in Sant'Apollinare, the ubiquitous tattoos over a Giotto Chapel, the enshrined hierarchies around a Gothic portal, even the illusionistic frescoes in a Venetian villa, all contain messages beyond their ornamental contribution to architectural space. The integration of the arts in Modern architecture has always been called a good thing. But one did not paint *on* Mies. Painted panels were floated independently of the structure by means of shadow joints; sculpture was in or near but seldom on the building. Objects of art were used to reinforce architectural space at the expense of their own content. The Kolbe in the Barcelona Pavilion was a foil to the directed spaces: The message was mainly architectural. The diminutive signs in most Modern buildings contained only the most necessary messages, like LADIES, minor accents begrudgingly applied.

ARCHITECTURE AS SYMBOL

Critics and historians, who documented the "decline of popular symbols" in art, supported orthodox Modern architects, who shunned symbolism of form as an expression or reinforcement of content: meaning was to be communicated, not through allusion to previously known forms, but through the inherent, physiognomic characteristics of form. The creation of architectural form was to be a logical process, free from images of past experience, determined solely by program and structure,

5.2 Pages 6 and 7, *Learning from Las Vegas*; © 1977 Massachusetts Institute of Technology, by permission of the MIT Press.

35. Streetlights, upper Strip

36. Upper Strip looking north

34. The order in this landscape is not obvious.

5.3 Pages 36 and 37, *Learning from Las Vegas*; © 1977 Massachusetts Institute of Technology, by permission of the MIT Press.

Muriel Cooper Gave Us a Duck

The "opportunity" to revise *Learning from Las Vegas* did not come about as the natural second stage in the life cycle of a book whose first printing had sold out, nor was the book reconceived in response to external criticism, economic disappointment, or the exigencies of new printing technologies. Rather, the idea of a radically different second edition was already insinuated in the negotiations over the first edition. Venturi and Scott Brown felt that Muriel Cooper's design of the first edition was so much in violation of their ideas that at one point they threatened to withdraw publication altogether. Although I have found no documents recording Steven Izenour's reaction to Cooper's design, one can infer from the evidence that does exist that the objections were voiced primarily, if not exclusively, by the other two authors. Rather than compromising Cooper's design in mid-process, an agreement was reached between Venturi and Scott Brown and the MIT Press whereby the publication of the first edition could proceed with Cooper's design fundamentally intact, but with Venturi and Scott Brown promised much more influence over the design of the second edition.[15] Although it took until 1975 for the revised edition to begin to move forward, such a book was imagined even while the first edition was advancing toward production. As Roger Conover explained to me, the revised edition "evolved as a kind of settlement of the two disappointed authors' reservations about the design of the first edition; rather than compromise Cooper's design, the Press agreed to give the Venturis their own uncompromised design in the second round."[16] Traces of the disagreement that Conover refers to are registered in letters written by Venturi and Scott Brown to the MIT Press, internal memos written by those involved in the book's production and design at the Press, and in an annotated copy of the first edition that contains written comments on the layout and design of the book in the hand of Venturi and Scott Brown, as well as responses by Muriel Cooper and Sylvia Steiner (among other editors and designers at the Press), on the subject of reprinting the first edition or the preparation of a revised edition.[17]

Although the first edition of *Learning from Las Vegas* is now celebrated in design circles, often illustrated alongside Cooper's famous design for Hans Wingler's monumental *Bauhaus* (MIT, 1969), Venturi and Scott Brown were not impressed with the results (figure 5.4). As Venturi wrote to Michael Connelly, then editorial director at the MIT Press, in the latter stages of the book's production: "we cannot have a book that for the sake of some design theories obscures the meaning by its format inside, and on the cover is the opposite of what we as designers, and of what the book itself, stands for."[18] After the book was finished, Scott Brown reiterated to Connelly: "The 'Swiss style' graphic design remains a disappointment to us."[19] For her part, Cooper characterized the conflict over the design of the first edition as a "battle of wits."[20] The authors' critique of Cooper's design is summed up by their query on the title page of their annotated copy of the book: circling the title on the upper left of the page and connecting it by a wobbly line to a drawn rectangle enclosing a written version of the title, placed axially at the center of the page, Scott Brown commented: "Could this page be revised because its composition is like a duck?" (figure 5.5).[21] Cooper, however, claimed she had given them what they asked for: "What they wanted most was a Duck, not a Decorated Shed. I gave them a Duck."[22]

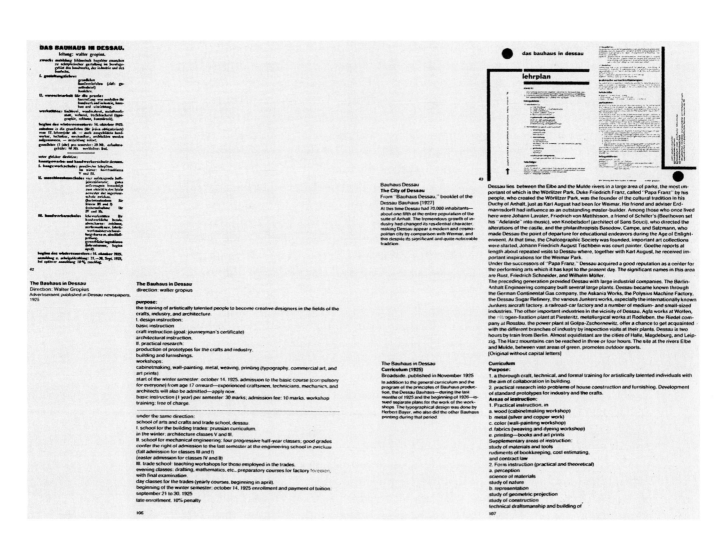

5.4 Hans Wingler, *Bauhaus*, design by Muriel Cooper; © 1969 Massachusetts Institute of Technology, by permission of the MIT Press.

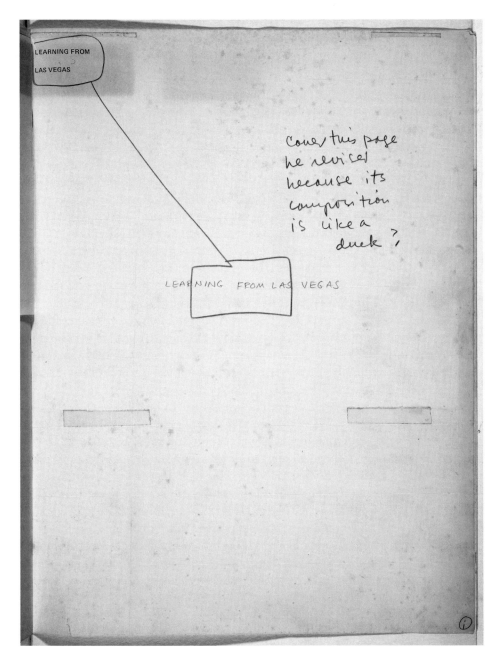

5.5 Title page from the annotated copy of *Learning from Las Vegas*; by permission of the Avery Architectural & Fine Arts Library, Columbia University.

Stripping Possession

The phrase "stripped and newly clothed" to describe the revised edition's undoing of the first edition suggests, among other connotations, a kind of violence done to the former. We might see the second edition as Scott Brown and Venturi's attempt to "strip possession" of the first edition from Muriel Cooper. If, as Roland Barthes claims, a "work," in contrast to a "text," has a clear filiation, then in the eyes of Venturi and Scott Brown the first edition was in many ways an "illegitimate work."[23] The revised edition by contrast, as Scott Brown put it to their editor, Barbara Ankeny, was "a great labor, done in the hope that together we shall produce a book we can all love."[24] By implication, the first edition was unlovable—perhaps an "ugly duckling." It is worth reiterating here that the status of "ugly duckling" is predicated on a certain kind of response—or more accurately, a lack of responsiveness or recognition. It is significant that Scott Brown in her preface twice refers to the revised edition as a "new" edition, further marking the two editions' separateness as their mode of coexistence.

The revised edition was literally "stripped" in the langue of graphic design; that is, the illustrations and copy were assembled anew on flats for the printing of each page of the revised edition, thus creating a new configuration of text and image.[25] The geological connotation of stripping—to mine a deposit by first taking off the overlying burden—would also seem to intersect with the idea of stripping possession; that is, it speaks to Venturi and Scott Brown's desire to have the form of their book more in keeping with the "core" of its content, which was "buried" in Cooper's design. Note, however, that the metaphor of stripping can suggest the continuity of a "body" of work that is then "newly clothed," or conversely can imply that there is no body as such, but rather that the work is exteriority and surface all the way down, without any "core." The struggle over the relationship between form and content is dramatically exemplified in the conflict between Cooper and Venturi and Scott Brown over the cloth cover and dust jacket of the first edition.

The Design Department at the MIT Press often did multiple takes for book jackets, no doubt exploring the perennial issue of the relationship between cover and text: that is, whether the cover had only a loose affiliation to the book, more akin to an expendable advertisement, or was meant as an expression of its contents. Was it, in architectural terms, a facade or a wrapping? The most controversial proposal for *Learning from Las Vegas* was Cooper's bubble-wrap jacket with fluorescent dots underneath, which she proposed for the first edition "in homage to Las Vegas Glitz." She said in an interview, "I thought: boy, this is wonderful material. I'm not gonna let them screw it. Hah! You should have seen it. Well, they hated it! I loved it."[26] A letter from Venturi and Scott Brown to Michael Connelly in February 1972 voiced their "extreme concern about some aspects of the design of *Learning from Las Vegas*," with their strongest objection being to the bubble-wrap jacket: "<u>The cover</u> as designed is absolutely unacceptable: leaving out questions of good or bad design, it is inappropriate. It is against the philosophy of the book; it is a duck—'heroic and original'—almost fruity in its appearance. This is a serious study with a serious text and deserves a dignified conventional image. The shock must come from the contents inside the book. . . . We have shown Muriel what we mean in sketches."[27] The cloth cover of the first edition that they did agree on suggests what Scott Brown was looking for. Its dark green hue, with the title and authors' names in Baskerville, stamped in gilt, is meant to recall traditional highbrow academic books, and thus offers a striking contrast with the crass Tanya paste-down above it (figure 2.5). This design clearly echoes that of Ed Ruscha's art books, such as *Every Building on the Sunset Strip,* which Scott Brown had admiringly described: "Deadpan, a scholarly monograph with a silver cover and slip-on box jacket, it could be on the piazzas of Florence, but it suggests a new vision of the very imminent world around us."[28] In contrast, Scott Brown felt that Cooper's bubble-wrap dust jacket had placed her deadpan cover, and the book as a whole, in an undignified package.

Scott Brown and Venturi's strongly worded letter to Connelly seems to have resulted in the authors' having a say in the design of the first edition's cover. A "compromise formation" of sorts was worked out with Cooper and the authors between March and June 1972. A glassine dust jacket was designed with the book's section headings—in black, sans serif letters—ranged across the front and back (figure 2.4). The design—and especially the red lettering of the title *Learning from Las Vegas,* on the second line of the jacket, which sets it off from the rest of the words on the jacket—is reminiscent of Cooper's aesthetic, such as her design for the cover of a 1964 exhibition catalog, *Communication by Design: Muriel Cooper, Malcolm Grear, Norman Ives, Carl Zahn,* in which different-colored typeface picks out selected letters spelling the word "communication" from a densely spaced wall of words in black typeface (figure 5.6).[29] It appears that the dust jacket was accepted, if not fully embraced, by Venturi and Scott Brown: "I have before me the table of contents. We think all the headings . . . are OK for the book jacket."[30] Yet, unlike Cooper's bubble-wrapped "Duck," this dust jacket does not really express anything. It surely does not express its contents as interior depth; rather, it literally ex-presses—stamps or extrudes the section headings as another surface.[31] No doubt the more "conventional" and "decorative" section headings, reminiscent of the snappy one-liners found on billboard signage, were more to Venturi and Scott Brown's liking, although Cooper's sans serif "Swiss style" typeface still masked the serif, gilt lettering on the cloth cover beneath.[32] Scott Brown's revised edition stripped *Learning from Las Vegas* of any traces of Cooper's designs *on* the book: the dust jacket was

5.6 Muriel Cooper, front cover, *Communication by Design: Muriel Cooper, Malcolm Grear, Norman Ives, Carl Zahn*, 1964; by permission of the Addison Gallery of American Art, Philips Academy, Andover, Massachusetts.

MOCMNUICTAINO
OCMUMNCIATNOI
CMONUMACINOIT
UICMOUNMTAINC
NOCMIUANCTIOM
TOUNMCIMANOIC
OUMMCCNAIITNO
UNICOMMTIONCA
COMMUNICATION
BY DESIGN

Muriel Cooper
Malcolm Grear
Norman Ives
Carl Zahn

removed, and the paperback cover reverted to her design for the cloth cover of the first edition. Thus, the conflict over the design of the book is literally hashed out on the cover of the first edition, before the book is even opened.

But the word "stripping" also suggests that what is being stripped is not simply an "outer" cover, which can be thought of in merely external or spatial terms; it can also imply an existential or skeptical "distancing." That is to say, Venturi and Scott Brown's connection to Cooper's design is progressively removed from their own cares, concerns, and connections to it. And this is where the phrase "stripped and newly clothed" converges with issues of skepticism. If the condition of skepticism, as I have argued throughout this book, is predicated on our attunement in our criteria—an acknowledgment of the conditions of possibility of our shared interests and concerns—then, as Cavell has noted, "to possess criteria is also to possess the demonic power to strip them from ourselves . . . to find that its criteria are, in relation to others, merely *outer*."[33] What I am trying to get at here is that issues of design are an exemplary way to explore these attunements, as they are deeply entwined with what we might literally call "forms of life"—the criteria, or (to use the language of book design) the "formats," that give sense to what communication and communicability, the inner and outer, control and freedom, might mean. This is precisely why Venturi and Scott Brown engage in a critique of "total design" as a certain vision of society (I will return to this issue shortly).

If the revised edition was undertaken to remove the conflict between Venturi and Scott Brown's critique of Bauhaus design and Cooper's "latter-day Bauhaus design" of the book, this is not simply a matter of a "stripped and newly clothed" book, but equally, and inextricably, an encounter with skepticism: the always present temptation to "strip" the criteria for our attunements in the shared conventions that regulate and give shape to the forms of life that we are willing to participate in. Thus, Venturi and Scott Brown's dissatisfaction with and eventual repudiation of Cooper's design—her way of regulating communicability as such—are the best indication that it is also "their" design, a matter of their response to and responsibility for it; theirs to own or disown as the case may be.[34] This is an appropriate point to turn to what I will call the problem of the "third," which makes further sense of what "merely outer" might mean here in relation to these issues.

The Third

I have always been struck by the wonderful photograph of Venturi and Scott Brown riding in a car during their trip to Las Vegas: Venturi's arm is extended, resting behind Scott Brown's shoulder. She is holding a camera gently in her hands (figure 1.1). The rearview mirror is prominently located between them, and slightly askew, but despite the multiple reflections circulating within this complex image, there is little or no trace in it of the photographer in the back seat who has captured this moment of shared adventure. This elision invites us to consider other individuals involved in the production of *Learning from Las Vegas*—including, but not exclusively, Steven Izenour, their coauthor—whose silent presence the book's cohesion relies upon. *Within* Venturi and Scott Brown's impressive articulations of new kinds of community, and despite their positive stress on inclusion, collaboration, and nonsexist practice, they still struggle with what I will simply call the "third"—that is, anyone or anything that disrupts the "internal" cohesion or communication of a system, group, or entity, and in response is given a supplementary status, disavowed, or deemed as "merely outer."

If we are willing to consider that love is a metonymy of community, there is always the risk—perhaps "dramatized" in the issues surrounding the design and publication of *Learning from Las Vegas*—that a community that is "not one" (to use Jean-Luc Nancy's phrase) can easily recuperate itself *as* one in a society of two. As Freud once said, a third can only be "superfluous or disturbing [for a couple], whereas civilization depends on relationships between a considerable number of individuals."[35] These issues of community are played out in relation to the dynamic of both studio and architectural collaboration. For example, Scott Brown was well aware that Robert Venturi's "Note on Authorship and Attribution," which followed the preface to the first edition, was problematic because, although it called attention to issues of misattribution and sexist practice in the deliberate overlooking of her contribution to their work, the very fact that it was written by Venturi accentuated Scott Brown's being "spoken for" and further excluded in her inclusion. Significantly, in the revised edition this "Note" is omitted and Scott Brown writes the entire preface to the second edition, speaking in her own voice of her own exclusion, and of the virtual ignoring of Venturi's request for fairness to his coauthors and coworkers. No doubt, Scott Brown's ire at the design of the first edition was inextricable from her increasing voice within their practice, and the fact that she felt that Cooper's "voice" in the book was overshadowing her own.

It is interesting to note that during the summer and fall of 1971, Venturi and Scott Brown were also planning to include a preface by Vincent Scully, which exists in multiple typescripts in the VSBA archives at the University of Pennsylvania (see figure 5.7, and the appendix to this volume).[36] One can speculate about why this introduction was not included in the published book. Scully certainly had reservations about the book's overemphasis on the symbolism of the Strip, which he thought narrowed and occluded the wide-ranging implications of its reintroduction of symbolism and representation into American architecture. (Scully is often very astute in recognizing how and when Venturi and Scott Brown contribute to their own misreading.) But one can also imagine that leaving out Scully's introduction allowed Scott Brown's distinctive voice to be heard within their collaborative work, and helped to further distance *Learning from Las Vegas* from Venturi's sole-authored *Complexity and Contradiction*, which prominently featured Scully's by now well-known and provocative introduction. After all, in the unpublished introduction to *Learning from Las Vegas*, Scully refers to the authors as "the Venturis," and only briefly acknowledges Steven Izenour.

What about other members of the firm, and Muriel Cooper herself? In the preface and "Note" to the first edition, Venturi and Scott Brown acknowledge John Rauch's and Steven Izenour's importance to them personally, to their work in general, and the latter's specific work on *Learning from Las Vegas*. They refer to these colleagues, however, in Latin terms: Izenour is their *sine qua non*

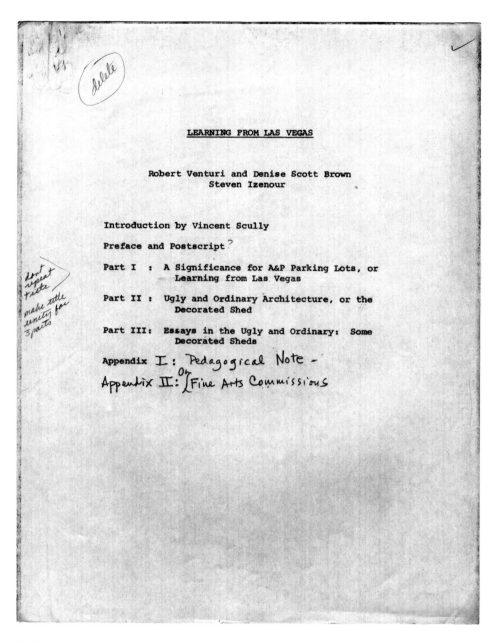

LEARNING FROM LAS VEGAS

Robert Venturi and Denise Scott Brown
Steven Izenour

Introduction by Vincent Scully

Preface and Postscript ?

Part I   : A Significance for A&P Parking Lots, or
            Learning from Las Vegas

Part II : Ugly and Ordinary Architecture, or the
            Decorated Shed

Part III : Essays in the Ugly and Ordinary: Some
            Decorated Sheds

Appendix I: Pedagogical Note -
             or
Appendix II: [Fine Arts Commissions

delete

don't repeat title / make title unity for 3 parts

5.7 Preliminary table of contents for the first
edition of *Learning from Las Vegas*; by permission of the Architectural Archives, University of
Pennsylvania, gift of Robert Venturi and Denise
Scott Brown.

and Rauch is their *paterfamilias*.[37] Both terms single the men out in a way that suggests essentialness and genealogy as that relates to *their* relationship. And although the book is supposedly coauthored by Izenour, only Venturi and Scott Brown sign the preface to the first edition. Also in light of the issue of the third, Cooper and her design could be seen as a kind of "scapegoat" within the production of *Learning from Las Vegas*: a convenient way of displacing "blame" onto a third party, in order to shore up a sense of group identity.[38] The price to pay for inclusion, it seems, was a willingness to make sacrifices for the group. This is attested to by a paragraph that Scott Brown wanted to include in the preface to the first edition, thanking their editor, Barbara Ankeny, personally: "And to Barbara Ankeny, our skill-friendly editor, who agreed to sacrifice grammar (and her credentials) to allow us the prose style we prefer."[39] Ankeny politely declined the offer, noting that "this Press prefers to omit individual editor recognition within the book."[40] But the "logic" of the third has ramifications far beyond any particular "third" person.

In a letter to Michael Connelly dated July 25, 1972, at the time when the book was ready to be bound, Scott Brown provided a list of "mistakes" that correspond quite closely to many of the inscriptions on the authors' annotated copy of the first edition. In the letter they are categorized as "mistakes of meaning" and "mistakes of layout," although the two categories are clearly intertwined. It is significant that all the problems listed in the letter are classified *as* "mistakes." Venturi and Scott Brown, however, are not specific about what they mean by mistake; in John Austin's words, they are unable to "distinguish between sheer, mere, pure, and simple mistake or inadvertence."[41] It is nearly impossible to make out whether Venturi and Scott Brown are talking about something done deliberately, in the sense of an intentional action; or done accidentally, in the sense of an unconscious error; or done inadvertently. Often it seems they are suggesting—in a grand telescoping of gradations of meaning—that Cooper literally mis-took; that is, pursued the wrong design. This lack of clarity seems to have ensured a cascade of insinuation, accusation, excuse, and justification on both sides. Both Venturi and Scott Brown and the editors and designers at the Press were aware of this at some level, and it deeply colored their (mis)communication. For example, at one point, Cynthia Ware, the copy editor for the revised edition, felt she needed to clarify to Scott Brown that some amount of deviation from the dummy constitutes common "error" and does not indicate "carelessness or any deliberate attempt to depart from the dummy."[42] As many of the images from the annotated copy confirm, at least part of the responsibility for these issues clearly stemmed either from Venturi and Scott Brown's own interventions and revisions or simply from the low quality of some images given to the Press (figure 5.8). Venturi and Scott Brown seemed unable to acknowledge that issues of illegibility and unreadability might be *internal* to issues of

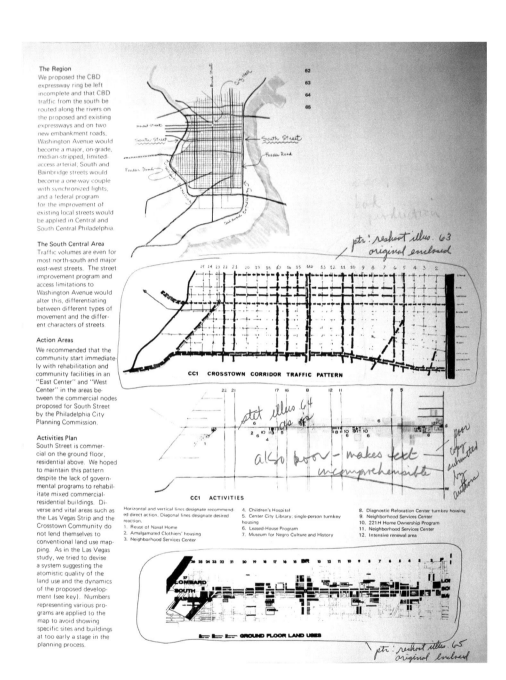

The Region
We proposed the CBD expressway ring be left incomplete and that CBD traffic from the south be routed along the rivers on the proposed and existing expressways and on two new embankment roads. Washington Avenue would become a major, on-grade, median-stripped, limited-access arterial; South and Bainbridge streets would become a one-way couple with synchronized lights; and a federal program for the improvement of existing local streets would be applied in Central and South Central Philadelphia.

The South Central Area
Traffic volumes are even for most north-south and major east-west streets. The street improvement program and access limitations to Washington Avenue would alter this, differentiating between different types of movement and the different characters of streets.

Action Areas
We recommended that the community start immediately with rehabilitation and community facilities in an "East Center" and "West Center" in the areas between the commercial nodes proposed for South Street by the Philadelphia City Planning Commission.

Activities Plan
South Street is commercial on the ground floor, residential above. We hoped to maintain this pattern despite the lack of governmental programs to rehabilitate mixed commercial-residential buildings. Diverse and vital areas such as the Las Vegas Strip and the Crosstown Community do not lend themselves to conventional land use mapping. As in the Las Vegas study, we tried to devise a system suggesting the atomistic quality of the land use and the dynamics of the proposed development (see key). Numbers representing various programs are applied to the map to avoid showing specific sites and buildings at too early a stage in the planning process.

CC1   CROSSTOWN CORRIDOR TRAFFIC PATTERN

CC1   ACTIVITIES

Horizontal and vertical lines designate recommended direct action. Diagonal lines designate desired reaction.
1. Reuse of Naval Home
2. Amalgamated Clothiers' housing
3. Neighborhood Services Center
4. Children's Hospital
5. Center City Library; single-person turnkey housing
6. Leased-House Program
7. Museum for Negro Culture and History
8. Diagnostic Relocation Center turnkey housing
9. Neighborhood Services Center
10. 221H Home Ownership Program
11. Neighborhood Services Center
12. Intensive renewal area

GROUND FLOOR LAND USES

5.8 Page 132, annotated copy of *Learning from Las Vegas*; by permission of the Avery Architectural & Fine Arts Library, Columbia University.

communicability as such, and not *external* disruptions of communication and/or the result of adherence to a particular design philosophy.

The whole issue of the "third" is exemplified in Venturi and Scott Brown's desire to include an "erratum" sheet with the first edition in order to call attention to, and correct, those mistakes. In a letter to Scott Brown, Ankeny wrote: "As I suggested on the phone, I am enclosing copy for an erratum sheet. I still feel very strongly that the only 'proper' entry is the fourth, purple for pink. The others are unusual entries for such a listing (Erratum sheets usually list only misstatements of fact)."[43] The sheet, which included seven errata, was inserted by hand into the book but, of course, was neither numbered nor bound within the main body of the text (figure 5.9). It remained a "loose leaf," but neatly pressed within the book's pages, both beyond the limits of the text yet embedded in it.[44] The "errant" text of the first edition of *Learning from Las Vegas* is an ex-foliation that still haunts the pages of the revised edition, just as the revised edition rewrites its way back to and beyond its progenitor. And here we come to Muriel Cooper's role in the design process.

5.9 Erratum sheet, *Learning from Las Vegas*, 1972; by permission of the Architectural Archives, University of Pennsylvania, gift of Robert Venturi and Denise Scott Brown.

Errata

Page vi, line 42:
For ≠, Delight *read* ≠ Delight

Page xv, Figure 71 credit:
For Yale University *read* Yale University, Evan Lanman

Page xv, Figure 72 credit:
For Yale University, Evan Lanman *read* Yale University

Page 6, Figure 8 caption:
For pink represents *read* purple represents

Page 60, line 7:
For meanings.233, 234 *read* meanings

Page 88, line 11:
For sciences of semeiology *read* science of semiology

Page 150, left column, line 57:
For aspirations of *read* aspirations or

Muriel Cooper, Swiss Design, and the MIT Press

Muriel Cooper joined the MIT Press in 1967 as its first art director in the Design Department, a role in which she designed over 500 books before she left to direct the Visible Language Workshop at MIT's Media Lab, which she had cofounded in the mid-1970s.[45] Cooper's roots were in the Swiss typographic tradition, as were those of most graphic designers in America and Europe in the sixties and seventies.[46]

The fifties saw the rise to dominance of Swiss typography, with such figures as Armin Hofmann, Herman Matter, Emil Ruder, Karl Gerstner, and Josef Müller-Brockmann providing both the intellectual underpinnings and technical advances that set the tone for graphic design well into the seventies. The dissemination of Swiss design was aided by key design and architectural journals such as *Graphis*, *Bauen + Wohnen*, *Typografische Monatsblatter*, *Werk*, and *New Graphic Design (Neue Grafik)*, and in America through educators such as Rob Roy Kelly and Alvin Eisenman, as well as in the corporate design work of Massimo Vignelli, Rudolf de Harak, and Ivan Chermayeff. The connection between Swiss design and modern architecture was quite strong, as exemplified by Max Bill's work on seminal publications in the field, including his editing and design of the third volume of Le Corbusier's *Oeuvre complète* in 1939.[47]

The beginnings of the Swiss design tradition at MIT date back to John Matill's creation of the Office of Publications in 1951 to handle all of the Institute's graphic work and design needs, including posters, brochures, prospectuses, and summer session material. Matill hired a select group of graphic designers to work with him, including Muriel Cooper, who had been recommended by Gyorgy Kepes, as well as Jacqueline Casey and Ralph Coburn.[48] To assist with the rush in January to produce graphic material for the MIT summer sessions, Matill invited the Swiss designer Therese Moll to work in the office, and she informally taught Cooper, Casey, and Coburn in the Swiss "method" of design. Over the years Matill invited other Swiss-trained designers, such as Paul Thalman, Walter Plata, and Dietmar Winkler, to work in the Office of Publications.

Cooper was director of the Office of Publications from 1952 to 1958 and became steeped in the tenets of Swiss design, with a strong interest in the work and theorizations of Ruder, Gerstner, and Müller-Brockmann. She was also exposed to Swiss design through the Boston design scene at this time. Carl Zahn, an important graphic designer in Boston and Cooper's close friend, had organized an early exhibition of Swiss graphic design at the Institute of Contemporary Art in 1961, for which Gerstner was invited to give a talk. Zahn also introduced Cooper to the important Swiss typographer Hermann Zapf in 1964, and at a later date Cooper and Casey invited Müller-Brockmann to speak in Boston.[49] Through these direct and indirect contacts, the Office of Publications developed a sophisticated program based on the principles of Swiss design. Its ability to forge a strong design identity was unique for university publications at this time, and its work was used as a model for that of other university public relations units.[50]

After leaving the Office of Publications in 1958, Cooper opened her own graphic design studio in Brookline and worked as a freelance designer from the early to mid-1960s, with the MIT Press as one of her clients, before being hired by the Press as art director in 1967. Under her guidance, the Press developed a strong but flexible house style and introduced ambitious design into academic publishing. It is not an exaggeration to say that Cooper put her stamp on almost every book published at the MIT Press, not only through her more than 500 designs but, more literally, through her design in 1963 of the MIT Press logo, which has appeared on the spine of every MIT Press book since then and is considered one of the publishing industry's most recognizable colophons. In 1982, she received the second AIGA Design Leadership Award, given in recognition of her work in Design Services (formerly the Office of Publications), the Design Department at the MIT Press, and the Visible Language Workshop in the Media Lab.[51]

The Grid, and Cooper's Layouts for _Learning from Las Vegas_

Cooper clearly inherited the most common and identifiable elements of Swiss design: the preference for sans serif fonts, such as Standard, Univers, and Helvetica, and the use of an underlying modular grid to organize text and image.[52] Although the modular grid is often regarded as a rigid typographic convention, it is actually quite flexible and no more constraining than any other kind of pictorial or graphic "convention."[53] It helps coordinate relationships and proportions, but allows for widely varied layouts of text and image.

From all reports, Cooper used the grid imaginatively, and never merely applied it in a rigid or slavish manner. This is attested to by the four layouts of her designs for Parts I, II, and III of _Learning from Las Vegas_ that exist in the VSBA archives at the University of Pennsylvania: the layout for Part I, a second layout that includes Parts I and II, and two variants for Part III (figures 5.10, 5.11, 5.12). These layouts were most likely produced between May and July 1971, except for one variant for Part III that is dated March 24, 1972.[54] The underlying grid provided a basic guideline enabling Cooper to rearrange the text and images, as the variant layouts for Parts I and II suggest. These layouts provide a general overview of the book's three parts in terms of flow, as well as the relationship between text and image on each page. The schematized text, indicated by arrows or chevron-like lines, suggests that these layouts are primarily concerned with the placement of the images in relationship to the text. The images are clearly indicated by relative size, type, and location on each page, with the corresponding text indicated by the section headings jotted at the bottom of each page. All of the layouts are rendered on gridded paper, the faint lines of which are seen below Cooper's design in pencil.

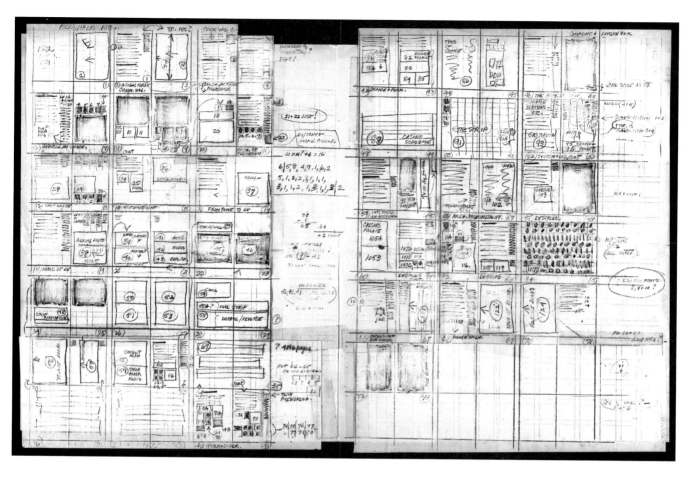

5.10 Muriel Cooper, layout of Part I, *Learning from Las Vegas*, 1971; by permission of the Architectural Archives, University of Pennsylvania, gift of Robert Venturi and Denise Scott Brown.

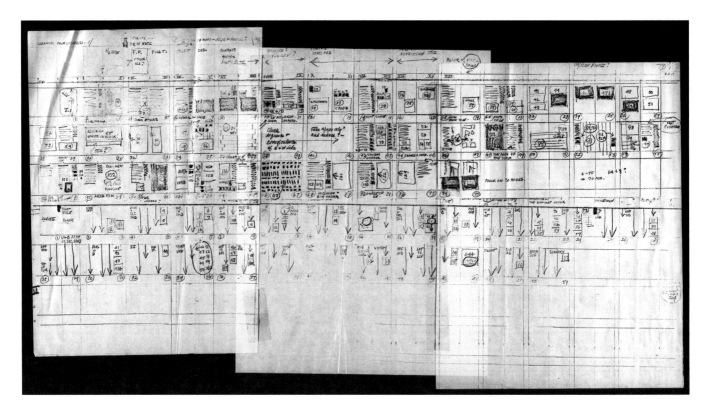

5.11 Muriel Cooper, layout of
Parts I and II, *Learning from
Las Vegas*, 1971; by permission
of the Architectural Archives,
University of Pennsylvania, gift
of Robert Venturi and Denise
Scott Brown.

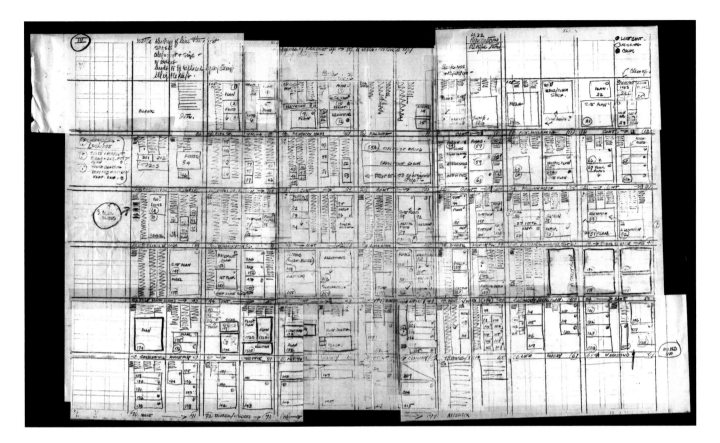

5.12 Muriel Cooper, layout of Part III, *Learning from Las Vegas*, 1971; by permission of the Architectural Archives, University of Pennsylvania, gift of Robert Venturi and Denise Scott Brown.

In the first edition of *Learning from Las Vegas,* Cooper used a basic five-column vertical grid, which is most clearly visible on page 11 where the columns of text and 35mm photographs correspond almost perfectly to the grid (figure 5.13). Each column is 11 picas wide with a 1-pica gutter between the columns, which works out to a text page measuring 59 picas wide and 78 picas high. Each of the three parts of the book follows a slightly different organization based on this grid, but dictated by the number of text columns: one column in Part I, two columns in Part II, and three columns in Part III. Whatever the particular dimensions of each combination of text column and gutters, they always add up to the text page dimensions laid out in the underlying five-column grid.[55]

Owing to the great number, variety, size, and relative importance of the images in the book, the images do not strictly adhere to the underlying grid, nor of course do the book's two-page spreads and broadside images. This also holds true for Cooper's design for Hans Wingler's *Bauhaus* (1969), in which she used a grid system as a starting point to deal with the plethora of visual and written documentation (figure 5.4). As Cooper recalled in an interview with Steven Heller, "The people and works of the Bauhaus were my conceptual and spiritual ancestors, so I felt a particular bond with the material. While the structure of the book evolved from the Swiss grid system, it was devised to be rich enough to encompass the complex panorama of the archival textual and visual material."[56] As with her layouts for *Learning from Las Vegas,* the Bauhaus layouts give a real sense of the implicit movement of the images as they range across and beyond the "confines" of the grid and the page, in a literal demonstration of the relationship between the *ergon* and *parergon*, the a priori and the a posteriori, the conceptual and the empirical. Cooper's grid seems to operate as a framework not to lock text and image into some rigidly predetermined format, but rather to explore the relationships between freedom and constraint, movement and stasis, legibility and visibility. Cooper's layouts for *Learning from Las Vegas* functioned as a kind of "synoptic dummy" for her, in that they showed how the pages related to each other in terms of rhythm and spacing, without one's having to flip through the actual pages of the book. Cooper was always interested in this implicit motion in the design of her books, and the mock-ups allowed her to "virtually" explore these issues on a single sheet of paper.[57]

Cooper's association with the design of the Bauhaus book was undoubtedly a striking exemplification for Venturi and Scott Brown of the supposed mismatch between her "latter-day Bauhaus design" for *Learning from Las Vegas* and the book's content.[58] Although there are close and verifiable connections between Swiss graphic design and modern architecture, these can easily devolve into loose analogies made between the "rational, objective methodology" of Swiss design—particularly its emphasis on underlying "grids"—and high modern architecture's modes of organization and assembly based on proportional grids

5.13 Sylvia Steiner, overlay of grid on page 11 of *Learning from Las Vegas*; © 1972 Massachusetts Institute of Technology, by permission of Sylvia Steiner and the MIT Press.

Although its buildings suggest a number of historical styles, its urban spaces owe nothing to historical space. Las Vegas space is neither contained and enclosed like medieval space nor classically balanced and proportioned like Renaissance space nor swept up in a rhythmically ordered movement like Baroque space, nor does it flow like Modern space around free-standing urban space makers.

It is something else again. But what? Not chaos, but a new spatial order relating the automobile and highway communication in an architecture which abandons pure form in favor of mixed media. Las Vegas space is so different from the docile spaces for which our analytical and conceptual tools were evolved that we need new concepts and theories to handle it.

One way of understanding the new form and space is to compare it with the old and the different. Compare Las Vegas with Ville Radieuse and Haussmann's Paris; compare the Strip with a medieval market street; compare Fremont Street, a shopping center, and the pilgrims' way through Rome. Compare a form that "just grew" with its designed equivalent and with "group forms" from other cultures.

Another way of understanding the new form is to describe carefully and then analyze what is there and, from an understanding of the city as is, to evolve new theories suited to twentieth-century realities and therefore more useful as conceptual tools in design and planning. This approach provides a way out of the CIAM grid. But how does one describe new form and space using techniques derived from the old? What techniques can represent the 60mph form and space of the Strip?

How does its desert site affect Las Vegas form and space?

Do Las Vegas public and institutional buildings show any influences from its recreational architecture?

25. Aladdin Casino and Hotel, Las Vegas. An asphalt landscape

Versailles

Parking lot of Caesars Palace, Vegas

Inflected highway signs on Strip

"The big sign and the little building . . ."

11 picas

11 picas

11 picas

11 picas

11 picas

1 gutter margin —
each gutter margin is 1 pica

11

and standardization, often resulting in tendentious comparisons between the underlying grid of a book page and the facade of a prismatic modernist building. To keep with loose analogies for a moment, one could hardly imagine Venturi and Scott Brown being more satisfied with a "postmodern" design of their book, along the lines of a Pushpin Studio aesthetic or in the style of William Longhauser's well-known poster for the 1983 exhibition "The Language of Michael Graves." In fact, Cooper's attempt to find a coherent yet flexible order within the complex amalgam of image and text in the book would seem to be in sync with *Learning from Las Vegas*'s attempt to find the "order" within the "chaos" of the Las Vegas Strip.

In other words, Venturi and Scott Brown's characterization of Cooper's work in terms of its "Swiss style" is a sweeping conflation of Swiss typography and Cooper's modifications of it. Under closer scrutiny, neither Swiss design nor Cooper's approach were, in fact, monolithic entities, nor were they isomorphic with one another. At the very moment that Swiss typography and design were becoming the lingua franca of 1970s corporate America, their tenets were being reworked and critiqued by many of those trained in Swiss design, including such figures as Wolfgang Weingert, Dan Friedman, April Greiman, Willi Kunz, and, to a degree, Muriel Cooper herself.[59] As Cooper described herself in an unpublished interview with Ellen Lupton, "I was a modernist, but I was an uneasy Swiss, if you know what I mean."[60] But she was not uneasy enough in the eyes of Venturi and Scott Brown, despite their similar claims "to extend the theory and principles of Modern architecture, 50–75 years after their initial development, for a new generation facing new realities."[61] Taken in this light, one might have expected a degree of overlapping interest between Cooper and Scott Brown rather than out-and-out conflict.

Although many characteristics of Swiss design are evident in Cooper's book designs for the MIT Press, her designs are also quite varied in their details. Constantinos Doxiadis's *Architectural Space in Ancient Greece* (1972) demonstrates some of the more typical traits of Swiss design in Cooper's work, with its sans serif typeface, asymmetrical images, and generous use of white space on the title page and around the photographs and plans (figures 5.14, 5.15). The first book she designed for the MIT Press (as a freelancer), in 1964, was *The View from the Road*, by Kevin Lynch, John R. Myer, and Donald Appleyard, a tall, rectangular book with double columns of sans serif text, paragraphs separated by line spacing rather than indentation, and generous areas of white space around many of the images. It also made use of margins for small diagrams and figures, and included flipbook images on the bottom left and right side of each page (figure 5.16). The book was intended to convey to engineers important views and reference points in the building of roads. Significantly, the flipbook images were trying to convey, and perhaps to equate, the rhythm

Architectural Space
in Ancient Greece

C. A. Doxiadis   Translated and Edited by Jaqueline Tyrwhitt

5.14 Title page, Constantinos Doxiadis, *Architectural Space in Ancient Greece*, design by Muriel Cooper; © 1972 Massachusetts Institute of Technology, by permission of the MIT Press.

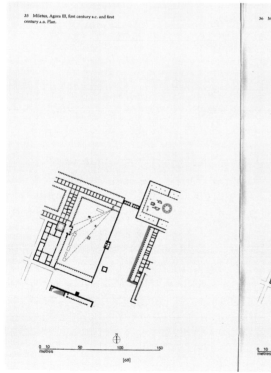

35 Miletus, Agora III, first century B.C. and first century A.D. Plan.

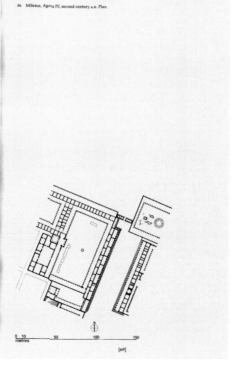

36 Miletus, Agora IV, second century A.D. Plan.

5.15 "Miletus, Agora III and IV," in Constantinos Doxiadis, *Architectural Space in Ancient Greece*, design by Muriel Cooper; © 1972 Massachusetts Institute of Technology, by permission of the MIT Press.

5.16 Kevin Lynch, John R. Myer, and Donald Appleyard, *The View from the Road*, design by Muriel Cooper; © 1964 Massachusetts Institute of Technology, by permission of the MIT Press.

32

A Trip on the Northeast Expressway

Let us describe a brief trip on this road, as it might impress a typical passenger. At the start, after rising up onto the road by a short ramp, there begins the first, or familiarization, phase. Attention is confined to the road itself, to the signs and accompanying traffic, to the fly-by of small close objects which give the basic sensation of speed. In the late afternoon in winter, when most of the trips were made, the road points at a low sun, and the glistening of the sky and of the road and car surfaces is a notable feature. The attention to silhouetted objects is heightened.

In the beginning there is little to orient the observer, and he has to trust the road for direction. The route lacks those elements of distant direction in which it is so rich farther on. A foretaste view of the Custom House tower, for example, or a sense of the water edge paralleling the route to the left, would be of great value.

Soon the original interest in the ordinary features of the road and in the basic sense of speed diminishes, while the outside landscape is still of weak quality. This part of the trip, from minute 1 to 1½, is most like the run of ordinary highway-driving. Attention still centers on the road ahead, but the tempo of observation falls off markedly. The tempo of the sketching by the sample group also slackened at this point.

As the road approaches the northern spur of Fennos Hill, the interest begins to rise again. At first it is not clear how, or if, the road will pass this barrier. The cut is turned at an angle to the road and is therefore invisible. The approaching ribbon of road that may point it out is obscured by a small mound and dip in the vertical alignment at minute 1½. This mound
67 passes over a road which is largely invisible to the observer, and so the hump is for him an inexplicable irregularity in the line. Changes of level can be quite exciting, but small variations, whose origins are not visually explained, act only as minor irritants.

Once past this hump, the approach to Fennos Hill suddenly becomes clear, and excitement mounts as the road plunges into the cut, under the two bridges overhead, and makes a sweeping left turn. Visual speed is intensified by the spatial confinement and the bridges passing overhead, and the cut marks the passage of an important edge in the orientation scheme. The turning of the road adds to the interest, conveying a sense of centrifugal force and apparently causing the far landscape (which is framed by the cut and the bridges) to move swiftly sidewise. This strong impression is reflected in the concentration and tempo of attention.

On bursting out of the cut, the observer's eyes sweep the far landscape and immediately pick up the next major event, Powder Horn Hill, whose principal landmarks (a hospital and a water tower) are seen in the framed view while the observer is moving through the first bridge. There is an apparent 90-degree turn to the left (actually the turn is
68 nearer 60 degrees), and the observer finds himself moving along the back side of Fennos Hill, whose rocks and slopes make a pleasant contrast to the urban scene at the right. This backward view of an orientation element al-

Read Up

67

Read Up

68

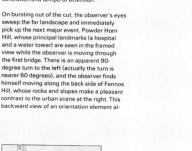

and tempo of moving through the city in a car with our way of "reading" books. Cooper's filmic approach to book design became a hallmark of her work and was unique to the MIT Press; she recalled that she "once . . . presented the Bauhaus book as a single-frame movie—showing all the pages in rapid succession."[62] The filmic approach also manifested itself in the texture and patterning of her design for *Learning from Las* Vegas (more on this to come). As Cooper readily admitted, Kevin Lynch disliked her design for his book, as it was "too big, and arty."[63] Interestingly, Venturi and Scott Brown admired it, and Cooper considered it one of her finest achievements.

One of Cooper's favorite designs was for Herbert Muschamp's first book, *File under Architecture* (1974). The book was bound in corrugated cardboard, printed on brown wrapping paper, and typeset on an IBM Composer, as was *Learning from Las Vegas* in 1972.[64] Besides allowing for "mise-en-page" typography, the IBM Composer enabled experimentation in different typefaces.[65] In contrast to Kevin Lynch, Muschamp felt that Cooper's design for his book expressed his ideas about the relationship between ephemerality and architecture even better than his own writings did.[66]

"White-Page Aesthetic"

Much of Denise Scott Brown's criticism of the first edition of *Learning from Las Vegas* centered on what she referred to as its "white-page aesthetic," that is, the preference in Swiss design to "implicate the unprinted white space as a design factor."[67] This design strategy seemed to work against Venturi and Scott Brown's critique of the emphasis on space as the "essential ingredient" in "purist architecture," as opposed to their own pursuit of an architecture of "mixed media." Venturi and Scott Brown interpreted Cooper's incorporation of white space into the design of the book to literally mean that she had emphasized "form in space before symbols in space," or "subtle expression over bold communication," to echo the language in *Learning from Las Vegas*. But it is not at all self-evident that Cooper equated the unprinted page—what Meyer Schapiro would call the "field" of the image-sign—with space as such, much less with a space that overshadowed individual images and text in expressivity or homogeneity.

Venturi and Scott Brown, however, seemed to believe that their very large schedules and images—already scaled down drastically for publication—would have been more visible, legible, and readable if issues of meaning and communication had not been sacrificed to Cooper's desire for an emphasis on space. The annotated copy of the first edition includes many such critiques of Cooper's layout (figures 5.17, 5.18). Yet in many cases the images, and the text in the images, are no more visible or legible in the revised edition than they are

90, 91. A schedule of Las Vegas Strip hotels: plans and sections and elements

	Panorama	Front	Side	Back	Parts	Entrance	Roof	Parking		Pedestrian	Oasis	Fountain	Foliage	Sign	Sculpture	Interior	Aerial	Style
Sahara																		
Riviera																		
Stardust																		
Caesars Palace																		
Dunes																		
Aladdin																		
Tropicana																		

39

5.17 "A schedule of Las Vegas Strip hotels: plans and sections and elements," in *Learning from Las Vegas*; © 1972 Massachusetts Institute of Technology, by permission of the MIT Press.

5.18 Comment on the "schedule of Las Vegas Strip hotels," annotated copy of *Learning from Las Vegas*; by permission of the Avery Architectural & Fine Arts Library, Columbia University.

If these could stretch to edge of page their details would be visible

NO.

in the first, as is the case in the two-page spread of the "schedule of Las Vegas Strip hotels," which they felt would show more detail if stretched to the edge of the page. The criticisms in the annotated copy correspond quite closely to those listed in the letter Denise Scott Brown wrote to the Press outlining the "mistakes" in the design of the book. Almost all of these refer to issues of "illegibility" and "unreadability": "Again, a 'white paper' aesthetic has this beautiful schedule smaller than it needs be and therefore almost illegible"; "illegible. [figure] 101 poorly printed"; "[figure] 70 still too small to read all lettering"; "[figure] 18 world's teeniest, weeniest elevation is unreadable; more 'white space' aesthetic"; "text almost illegible"; "pictures illegible."

In many ways, the conflict over the "white-page aesthetic" was a struggle over what the expanse of the white page stood for: is it homogeneous space, in which images are "placed," or are those images "places" in and of themselves, and thus never merely placed, but rather dis-placed, *partes extra partes* in and as the texture of the page? Was the page understood as a "frame" that isolated the field of representation from the surrounding surface, or was it a frame that functioned as the pictorial milieu of the image? Or was the page the very ground for rethinking the division between "figure" and "ground" in the first place?[68] Venturi and Scott Brown believed that Cooper's "white-page aesthetic" worked against their problematizing of the figure/ground relationship within new urban environments like Las Vegas. The "good gestalt" patterns that cut themselves out from the fabric of the city were less relevant to the new Vasarely-like, shifting patterns that were weaving and unweaving a new rhythm of the city's warp and weft. This would seem to call for a different approach to the relationship of image and text on the page.

But Cooper was quite intent on exploring such an approach in her design for *Learning from Las Vegas;* thus it is an oversimplification to categorize her entire approach to design as a "white-page aesthetic." She expected that her design would be consonant with the subject matter of *Learning from Las Vegas*: "*Learning from Las Vegas* . . . was an exercise in using design to resonate content with subject. The visual materials were not only graphically rich, but as content-laden as the text, so the interdependent rhythms of those relationships were important."[69] Her attempt to account for the interdependent rhythms of image in text, and text in image, and her desire to arrange these materials spatially "in a non-linear way," would seem to suggest that she was interested in a conception of design in which, as Nancy has so nicely put it, "a form is the force of a ground that sets apart and dislocates itself, its syncopated rhythm."[70] This understanding of the relationship of "figure" *as* a "ground" that is of a piece with its own dislocation would seem to resonate with Venturi and Scott Brown's critique of the "good gestalt patterns" that were inadequate for such urban environments as Las Vegas. In fact, Venturi and Scott Brown referred to

5.19 Mylar overlay, presentation board for the Learning from Las Vegas studio, Yale University; by permission of the Architectural Archives, University of Pennsylvania, gift of Robert Venturi and Denise Scott Brown.

these new environments as "textures," suggesting a connection between the warp and weft of those "information landscapes" (a phrase coined by Muriel Cooper) and the possible designs for the "text" of *Learning from Las Vegas*.[71] But neither Cooper nor Venturi and Scott Brown were able to recognize where their interests did coincide, and they tended to focus solely on where they did not. One might say that they were "mutually unattuned."

Cooper's interest in the translation and transformation of content across different media and genres might have resonated well with the Learning from Las Vegas studio's exploration of different graphic means for registering and conveying complex patterns of action. And her interest in layering and translucency—an approach that she further explored at the Visible Language Workshop—recalls the use of such techniques as Mylar overlays in the Las Vegas studio presentation boards in order to convey the temporal and spatial dimensions of movement patterns on the Strip (figure 5.19). Even Cooper's early interest in the computer's role in book and information design is echoed by Venturi and Scott Brown's fascination with the early experimentations with SYMAP and OTOROL in the work of Carl Steinitz and Richard Saul Wurman, which they used to organize and map patterns of activity in "significant" form.[72] This is all to say that the conflict between the designer and the authors was caused not only by differing design sensibilities, but also by misreadings and missed opportunities on both sides. Furthermore, issues of design were at the heart of the Las Vegas studio, and thus Venturi and Scott Brown were heavily invested in their book's layout and design.

Graphic Design and the Learning from Las Vegas Studio

Issues of graphic design were always central to VSBI's conceptualization, research, and final presentation of the Learning from Las Vegas studio. One of the studio's central premises was to find new graphic means to register the activity and intensity of Las Vegas as an exaggerated example of their typologies of the Strip and Sprawl City. As Venturi and Scott Brown put it, "Particular emphasis will be placed on the evolution of new descriptive graphic techniques to augment the conventional maps and drawings inherited from architecture and city planning."[73] Simply put, they saw the Strip's configuration and mode of impact as predominantly "graphic" in nature.

To confirm the importance of these issues, two graphic design students participated in the studio, in addition to the students from architecture and urban planning. One of the twelve research topics for the studio was "Graphic and Other Techniques of Representation," but this issue, in fact, permeated all the other research topics as well. And the importance of this component to the entire studio as such is attested by "Phase V" in which, after returning from

Las Vegas, the group addressed the problem of how "to make the material we have graphically meaningful and instructive to ourselves and others."[74] This effort resulted in the large-scale schedules, plans, 16mm films, and sequence of 35mm slides shown at the studio's final "multi-media event" presentation.[75] VSBI emphasized to prospective publishers that the winnowing down of the plethora of statistical, economic, and planning documentation they had accumulated during their studio—not to mention the 5,000 color slides and 10,000 feet of 16mm color film—to the approximately 80 maps, schedules, diagrams, and movie/slide sequences for the final presentation should be seen as "the first editing of the book."[76]

The amount of cumulative material from the studio research, including massive amounts of film reel; the necessity of multiple stages to edit that material; and the problems in negotiating issues of radical changes in scale from primary shooting, to studio presentation, to book format suggest that the authors' approach to producing the first edition of *Learning from Las Vegas*, as well as its 1977 "redux," might have been closer to the pace and feel of film editing than that of book editing. Indeed, the production of the first and revised editions required a complex dance of cutting, splicing, and reweaving; the multiple viewing of "dailies" at different stages of production; and a distillation of the myriad possible narrative lines latent in that material. As Walter Murch has so well put it, "editing—even on a normal film—is not so much a *putting together* as it is a *discovery of a path*."[77] And of course, the more material there is to work with, the more pathways there are to consider. Simply put, the first edition had to be worked *through* and not simply against, in order for Venturi and Scott Brown to get to where they wanted to be with the revised edition, which might suggest that the former was not as "other" to them as they imply. The first edition was not inimical to their intentions, as if they had played no part in it or were simply dissatisfied with it; it was partially their "production." This situation suggests another point of connection and conflict with Muriel Cooper. She also approached her book design and layouts in terms of film editing, and was clearly arriving on the scene after the "directors" of *Learning from Las Vegas* had already initiated a process of "post-production."

The First Edition and Its Preconceptions

VSBI were clearly thinking about publishing a book based on the Las Vegas studio well *before* the studio ended, and perhaps even before it began in September 1968.[78] Between May and September 1969, they began to contact publishers in an effort to secure a contract for their proposed book. VSBI eventually chose the MIT Press over Praeger, a decision most likely influenced by the MIT

Press's reputation for innovative graphic design and their impressive list of books on architecture and urbanism. The choice was also dictated by a brute monetary reality: in order to publish the extensive and expensive material they wanted to include—much of it in four-color reproduction—the authors needed external subsidies, which would be awarded only if they published with a nonprofit academic press.[79] The MIT Press was enthusiastic about the book and approved publication in October 1969, although the official contract was not formally signed and returned to the Press until February 1970.[80]

In an interview with Janet Abrams, Muriel Cooper seemed to think that Venturi and Scott Brown's "pre-conceptions" about the design of the first edition were at the root of their conflict with her: "After several years gestating a text, authors tend to have their own view of what their book should look like, which can lead to some interesting battles of wits. I had that experience in spades with Denise Scott Brown and Robert Venturi."[81] While it is difficult to tell exactly how much of a (pre)conception Venturi and Scott Brown had about how the book should be designed, there are clear indications that they were thinking very hard about reproduction costs and possible layouts well before they landed a contract. In a letter of June 12, 1969, Venturi wrote to Carroll Bowen, then the director of the MIT Press, that "Steve [Izenour] has put together the enclosed minimum schedule of drawings and illustrations divided by program topic and type of reproduction. We have also done some sketches to show relative size and importance of the different illustrations."[82] At this point VSBI were thinking about a book of somewhere between 60 and 80 pages, with approximately 25 to 50 pages of text (15,000–20,000 words) and 30 to 65 pages of images. Yale University Press, to whom the authors had also submitted their proposal, interpreted Izenour's sketches—perhaps not the same ones sent to the MIT Press—to suggest that the manuscript would include 25 pages of text, four pages of two-color illustrations, one of four-color illustrations, plus 29 black-and-white line cuts and halftones.[83] The final contract with MIT called for a manuscript of between 20,000 and 25,000 words and between 71 and 105 images, of which 25 would be four-color illustrations. It seems that VSBI were also exploring some basic configurations and layouts for these images, akin to something like a filmic "rough edit."

All of these details are at odds with Venturi and Scott Brown's claim to the presses they were contacting that the "only preconception we have about layout . . . is that the four color slide illustrations should be kept small so as not to overwhelm the drawings."[84] Although they did not have a detailed layout in mind for their book at this time, they clearly had more ideas about it than they were willing to admit.

Although Venturi and Scott Brown might not have wanted to design the first edition of *Learning from Las Vegas*, they did want extensive control over the design process. In a letter from Venturi to Michael Connelly, written in December 1969, Venturi asked for the following crucial sentence to be added to paragraph six of their letter of agreement with the Press: "MIT Press shall submit all matters of manner and style; including layout and graphic design of the book to the authors for comment prior to publication."[85] Their request was granted, and the sentence was added to their contract.[86] No doubt Venturi and Scott Brown had this agreement in mind while they were struggling with Muriel Cooper over the design of the first edition.[87]

But one might expect that the struggles for control over the design process would have ended with the first edition; after all, Scott Brown was now the principal designer of the revised edition.[88] But Venturi and Scott Brown's experience with the first edition seemed to heighten their desire for control over the revised edition. In fact, an even more detailed set of "procedures" were put in place for the revised edition, which gave Venturi and Scott Brown the right to see sample pages, the edited manuscript, galley proofs, page proofs, and the blueprints of the illustration signature during preparation and publication of the manuscript.[89] Thus, despite Scott Brown's redesign of the revised edition, many of the same issues about control continued, which suggests that there were other forces, beyond differing design sensibilities and philosophy, going on in relationship to the production of both editions of the book.

A July 1976 memo written by Mario Furtado, a designer at the MIT Press working with Sylvia Steiner in implementing Scott Brown's design for the revised edition, noted that "67 total design hours have thus far been spent in the rough dummying and preparation of sample pages (and revised sample pages). This represents twice the time spent on a comparable book."[90] The extra time expended was due, in large part, to the numerous rewrites and revisions requested by Venturi and Scott Brown, which led to delays that were further exacerbated by their constant requests to see page proofs, mechanicals, and book blues.[91] Letters written late in the publication process of both editions make it clear that their level of involvement at every stage of production—well beyond what most authors are allowed—never abated.[92] In fact, there was concern at the Press about their continuous intervention right up to the point when the revised edition was sent off to the binder.[93] At times these interventions involved minute details, literally down to the last millimeter: "Captions, I think are a smidgeon too close to the figures—perhaps 1mm . . . I think Mario should try to drop them very slightly if he can."[94] This paper trail of delaying interventions is in striking contrast to a "Launching Report" produced at the start of the publication process for the revised edition in May 1976, which anticipated minimal work to be done aside from copyediting the new material. The level of difficulty for producing the book was rated a 3 out of 5, with an estimate of 30 total editorial hours.[95] One can assume that at the very least, twice this time was needed in the end.

This is all to say to that there is a striking contrast between Venturi and Scott Brown's critique of the ideology of "total design," in both the first and revised editions, and their dogged attempts to control all aspects of the design process of the book. A letter written by Lee Ewing, a production staff member of the MIT Press, after the publication of the revised edition states this in the starkest terms possible: "the decision to allow the author complete design control over the project from sample pages to blues set the tone of the whole project. I do not think it an exaggeration to characterize that tone as one of intimidation. Even in the middle of the project when the author's own design began to produce serious production problems (albeit unexpected), the attitude engendered by this tone was one of placating the author at all costs. . . . The amount of quibbling by the author over figures being moved ¼₆″ to ⅛″ was remarkable and did not encourage a cooperative or trusting atmosphere."[96] Although the first edition appears to be more designed—"too-much design," as Venturi and Scott Brown would say—and the revised edition appears "less" designed, the degree of "design control" to get to that point of "less design" is indeed striking.

If Venturi and Scott Brown's equation of the megastructure with total design in *Learning from Las Vegas* allegorizes the inability to acknowledge issues of limitation and separateness, resulting in a drive for total control, their critique would appear countermanded by the very act of producing the book itself. Their *own* investment in total design is clearly something they had difficulty acknowledging. No doubt they interpreted this struggle in precisely the opposite way; to them, it was Cooper who was arrogantly imposing her preconceived design on them, in the face of their critique of "total design." Thus, in contrast to their admirable and, at times, radical proposals for a reconfigured sense of community in the book—such as the discussion about the Duck and the Decorated Shed, or the issues raised in the "recommendation for a monument"—there are clearly aspects of their work that simply reconstitute the very positions they are critiquing. But it is equally true that although Muriel Cooper had a reputation for being collaborative and for encouraging other people's ideas, including the many women designers she mentored, she also believed strongly in design autonomy; indeed, she was known for being possessive of her projects, and had no problem fighting for them in the face of opposition. The first edition was indeed a "battle of wits" between three very intelligent, creative, and accomplished designers.

But one also gets the sense that their conflict was not only over supposed "big" differences in design philosophy but was also marked by what we might call, in Freud's words, a "narcissism of small differences," in which "it is precisely communities with adjoining territories, and related to each other in other ways as well, who are engaged in constant feuds and in ridiculing each other."[97] After all, Venturi and Scott Brown clearly considered themselves "designers"[98]—and referred to themselves as such in the book, as well as in their letters to Connelly about their dissatisfaction with Cooper's design of the first edition—while Cooper felt that her background gave her a certain understanding and affinity with architectural matters. Some of her closest interlocutors at MIT were architects and professors of architecture, not to mention her many architect-clients; she began teaching a course, "Messages and Means," in the School of Architecture at MIT, and in 1977 she became its first female tenured faculty member.[99] Yet neither party could take the measure of either the large or small issues that both linked and separated them. Some of these incompatibilities were real, while others were retrospectively constructed and exaggerated. The format of the book was just such an after-the-fact conflict.

A Large Book

From the beginning, Venturi and Scott Brown wanted what they called a "large book," particularly in the horizontal dimension, in order to accommodate, in their words, "the size of the original drawings and the scale of reduction."[100] The latter phrase refers to the many schedules and plans produced at a very large scale for the huge presentation boards—some over twenty feet in length—shown at the final presentation of the Learning from Las Vegas studio, which had to be drastically reduced in scale for publication.[101] Between January and September 1970, VSBI envisioned a large-format book with dimensions of 12 x 9 or 12 x 15 inches, and at one point they even expressed the desire for a 24 x 12 page format.[102] The placement of some schedules and plans over a double-page spread in the first edition, and others running broadside (rotated 90 degrees), gave them a 21- or 14-inch width, which comes quite close to the horizontal dimensions they were looking for (figures 3.12, 3.21, 5.17).[103]

Thus, the large format of the first edition was never inimical to Venturi and Scott Brown's "original" intentions, as the preface to the revised edition seems to imply. The small size, portability, and reduced cost of the revised edition did not simply and belatedly fulfill their intentions for their ideal book design. The whole issue of the format of the first edition might caution us to avoid the temptation to make "teleological explanations"; that is, assumptions of some design goal that is then read back into the process in order to provide the narrative for that very goal. Here, as elsewhere, the two editions were worked out over a span of time in which they served differing needs at different points. Any intentionality that we might care to talk about was produced in, as, and through the very process of design and was never simply hovering over it, neither at the "beginning" nor at the "end."

Venturi and Scott Brown's writing of the text and organization of the images do not appear to have begun in earnest until 1971, even though the manuscript was originally due in June 1970.[104] The basic tripartite organization of *Learning from Las Vegas* seems to have been decided on at an early stage. Part I was based on Venturi and Scott Brown's article "A Significance for A&P Parking Lots, or Learning from Las Vegas," published in 1968 in *Architectural Forum*, with additional material from the Yale studio; Part II, the "theorization" of the material in Part I, was written in 1971 and first appeared in article form that year as "Ugly and Ordinary Architecture, or The Decorated Shed," in the same journal, while they were working on the book for the MIT Press; and Part III consisted of Venturi and Rauch's work exemplifying the theorizations in Part II.[105] Two marked-up versions of the 1968 "A&P" article in the VSBA archives at the University of Pennsylvania confirm that the first step in preparing the book for publication was a light reworking of this essay, with the addition of images from the Las Vegas studio keyed to the text. Venturi and Scott Brown were primarily responsible for the writing and rewriting of the text, and Steven Izenour for preparing the images. One can assume that any design decisions were shared in some way between the three, with Venturi and Scott Brown having the final say.

Venturi, Scott Brown, and Izenour's Preliminary Mock-Up

A preliminary mock-up of Part I of *Learning from Las Vegas*, with text and images, is dated February 23, 1970.[106] From all indications, this preliminary mock-up was produced in the office of Venturi and Rauch. It consists of thirteen 22 x 30-inch boards, divided in half by a dotted blue line, and numbered 1–1A (left and right side of the boards) up to 13–13A (figures 5.20, 5.21, 5.22). The size of the boards works out to a trim size of 22 x 15 inches, which seems to reflect Venturi and Scott Brown's desire for a large-format book (but now one that is longer in the vertical dimension). The first board contains the "introduction" to the book on the left side of the board, which corresponds quite closely to the preface of the first edition, and the right side has affixed photographs of the Learning from Las Vegas studio poster and a collage of newspaper articles about the studio in

5.20 Board 1–1A, preliminary mock-up for Part I of *Learning from Las Vegas*, 1971; by permission of the Architectural Archives, University of Pennsylvania, gift of Robert Venturi and Denise Scott Brown.

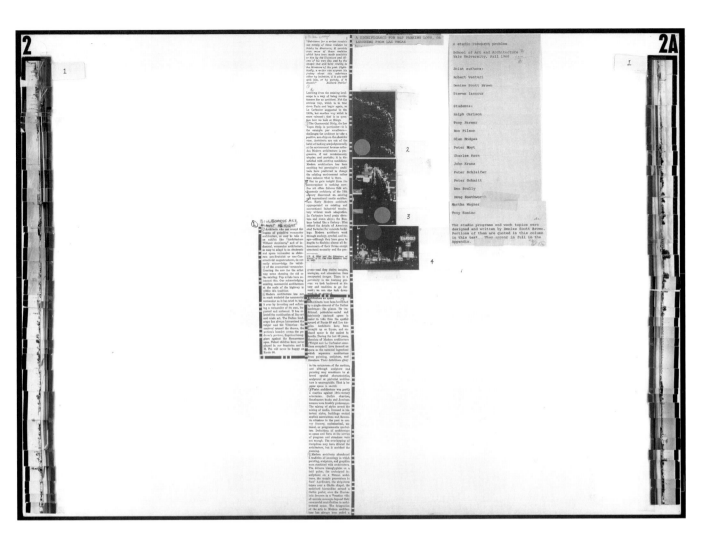

5.21 Board 2–2A, preliminary mock-up for Part I of *Learning from Las Vegas*, 1971; by permission of the Architectural Archives, University of Pennsylvania, gift of Robert Venturi and Denise Scott Brown.

5.22 Board 3–3A, preliminary mock-up for Part I of *Learning from Las Vegas*, 1971; by permission of the Architectural Archives, University of Pennsylvania, gift of Robert Venturi and Denise Scott Brown.

Yale and images of them in Las Vegas, simply called "The Trip" (figures 5.23, 5.24). Both of these appear as unnumbered images in the front matter of the first edition as published. Beginning on board 2, a photocopy of the text from "A Significance for A&P Parking Lots" has been cut and pasted onto the gutter margins of the left half of the boards, with sequentially numbered schedules and maps from the Learning from Las Vegas studio arranged to the left and right of the text.[107]

Beginning with board 3A, the right side of each board contains text, in different font size and leading, that corresponds to what would become the "Studio Notes." These notes are derived from Scott Brown's summaries of the different research topics and phases of the Las Vegas studio assigned to the students, including some written material from the students themselves. To the right of the studio notes are predominantly 35mm color photographs taken in Las Vegas. This arrangement—with the schedules and maps on one side, and the color photographs on the other—seems to reflect Venturi and Scott Brown's previously stated desire to have a layout in which the color photographs would not overwhelm the schedules and maps. This is an important point, in light of their later dissatisfaction with the lack of clarity and small size of the photographs in Cooper's design of the first edition. The majority of the 160-odd images in the mock-up of Part I would appear in the first edition as published, but in very different arrangements and locations. It is also interesting to note that despite the plethora of images in the mock-up, there is also quite a bit of "white-space aesthetic," as many of the images are grouped together, leaving large expanses of empty board.[108]

The first typescript of *Learning from Las Vegas* was submitted to the Press on May 7, 1971.[109] The multiple copies of the typescripts for Parts, I, II, and III in the VSBA archives indicate that they were continually reworked and adjusted throughout the fall. The May submission also includes a reference to "some photos of the layout sheets" for Muriel Cooper.[110] This probably corresponds to a set of Photostats of the preliminary mock-up boards that are also located in the VSBA archives.[111] In addition to those mock-up boards and Photostats, there is another set of Photostats of a variant mock-up in the archives that consists of seven boards, numbered 1–7A; that is, five fewer boards (or ten pages) than the mock-up discussed above (figure 5.25).[112] It also has a significantly different arrangement of images, and the studio notes do not appear on the "A" side of the boards.

What is striking about both mock-ups is the placement of the "Edward Ruscha elevation of the Strip" along the vertical edges of the left- and right-hand side of each panel, beginning on board 2 and ending on board 9A on the preliminary mock-up, and running along all the boards in the Photostats of the variant mock-up (figures 5.20–22, 5.25). The original "Edward Ruscha elevations"

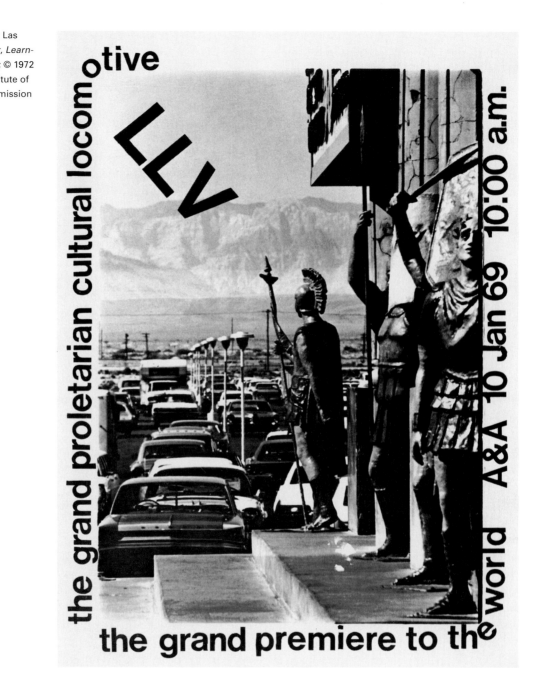

5.24 "The Trip," *Learning from Las Vegas*;
© 1972 Massachusetts Institute of Technology,
by permission of the MIT Press.

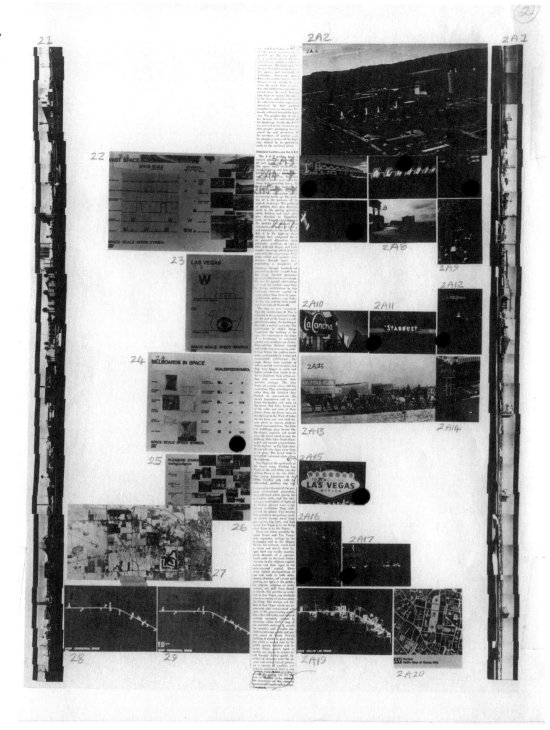

5.25 Photostat of alternate mock-up for Part I of *Learning from Las Vegas*; by permission of the Architectural Archives, University of Pennsylvania, gift of Robert Venturi and Denise Scott Brown.

5.26 Presentation boards for the "Edward Ruscha elevations of the Strip," photograph by the author; by permission of VSBA, Inc.

are still located in the VSBA office at Manayunk. As is the case with most of the Las Vegas studio presentation material, these eight narrow boards are extravagant in size, each approximately fourteen feet high and ten inches wide (figure 5.26). When the first edition was finally published, the eight "Ruscha elevations" appeared with each alternating band showing one side of the street, and then the opposite side, running down two full-page spreads (figure 3.12).[113] Some of the actual footage of the "three-camera deadpan" film made during the trip to Las Vegas can be seen on video transfer from the original 16mm film; this film was shown in three installments during the final presentation of the studio.[114]

As I argued in chapter 3, the deadpan attitude and aesthetic was central to the Las Vegas studio, as well as to Venturi and Scott Brown's approach to the book itself. As Venturi phrased it in a series of brief notes to their closest interlocutors and supporters shortly after the final studio presentation: "We think it went well in general, but I am still a little unbelieving that some people can't understand we just wanted to look at Las Vegas in a dead-pan way."[115] The two early mock-ups for the first edition clearly demonstrate that they wanted their deadpan approach to Las Vegas to register in the design of the book. Two years later, in Venturi and Scott Brown's early designs for their 1976 "Signs of Life" exhibition at the Renwick Gallery, they proposed a gallery layout for the "Symbols & Signs on the Strip" section that was, in many ways, a huge, kinetic, three-dimensional instantiation of the preliminary mock-up boards:

In this room you experience one large, moving, linear image of the strip. You walk the length of the room along a moving "Ruscha" elevation of a major strip. . . . At eye level to your right is the right side of the strip; to your left the left side. The Ruscha elevation is 12" to 18" high, 40' to 50' long. Its movement in the opposite direction from the visitors' increases its speed of passing and simulates the experience of perception from an automobile. It is in color and rear-illuminated for brilliance and sparkle; by means of motor drives, it changes from day to night and back again every two to three minutes. . . . Along the "strip" and over it, perpendicular to the "Ruscha" are real signs; neon, rear-illuminated, painted, animated, hung from above and mounted on the floor.[116]

This design was never implemented owing to its cost. The final design for this room was eventually configured into an oversized book, with the title of that section of the exhibition written vertically on the "book spine" and the long, horizontally splayed back and front covers functioning as walls with backlit photographs of Strip signage (figure 5.27). Although there was a small catalog produced for the Renwick exhibition by Aperture, here it would seem that the book and the exhibition design had merged into each other. This dramatizes what I have hinted at previously: that there is a complex and overlapping, if asymmetrical, relationship between Venturi and Scott Brown's "exhibition" work—including formal museum exhibitions as well as quasi-formal studio presentations—and their ideas about book design.

The difficulty in negotiating this relationship—the degree and kind of their family resemblance—was part of the problem any graphic designer would have in producing a book based on their work. To further complicate this relationship, Cooper also had to negotiate what I would call Venturi and Scott Brown's "comico-aesthetic doublet" that was central to both their exhibition and book design: the attitude of the jester—with an emphasis on sensory overload, excess, and motley presentation—coupled with their deadpan approach, with its emphasis on restraint, modest design, and low-key presentation.[117] Both components were integral to the final studio presentation: the deadpan films

5.27 "Signs of Life: Symbols in the American City," Bicentennial exhibition, Renwick Gallery, National Collection of Fine Arts of the Smithsonian Institution, Washington, D.C.; by permission of VSBA, Inc.

coexisted cheek by jowl with an atmosphere of sensory overload, through the large-scale presentation boards, films, and their coordination into a "multimedia presentation." In the words of one attendee of the final presentation: "It had all the blatant, proliferating affluence of the strip itself."[118]

Cooper was unable to capture the configuration of the two approaches that Venturi and Scott Brown wanted, but that was undoubtedly a Sisyphean task, as their conception of the comico-aesthetic doublet changed over time, particularly in regard to different genres of display, exhibition, and format. For example, they enjoyed using radically different typefaces and font sizes for the wall text and signage in their exhibitions, but they didn't seem to want these kinds of irregularities in their books. It is easy to imagine why Cooper thought that her own experimentation with different typefaces and interleaved narratives in *Learning from Las Vegas* might have appealed to them.[119]

Likewise with the "filmic" deadpan. Venturi and Scott Brown's "Ruscha elevations" along the edges of the boards in the mock-up of the first edition would seem to resonate with Cooper's filmic approach to book design: "I thought about books as being like a movie. Once I presented the Bauhaus book as a single-frame movie—showing all the pages in rapid succession."[120] In her design for Lynch's *The View from the Road*, she included flipbook images that gave an "animated" sense of moving through the city; these images also echoed her approach to editing, in which she would do "a flip" on a dummy to check for flow (figure 5.16). In fact, the Ruscha elevations along the side of the pages in the Venturi and Scott Brown mock-up would have set them apart from the rest of the images, as they would have been placed broadside, requiring the viewer to rotate the book. With a rapid turning of the pages, the Ruscha elevations would have operated like a flipbook, not far in conception from *The View from the Road*.

However, during the design process, the Ruscha elevations were edited down and isolated to a few pages.[121] By the time Scott Brown designed the revised edition, the first two figures—"The Las Vegas Strip, looking Southwest" and "Map of Las Vegas Strip"—were meant, at the outset, to give the reader an eyeful of the Strip without, as Scott Brown put it, "the pizzazz" of vibrant neon lights.[122] That is to say, by the time of the revised edition, the deadpan itself had become less dramatic, and less "expressive," and now permeated the book as such. This edition's "boring" appearance—its literal and metaphoric "de-coloring"—is meant to contrast with the "interesting" styling of the first edition, just as its uniformly spaced and weighted typeface—its "colorless writing of degree zero"[123]—is meant to contrast with the highly "textured" pages of the first edition.

Beyond Within

In the first edition of *Learning from Las Vegas*, one gets a real sense of experimentation in the literal meaning of that word: an exploration of (shared) experience at the limit of sense.[124] There is more "noise" in the first edition, despite the "white-page aesthetic" and "Swiss styling" that Venturi and Scott Brown disliked. One can sense the buzz of excitement in the pleasure of trying to account for a new sense of the city, but not quite knowing how to frame that in terms of words or images, or even whether those very categories, and their strict separation, were part of the problem. If a more traditional relationship between word and image was incapable of showing the Strip's intensity—merely "representing" it, one might say, with the "re-" operating as a repetition or doubling in the sense of a signifying practice that simply referred to "presentation"—then the first edition was clearly after a mode of representation that understood the "re-" as an intensification of presentation.[125] That is, our fundamental access to this new urban language is not one of knowing, but a way of responding to its particular exposure and insistence of sense. Thus an essential task of the first edition of *Learning from Las Vegas* was to reorient the reader's sensibilities to this new condition, and not merely refer to or codify it.

If we do "read" the first edition, it is a reading that is less concerned with issues of decoding or signification and more concerned with taking a reading, as one might verify a temperature by a thermometer, but without any predetermined meter or standard to take the measure of that reading as such. The design of the first edition *shows* that whatever we want to know or say about signs and symbols cannot be said apart from their "stimulus ecology": the conditions of their realization in sound, light, atmosphere, and contact.[126] If the revised edition is what Barbara Ankeny called "a book of ideas," then the first edition is to a great degree inimical to that bookish condition, for "experience," as Jean-Luc Nancy has argued, "does not lead us to what is usually termed an 'idea' or 'view of things.'"[127] The first edition explores what it is like to think, make, and present architecture in which the "reciprocal supplementation" of word, world, and architecture gives free play to their mutual interference before any rigid cod(ex)ification.[128]

The revised edition, published five years later, had indeed revised itself into quite a different scene of instruction. It is a book that is seemingly at odds with the first edition, yet still tethered to it in its very disavowal. What is immediately noticeable is that the revised edition distances itself from the "stimulus ecology" of the Las Vegas "Trip" (and the reference to psychedelic experience in the students' way of referring to their ten-day visit to Las Vegas is significant).[129] But perhaps more importantly, it distances itself from the studio experience, in which the first edition was deeply steeped (figure 5.28).[130] For example, the Learning from Las Vegas studio logo, the small square "LLV" in sans serif font, which is on every board shown in the final presentation of the studio, and clearly in evidence on the schedules and plans in the preliminary mock-up for Part I, is slowly cropped out of the images from the first edition, and is completely absent from the revised edition (figure 5.29). Furthermore, the two unnumbered images that the reader immediately encountered in the first edition—the students' poster for the Las Vegas studio, which included the time and date of the final presentation, and the "Trip" collage—are omitted from the revised edition (figures 5.23, 5.24).[131] And with them, so are the marks of political ferment and war so apparent in the students' renaming of the studio from "Learning from Las Vegas, or Form Analysis as Design Research" to "Learning from Las Vegas: the grand proletarian cultural locomotive," which is boldly printed on their poster (not to mention the barely visible poster for an antiwar demonstration incorporated into the last collage image in Part I).

Scott Brown felt, however, that the studio's pedagogical aspects gained in prominence in the revised edition with the gathering of the studio notes into a separate section now keyed to Part I, rather than existing parallel to the body of the text in the first edition (figures 5.30, 5.31).[132] It is true that in their original placement the studio notes were at times hard to identify, as they were competing for space with other material in the margins, including small photographs, footnotes, and figure numbers. Furthermore, the placement of the studio notes

5.28 The Learning from Las Vegas studio; by permission of the Architectural Archives, University of Pennsylvania, gift of Robert Venturi and Denise Scott Brown.

5.29 Logo of the Learning from Las Vegas studio; by permission of the Architectural Archives, University of Pennsylvania, gift of Robert Venturi and Denise Scott Brown.

on the page was not consistent throughout Part I. But at the same time, the notes in the first edition were printed in bold Univers, with tight lateral and vertical spacing, which contrasted well with the triple spacing in the body of the main text. Most importantly, their placement within the flux of Part I gave more of a sense of the Las Vegas studio as a "group work and a sense of shared investigation between faculty and students."[133] What the notes gained in autonomy in the revised edition, they lost in the sense of shared conversation that is intrinsic to the studio condition. If the ideal culture is one in which we are all teachers *and* students, one gets a better sense of that condition in the first edition.

The participants in the Learning from Las Vegas studio weren't quite sure what they had "learned," but they were all aware that they were involved in a meaningful event.[134] To put it in McLuhanesque terms, the learning process in the first edition is still suspended between the acquisition of data and the plane of discovery.[135] It is precisely within this suspension that one might delay judgment in order to heighten sensitivity, and prolong the state of making sense before undertaking any critical action or normative judgment. In Freud's essay "Negation," affirmation is intimately linked with *eros*, or the pleasure principle, and the first edition of *Learning from Las Vegas* is deeply committed to lingering in that state and deferring the point of negation, or critical judgment. Not— as Venturi and Scott Brown are quick to note—to avoid judgment, but rather to delay it awhile in order to render judgment more sensitive. That is to say, their quest is for a mode of judgment that is more interested in heightening and reconfiguring our experience of the world, a criticism that, in the words of Foucault, "would not try to judge but to bring an oeuvre, a book . . . to life."[136]

In this pursuit of "signs of life," the "pleasure principle" is not at odds with the "reality principle"; in fact, the pleasure (principle) of research and shared studio experience is enabled by the reality principle of the given world—the imminent world around us—under investigation. "The reality principle imposes no definitive inhibition, no renunciation of pleasure," as Derrida notes, "only a detour in order to defer enjoyment."[137] One might say that the first edition of *Learning from Las Vegas* proposes "pleasure without a concept," which is reminiscent of a Kantian "reflective judgment"; that is, an aesthetic judgment in which pleasure has no predetermined "bounds," nor any a priori "concepts," that would assure us of its claims for assent. Any claims made for the exemplarity or universality of its judgments have no firmer ground than perception reflected upon, and the subjective voice of that reflection. Although it would be an exaggeration to say that the structure of the revised edition is more akin to a Kantian determinate judgment, the revised text is clearly more assured of its claims, as if it were confident that it already knew the bounds of pleasure and sense, and their reasoned relation to the world.[138] With the revised edition in mind, we should also note that in contrast to the accumulated tension,

5.30 "Studio Notes," *Learning from Las Vegas;* © 1977 Massachusetts Institute of Technology, by permission of the MIT Press.

STUDIO NOTES

§ A SIGNIFICANCE FOR A&P PARKING LOTS, OR LEARNING FROM LAS VEGAS: A STUDIO RESEARCH PROBLEM

School of Art and Architecture, Yale University, Fall 1968

Joint authors:
Robert Venturi
Denise Scott Brown
Steven Izenour

Students:
Ralph Carlson
Tony Farmer
Ron Filson
Glen Hodges
Peter Hoyt
Charles Korn
John Kranz
Peter Schlaifer
Peter Schmitt
Dan Scully
Doug Southworth
Martha Wagner
Tony Zunino

The studio programs and work topics were designed by Denise Scott Brown. Portions of them are quoted in these notes. Excerpts from writings by students have their names appended.

§ COMMERCIAL VALUES AND COMMERCIAL METHODS

This has been a technical studio. We are evolving new tools: analytical tools for understanding new space and form, and graphic tools for represent-

§ See material under the corresponding heading in Part I.

ing them. Don't bug us for lack of social concern; we are trying to train ourselves to offer *socially* relevant skills.

§ SYMBOL IN SPACE BEFORE FORM IN SPACE: LAS VEGAS AS A COMMUNICATION SYSTEM

WELCOME TO FABULOUS LAS VEGAS, FREE ASPIRIN—ASK US ANYTHING, VACANCY, GAS.

All cities communicate messages—functional, symbolic, and persuasive—to people as they move about. Las Vegas signs hit you at the California border and before you land at the airport. On the Strip three message systems exist: the *heraldic*—the signs—dominates (Fig. 1); the *physiognomic*, the messages given by the faces of the buildings—the continuous balconies and regularly spaced picture windows of the Dunes saying HOTEL (Fig. 3) and the suburban bungalows converted to chapels by the addition of a steeple (Fig. 4)—and the *locational*—service stations are found on corner lots, the casino is in front of the hotel, and the ceremonial valet parking is in front of the casino. All three message systems are closely interrelated on the Strip. Sometimes they are combined, as when the facade of a casino becomes one big sign (Fig. 5) or the shape of the building reflects its name, and the sign, in turn, reflects the shape. Is the sign the building or the building the sign?

Symbol in Space Before Form in Space: Las Vegas as a Communication System

The sign for the Motel Monticello, a silhouette of an enormous Chippendale highboy, is visible on the highway before the motel itself. This architecture of styles and signs is antispatial; it is an architecture of communication over space; communication dominates space as an element in the architecture and in the landscape. But it is for a new scale of landscape. The philosophical associations of the old eclecticism evoked subtle and complex meanings to be savored in the docile spaces of a traditional landscape. The commercial persuasion of roadside eclecticism provokes bold impact in the vast and complex setting of a new landscape of big spaces, high speeds, and complex programs. Styles and signs make connections among many elements, far apart and seen fast. The message is basely commercial; the context is basically new.

A driver 30 years ago could maintain a sense of orientation in space. At the simple crossroad a little sign with an arrow confirmed what he already knew. He knew where he was. Today the crossroad is a cloverleaf. To turn left he must turn right, a contradiction poignantly evoked in the print by Allan D'Arcangelo. But the driver has no time to ponder paradoxical subtleties within a dangerous, sinuous maze. He relies on signs to guide him — enormous signs in vast spaces at high speeds.

The dominance of signs over space at a pedestrian scale occurs in big airports. Circulation in a big railroad station required little more than a simple axial system from taxi to train, by ticket window, stores, waiting room, and platform — all virtually without signs. Architects object to signs in buildings: "If the plan is clear, you can see where to go." But complex programs and settings require complex combinations of media beyond the purer architectural triad of structure, form, and light at the service of space. They suggest an architecture of bold communication rather than one of subtle expression.

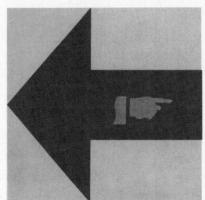

2. The trip. Allan D'Arcangelo

LAS VEGAS AS A COMMUNICATION SYSTEM 3-6

WELCOME TO FABULOUS LAS VEGAS, FREE ASPIRIN — ASK US ANYTHING, VACANCY, GAS.

All cities communicate messages — functional, symbolic, and persuasive — to people as they move about. Las Vegas signs hit you at the California border and before you land at the airport. On the Strip three message systems [7] exist: the heraldic (the signs) dominates; the [8] physiognomic, the messages given by the faces of the buildings (the continuous balconies and regularly spaced picture windows of the Dunes say- [9] ing HOTEL and the suburban bungalows converted to chapels by the [10] addition of a steeple); and the locational (service [11, 12] stations are found on corner lots, the casino is in front of the hotel, and the ceremonial valet parking is in front of the casino). All three message systems are closely interrelated on the Strip. Sometimes they are combined, as when the facade of a casino becomes one big sign or the shape of [13, 14] the building reflects its name, and the sign, in turn, reflects the shape. Is the sign the building or the building the sign?[15] These relationships, and combinations between signs and buildings, between architecture and symbolism, between form and meaning, between driver and the roadside are deeply relevant to architecture today and have been discussed at length by several writers. But they have not been studied in detail or as an overall system. The students of urban perception and imageability have ignored them, and there is some evidence that the Strip would confound their theories. How is it that in spite of "noise" from competing signs we do in fact find what we want on the Strip? Also, we have no good graphic tools for depicting the Strip as message giver. How can the visual importance of the Stardust sign be mapped at 1 inch to 100 feet?

4

5.31 Studio notes, *Learning from Las Vegas;* © 1972 Massachusetts Institute of Technology, by permission of the MIT Press.

excitement, and exorbitance of the first edition, eventually, according to Freud, the pleasure principle consists in a discharge of energy in order to return the psychical apparatus to a state of minimal excitation.

Text, Readability, and the Skeins of Sense

This sense of experimentation and delayed judgment in the first edition of *Learning from Las Vegas* is attested to by the fact that it is difficult to categorize as a traditional book that is meant to be read. By its own self-definition, it is a monster of a book: at once catalog and travelog; unfinished collage; and picture, pattern, sketch, or coffee-table book.[139] Although the revised edition was, as Scott Brown put it, an attempt to "shift the book's emphasis from illustrations to text," one is tempted to say that the first edition is more like a "text," in Roland Barthes's sense of that term; that is, a plural entity that is in excess of the "book," and thus not isolated to any particular genre, format, or clear "filiation."[140] And if we are willing to consider that a text is, as Jean-Luc Nancy writes, a certain "meshing and weaving together of a sense," we can then see the first edition as still caught up in the midst of its own weaving, as if it were trying to find the right warp and weft of image and text, its skeins of sense.[141] Seen in this light, the generous white spaces in Cooper's design might suggest a state of loose weave before the skeins of text and image were "tightened up" in Scott Brown's design of the revised edition.

We might consult the first edition or flip through it, as if we are too caught up in the work of weaving together text and image, the visible and legible, and thus leaving no time for reading that texture. It is much easier to imagine the first edition placed open on a flat surface than held between the hands in a relaxed, informal act of reading. To use Steinberg's imagery, it echoes any "hard receptor surface" on which information "may be received, imprinted, or impressed."[142] Thus, the first edition's mode of imaginative confrontation no longer takes place solely within the realm of reading, but rather within the labor and act of moving through its realm of information. This is epitomized in the many two-page spreads and broadsides that encourage the viewer to imagine they are unfolding and reorienting large sheets of information *as* their mode of turning the pages of the book.

But Venturi and Scott Brown clearly did not appreciate Muriel Cooper's way of moving through the material, her approach to the pacing and texture of the page layouts, or the patterning of its punctuation. In terms of typography, they thought that she had overemphasized the nonmimetic elements of the "sign-bearing matter" in the book—its texture, weight, and patterning—at the expense of its "semantic" function.[143] Venturi and Scott Brown disliked the use of boldface for quotations and figure numbers, and the odd placement of

Maps of Las Vegas

A "Nolli" map of the Las Vegas Strip reveals and clarifies what is public and what is private, but here the scale is enlarged

by the inclusion of the parking lot, and the solid-to-void ratio is reversed by the open spaces of the desert. Mapping the

34
Nolli components from an aerial photograph provides an intriguing crosscut of Strip systems. These components,

35-39
separated and redefined, could be undeveloped land, asphalt, autos, buildings, and ceremonial space. Reassembled, they

40
describe the Las Vegas equivalent of the pilgrims' way, although the description, like Nolli's map, misses the iconological

41
dimensions of the experience.

A conventional land-use map of Las Vegas can show the overall structure of commercial use in the city as it relates to

42
other uses but none of the detail of use type or intensity. "Land-use" maps of the insides of casino complexes, however,

43   **44**   **45**
begin to suggest the systematic planning that all casinos share. Strip "address" and "establishment" maps can depict both

46   **47**
intensity and variety of use. Distribution maps show patterns (of churches and food stores) that Las Vegas shares with

48   **49**
other cities and those (wedding chapels and auto rental stations) that are Strip-oriented and unique. It is extremely

52
hard to suggest the atmospheric qualities of Las Vegas, because these are primarily dependent on watts, animation, and

50, 51   **53**   **54**
iconology; however, "message maps," tourist maps, and brochures suggest some of it.

The representation techniques learned from architecture and planning impede our understanding of Las Vegas. They are static where it is dynamic, contained where it is open, two-dimensional where it is three-dimensional — how do you show the Aladdin sign meaningfully in plan, section, and elevation, or show the Golden Slipper on a land-use plan? Architectural techniques are suitable for large, broad objects in space, like buildings, but not for thin, intense objects, like signs; planning techniques are able to depict activity (land use), but in excessively general categories, for the ground floor only, and without intensity.

We need techniques for abstracting, for example, to represent "twin phenomena" or to demonstrate concepts and generalized schema — an archetypal casino or a piece of the urban fabric — rather than specific buildings. The pretty photographs that we and other tourists made in Las Vegas are not enough.

How do you <u>distort</u> these to draw out a meaning for

the latter over the lines of text, like so many signs dotting the side of the road. Yet I see this patterning as one of the best instantiations of their own argument about the contrast between the system and order on the Las Vegas Strip, in which the "continuous" and "constant rhythm" of the highway contrasts effectively with the "uneven rhythm of signs behind it" (figure 5.32).[144] For Venturi and Scott Brown, these idiosyncratic design elements impeded the readability and legibility of the text, whereas Cooper felt they enhanced readability, and that the very patterning and texture of her page exemplified movement through the city. But Venturi and Scott Brown were clearly after some other way of blocking together these issues.

Scott Brown characterized what they wanted as "a more 'traditional' relation between blocks of text, subtitles, titles, and page dimensions."[145] In order to demonstrate what they were looking for in the revised edition, she sent the Press copies of the layouts of an old Italian touring book, *Piemonte, attraverso*

5.32 Text with figure numbers, *Learning from Las Vegas*; © 1972 Massachusetts Institute of Technology, by permission of the MIT Press.

l'Italia, published in 1941 (figure 5.33).[146] Venturi and Scott Brown liked its "retardaire aesthetic," which seemed to reflect a "true monograph format" and the "standard textbook design" they were looking for.[147] Scott Brown also referred to the revised edition as a "treatise," by definition a systematic and comprehensive analysis of a subject.[148] This seems to entail a significant step beyond the motley text of the first edition, toward a "proper" book that is meant to be "read," and with its signification under the control of clearly identifiable authors. One might say that in the first edition legibility is lodged within visibility and visibility within legibility, whereas in the revised edition they seem to be prised apart into a condition in which visibility is now the condition, if not the a priori condition, for legibility as such. But it would be equally correct to say that legibility is now the condition for visibility as such: any sense of reciprocal supplementation between legibility and visibility is no longer a primary concern, or even pertinent, in the revised edition. One might say that the *shift* from the first edition was from the "sense" of text to an "idea" of text, keeping in mind the close relationship between idea, vision, and theory.

It is hardly surprising then that the argumentative, comparative, and binary structure that was not as prominent in the first edition comes to the fore in the revised edition. Although Venturi and Scott Brown have always been interested in what they call a "mild polemic," the revised edition is more didactic in its pedagogy, and tends toward focused argument rather than conversation or shared adventure. In Part II of *Learning from Las Vegas*, Venturi and Scott Brown wrote that their argument depends on bold comparisons, "because it is simple to the point of banality. It needs contrast to point it up."[149] These bold comparisons are further emboldened by the reconfiguration of the images into separate signatures in the revised edition, not to mention the resetting of the two "comparative tables" in Part II, which now occupy an entire page rather than only part of it as in the first edition. In the words of Scott Brown, "I have recast the dummy in a much more condensed form because . . . comparability is of the essence here and this makes the figures more comparable."[150] The condensation and reconfiguration of images resulted in even starker comparisons than in the first edition. For instance, the comparison between the Duck and the Decorated Shed, and their exemplification in Rudolph's Crawford Manor and Venturi and Rauch's Guild House, is awkward in the first edition owing to the vertical arrangement of the images (figure 5.34). In the revised edition, the new layout facilitates the comparison, in true Wölfflinian fashion, as the two buildings face each other on opposite pages, separated by the cleft of the spine and drawn to the same scale (figures 3.3, 3.4).[151]

Although the revised edition of *Learning from Las Vegas* established Venturi and Scott Brown's reputation and fame, like all important books it contributes to its own misreading. And this was due, in no small part, to the design of the

73

74

75

76

73. *Palazzo Saluzzo-Paesana*, in via della Consolata. Venne edificato per i Marchesi di Saluzzo-Paesana dall'architetto Planteri (sec. XVIII) ed è uno dei più sontuosi palazzi privati di Torino; il cortile d'onore, spaziosissimo, gareggia in magnificenza con quello dell'Università. Foto Alinari

74. *Il palazzo Balbo Bertone*, sito in via Stampatori 4, di cui riproduciamo il cortile, venne edificato dagli Scaglia di Verrua e passò poi al ramo dei Balbo Bertone di Sambuy, marchesi di Breme, attuali possessori, nel quale si estinse la famiglia Scaglia. L'insieme architettonico del cortile e dei loggiati del palazzo si può far risalire alla fine del regno di Emanuele Filiberto, per quanto le vôlte a vela molto depresse dei porticati, risentano ancora dell'influenza del Quattrocento.

Le figure a fresco della facciata esterna ed interna subirono indubbiamente nei motivi architettonici l'influsso di quanto costruivasi allora nel Genovesato, e si palesano alquanto posteriori all'edificio.

Il palazzo, tra i più notevoli della città, è unico perchè rappresenta la prima manifestazione del Rinascimento in Torino, e si distacca completamente da quanto sino allora si era edificato in Piemonte.

75. *Il palazzo della Corte d'Appello*, che sorge nella via omonima, venne iniziato nella prima metà del Settecento per ordine di Vittorio Amedeo II: diede i disegni il Juvara. Sospesa la costruzione, questa fu poi proseguita dall'Alfieri; ma il palazzo non fu terminato che nel secolo scorso. È sede della Corte d'Assise, della Corte d'Appello e del Tribunale.

76. *Palazzo Barolo : Atrio*. Di fianco al palazzo di Giustizia s'erge nella via delle Orfane il palazzo Barolo, di cui qui illustriamo l'atrio e lo scalone. Fu fatto costruire su disegni del Baroncelli (1692) da Ottavio Provana di Druent; passò poi ai marchesi Falletti di Barolo. Fot. Guido Cometto, Torino

77. *La marchesa Giulia Colbert di Maulévrier*, qui a fianco raffigurata, vedova dell'ultimo Falletti di Barolo, creò un'Opera pia alla quale lasciò il suo cospicuo patrimonio e che alla sua morte, nel 1864, fu eretta in Ente morale. L'Opera pia Barolo amministra le sostanze ereditate e tiene in vita le benefiche istituzioni dalla marchesa create, vale a dire educatori, asili, collegi, ecc.

Nel palazzo Barolo morì Silvio Pellico il 31 gennaio 1854. Fot. Guido Cometto, Torino

77

5.33 *Piemonte, attraverso l'Italia*, vol. 1
(Milan, 1941).

5.34 Comparison of Venturi and Rauch's Guild House with Paul Rudolph's Crawford Manor (by permission of the photographer, Robert Perron), in *Learning from Las Vegas*; © 1972 Massachusetts Institute of Technology, by permission of the MIT Press.

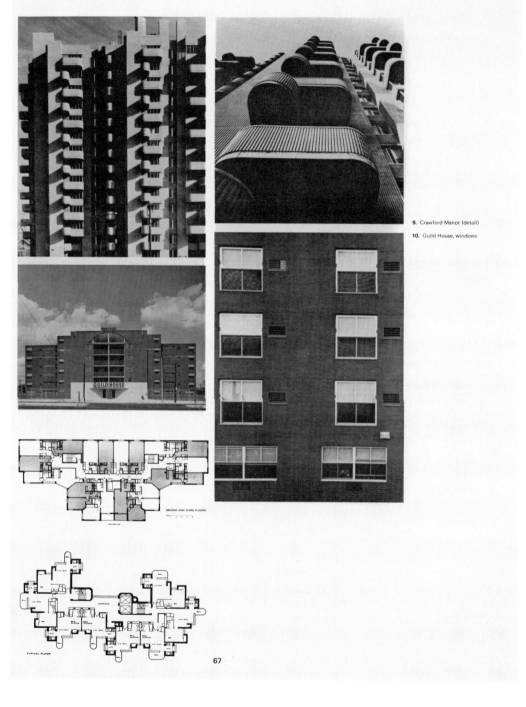

9. Crawford Manor (detail)

10. Guild House, windows

67

revised edition. The dramatized comparisons and amplified polemic no doubt contributed to the interpretation of *Learning from Las Vegas* as a "manifesto" of postmodernism, or at the very least its most "exemplary" text. Furthermore, its cleaving apart of legibility from visibility, rather than their mutual supplementation as in the first edition, and the separation of signs and symbols from their existence in and as a "stimulus ecology" encouraged the idea that *Learning from Las Vegas* initiated a "linguistic turn" in architecture. Venturi and Scott Brown clearly wanted the revised edition to be a book that looked like a book, and one that could take its place as a classic alongside other influential and widely disseminated paperbacks at the time, such as Jane Jacobs's *The Death and Life of Great American Cities* (1961), Kevin Lynch's *The Image of the City* (1964), or Yona Friedman's *Towards a Scientific Architecture* (1975). It certainly accomplished that goal in spades.

While the revised edition is supposedly "a treatise on symbolism in architecture," it is also a treatise on departure—a learning "from" the first edition of *Learning from Las Vegas*. Thus, the revised edition is equally what Derrida would call a "treatise on unleashing, on detaching, on unbinding. On destricturation."[152] But it achieves this departure precisely by leashing, attaching, binding, and restricturation. If we are willing to consider that possibility, then perhaps the "text" of *Learning from Las Vegas* is located somewhere between the lines of both editions, traversing them as it perpetually rewrites their affiliation. It is up to us to find our own point of departure from that text, and this is predicated on our finding new ways to read and write the first and revised editions together. The criteria for how to do so are up to us, and our claim to speak for *Learning from Las Vegas*'s inheritance can begin only with our participation in the conversations it initiated, acknowledged, and avoided.

APPENDIX: VINCENT SCULLY, UNPUBLISHED INTRODUCTION TO
LEARNING FROM LAS VEGAS

Vincent Scully's unpublished introduction to *Learning from Las Vegas* exists in three copies with slight variations, located in the VSBA archives at the University of Pennsylvania. During the summer and early fall of 1971, Venturi and Scott Brown planned to include Scully's introduction in the first edition of *Learning from Las Vegas*, but for unspecified reasons it was never published (see chapter 5 for my speculations). Scully's note in pen at the top of the first page suggests that this introduction was also being considered as a text for an exhibition of the works of Robert Venturi and Denise Scott Brown. Scully indeed published a version very close to this one for a brochure that accompanied the exhibition entitled "The Work of Venturi and Rauch, Architects and Planners" that took place at the Whitney Museum of American Art from October 1 to 31, 1971. Considering this text thirty-six years after it was written, Vincent Scully requested that I include the following note: "In 2007 these footnotes seem a little petulant but no more than half wrong."

It is no pleasure to write another introduction to a book by

and Steven Izenour *One's*

Robert and (in this case) Denise Venturi. ~~My own~~ paranoia ~~needs little~~

~~encouragement from theirs, and it~~ cannot help but flare up as the

classic pattern of lost competitions and sinister Design Review Boards

archetypally unfolds. In a previous Introduction I apparently annoyed

a few people by comparing (actually, contrasting) Venturi with Le Cor-

busier. I must now repeat the offense. The Venturis' paranoia is as

justified as Le Corbusier's was, and springs from the same real cause:

the venomous opposition to their work exhibited by much of the profes-

sion and, especially, ~~by~~ a few little men who are temporarily in a posi-

tion to block architectural change! No architect since the Le Corbusier

the profession

of the twenties has so driven ~~such~~ mediocrities to fury, which is per-

the firm Venturi and

Rauch

haps one of the most reliable touchstones to the fact that ~~Venturi~~ has

something important, even revolutionary, under way.

managed to

That something is, I think, largely this: Venturi has ~~finally~~

jettison

~~broken up~~ a wornout model of reality and has found, or revived, another

presently

and more relevant one. He has, in fact, broken through a haze of superficial idealism to the core of what is real in the present day.

He has done so, most of all, in that area which somehow always turns

out to be the critical one, the area wherein men would rather fight *apparently*

than switch: the area, that is, of symbol. He has found a way to make

his work symbolize the reality of things as they are in contemporary

America, and those who have lived under the protection of self-delusion

(as most of us do) cannot forgive him that act.

The historical process out of which Venturi evolved goes some-

thing like this: By the late nineteen-fifties the *rather tired formalistic* idealism of the late

International Style *in America* was modified, for a critical period by Louis I. Kahn

who succeeded in deriving fresh architectural forms from *two kinds of reality: from* struc-

ture, as in the Richards Laboratories; and, second, from function, as

in the Unitarian Church in Rochester. *That achievement was an enormous one,* But Kahn's buildings *tended to* re-

mained abstractly "expressive" -- of structure and space -- rather than

symbolic. "That doesn't look like a church," said the Vice-Mayor of

Leningrad, in a way rightly, when he saw an exhibition of the Rochester

building. It is in fact symbolically inert. One should contrast it, say, with Venturi's Fire Station in Columbus, which is symbolically

active.

But Venturi's work comes out of Kahn's, and the ~~anguished~~ re-

lationship between the two men is characteristic of such connections

between equals of different ages; it recalls that between Sullivan and

and ~~~~ it marks the first time *since Sullivan and Wright* *that one major innovator has un-*

Wright, for example. Venturi simply takes the last step -- but a giant

abstract *full architectural*

one -- away from idealism to realism: the step to symbol. It is the

the symbolic one; *it*

ultimate humane stance, ~~the one which~~ Michelangelo achieved in another

context in Renaissance architecture. It is not materialistic -- hence

structure becomes purely a servant, never a fetish, in it -- but human-

istic, man-centered; and function rises in it to a state of eloquent

declamation.

Venturi and Rauch

Such rhetoric is indeed eloquent in ~~Venturi's~~ buildings, but

the Venturis *their*

~~his~~ writing has sometimes functioned as ~~his own~~ worst enemy in terms

of the public recognition of that fact, because, in trying to make *their* ~~his~~

Venturi they

realistic, anti-heroic, and ironic points, ~~~~ persistently refers to

their

~~his~~ buildings as "dull," "boring," and "ugly." They are, of course,

Here is a second massive achievement on Kahn's part, perhaps the climax of Lou's career as a teacher

(should be ugly or boring,) but

never any of those things, though they probably look that way — because they are truly new — to people who have been brought up on the late International Style. ~~Here, too,~~ (Nor does the Venturis really believe that architecture) they ~~Venturis~~ (again) have sometimes overreacted, as in their praise of Coop City and of some suburban practices, so that ~~the~~ critics who will not really look at their work feel sanctioned in regarding it as consciously anti-architectural or anti-beautiful — which, of course, it is not.

But Venturi has committed another act of destruction, one equally difficult for many members of the profession to forgive. He has destroyed the precious, sub-Romantic myth of "invention," to which all the most uninventive among us have been so pathetically eager to cling. Indeed, to live within a model of work which ~~is~~ was a good two-generations old, but to believe at the same time that one ~~is~~ was at bottom wholly inventive and original, (is a fair description of the stance of most American architects a few years ago.) ~~must be the most paradis... and least demanding of all possible worlds.~~ It is that sterile dream world which Venturi has thrown away. He neither takes refuge in a "style" nor troubles to "invent." He still uses many of the same simple forms, historical and

and has its own kind of inner growth, but it strives neither for variety, where in-applicable, nor for any overall personal developmental order. It faces what is, every time. 5

vernacular in origin, with which he began. So his work gets better, ∧

~~but it does not "develop," precisely because~~ *Therefore* each project is at once

at the same time ∧

absolutely unique and ~~part of~~ *plugged into* a governing tradition of human use and

meaning. That is what the majority of the /ury failed to perceive at

Brighton Beach ∧, or failed to perceive as a virtue; but the tormented

cries of some of the jurors show how directly Venturi's forms grow out

social and psychological

of the American tradition and how close to the ∧ bone his symbols can cut.

Those symbols release architecture from postur~~ing~~ into content.

Hence vernacular architecture returns to us as usable reality, and the

whole past can play its proper part in our present. All the multiple

too,

facts of the present ∧ become usable ~~as well~~ when reality ~~rather than~~

~~dream~~ is the goal. So the Strip, with the gestures of its signs, makes

possible the Fire Station in Columbus (Function: each opening the shape

overrides the openings

it needs to be; symbol: the white paint that ~~stays away from archi-~~

∧

~~tonic boundaries~~ and so causes the whole façade to gesture upward to

and in his lat

its ringing Number 4). <u>Façade libre</u>, Le Corbusier had said; ~~Venturi~~

work he had *his* *as sculptural forces. Venturi*

∧ utilize~~d~~ that freedom to make ~~the~~ façade~~s~~ act, ~~or, better, to let it~~

∧ ∧

flattens them back out to make them

6

as signs.

speak The building tells us what it is about, and in this the tor-

mented semantic analogies of the present crop of semiological critics

should find an easy and wholly architectural fulfillment.

Again, however, we should not permit the polemics of the

Venturis to keep us from perceiving the range of their work. The Strip,

for one, is not their only resource, just as it is only part of the con-

temporary American scene. They use and symbolize whatever the program

is about, and they are able to comprise an enormous range of American

reality, from New York's *Bronx-like* ~~burly~~ Brighton Beach to California City's

mirror blazing in the desert; from the *civilized,* tragically baffled Transporta-

tion Square Office Building for Washington to the *luminous* Mathematics competi-

tion winner for Yale (now the focus, like Le Corbusier's League of

Nations winner of 1929, for all the *disaffected* ~~jackals'~~ howl~~ing~~; and finally to

the haunting Trubek *and Wislocki* Houses, wherein the ~~noble~~ American tradition of

wooden vacation dwellings by the sea is distilled into ~~one terrible~~ *thunderous,*

the ultimate mythic vision of this island and this Atlantic sky. ✳

✳ *It ... for paranoiacs:* As this goes to press one of the members of the Nantucket Historical ~~commission~~, a reti[red?] arch[itect] has taken it upon himself to redesign the fenestration of the entrance façade of the Trubek House and threatens to prevent construction unless ... He will offer three

[left margin, vertical handwritten:] a house on its generous plot of land could turn the most ... of Nantucket islands a suburb, for example.

should find an easy and wholly architectural fulfillment.

Again, however, we should not permit the polemics of the

Venturis to keep us from perceiving the range of their work. The Strip,

for one, is not their only resource, just as it is only part of the con-

temporary American scene. They use and symbolize whatever the program

is about, and they are able to comprise an enormous range of American

reality, from New York's ~~burly~~ Bronx-like Brighton Beach to California City's

mirror blazing in the desert; from the civilized, tragically baffled Transporta-

tion Square Office Building for Washington to the luminous Mathematics competi-

tion winner for Yale (now the focus, like Le Corbusier's League of

Nations winner of 1929, for all the ~~jackals'~~ disaffected howl~~ing~~s); and finally to

the haunting Trubek and Wislocki Houses, wherein the ~~whole~~ American tradition of

wooden vacation dwellings by the sea is distilled into ~~one~~ ~~terrible~~ ~~thunderous~~ the ultimate mythic

vision of this island and this Atlantic sky. *

---

* Note for paranoiacs: As this goes to press one of the
members of the Nantucket Historical Commission, a retired
architect, has taken it upon himself to redesign the
fenestration of the entrance façade of the Trubek
House and threatens to prevent construction unless
his whims are complied with. He will offer three
alternate solutions, he says.
¶ Evidence of this type against the desirability of
Design Review Boards is building up impressively
throughout the nation. Communities are acquiring too much
captious power over individual buildings and not enough—
the proper laws having not yet been written—over the
grouping of buildings. The present laws, based upon the

[left margin, rotated:] a house on its generous plot of land could turn most of Nantucket's individual islands into a suburb, for example.

NOTES

Introduction

1   Andreas Huyssen, "Mapping the Postmodern," in *After the Great Divide: Modernism, Mass Culture, Postmodernism* (Bloomington: Indiana University Press, 1986), p. 187.

2   Fredric Jameson, "The Vanishing Mediator; or, Max Weber as Storyteller," in *The Ideologies of Theory: Essays 1971–1986*, vol. 2 (Minneapolis: University of Minnesota Press, 1988), pp. 3–34.

3   Chapter 1 investigates this departure and leave-taking in terms of the word "from" in the title of *LLV*. Unless otherwise indicated, all references to *LLV* are to the revised edition (Cambridge: MIT Press, 1977).

4   Mary McLeod, "Architecture and Politics in the Reagan Era: From Postmodernism to Deconstructivism," in *Architecture Theory since 1968*, ed. K. Michael Hays (Cambridge, Mass.: MIT Press, 1998), pp. 678–703.

5   Denise Scott Brown, "Room at the Top? Sexism and the Star System in Architecture," in *Gender, Space, Architecture: An Interdisciplinary Introduction*, ed. Jane Rendell, Barbara Penner, and Iain Borden (London: Routledge, 2000), pp. 258–265. The collaborative nature of architectural work has been the subject of Beatriz Colomina's writing on Charles and Ray Eames. See, for example, Colomina, "Reflections on the Eames House," in *Anyhow*, ed. Cynthia Davidson (New York: Anyone Corporation, 1998), pp. 190–211.

6   The studio included thirteen students, from architecture, urban planning, and graphic design. The Learning from Levittown studio, a companion to the Learning from Las Vegas studio, took place a year later in the Graduate Department of the School of Architecture at Yale, and concentrated on the residential rather than the commercial

dimensions of urban sprawl. It utilized similar visual and analytical methods as the Learning from Las Vegas studio, and there are important references to this studio in *LLV*. In fact, Venturi and Scott Brown intended to publish it with the MIT Press as a sequel to *LLV*. The book was to be coauthored by Denise Scott Brown, Robert Venturi, and Virginia Carroll (a student on the project). See "Learning from Levittown Project," AAUP, box 453.

7   Stanley Cavell, "The Avoidance of Love: A Reading of *King Lear*," in *Must We Mean What We Say?* (Cambridge: Cambridge University Press, 2002), p. 330. This sentence also reminds me of the beautiful pages on the "transcendental-empirico doublet" in Foucault's *The Order of Things*.

8   As Cavell has put it, "the ordinary is precisely what it is that skepticism attacks." See Stanley Cavell, *Contesting Tears: The Hollywood Drama of the Unknown Woman* (Chicago: University of Chicago Press, 1996), p. 89.

9   On acknowledgment, see Stanley Cavell, "Knowing and Acknowledging," in *Must We Mean What We Say?*, pp. 238–266; and "Part Four: Between Acknowledgment and Avoidance," in *The Claim of Reason: Wittgenstein, Skepticism, Morality, and Tragedy* (Oxford: Oxford University Press, 1979), pp. 329–496. The issue of acknowledgment is woven throughout his writings, but these two citations are the most thematic and sustained explorations of the concept.

10   Cavell's favorite way of characterizing the beginning of the skeptical dilemma is the "conversion of metaphysical finitude into intellectual lack." See Stanley Cavell, *Disowning Knowledge in Six Plays of Shakespeare* (Cambridge: Cambridge University Press, 1987), p. 138; and Cavell, "Knowing and Acknowledging," p. 263.

11   Hilary Putnam has put this nicely: "ordinary does not mean going to the post office and mailing a letter, it means faith that the way we think and live isn't all a fiction or an illusion, that the illusion is rather all these tremendous intellectual constructions that make the way we think and live look like an illusion. This is what Wittgenstein was trying to make room for." See Hilary Putnam, "Between the New Left and Judaism," in Giovanna Borradori, *The American Philosopher: Conversations with Quine, Davidson, Putnam, Nozick, Danto, Rorty, Cavell, MacIntyre, and Kuhn* (Chicago: University of Chicago Press, 1994), p. 128.

12   As I point out in chapter 2, they are not arguing against space in architecture, but against a kind of medium specificity that would view space as the sole and defining essence of architecture, differentiating it from painting, sculpture, and literature. But there is, I believe, more going on here than just a critique of medium specificity in favor of mixed media. Venturi and Scott Brown seem to recognize that each new definition of an art or practice will have to come to terms with how that art touches on all the other arts, and in that touching, how it enacts a new redistribution and partition of sense. In philosophy, this "museology" has been most thoroughly pursued by Jean-Luc Nancy and Stanley Cavell. See Nancy, "Why Are There Several Arts and Not Just One," in *The Muses*, trans. Peggy Kamuf (Stanford: Stanford University Press, 1996), pp. 1–39; and Cavell, *The World Viewed: Reflections on the Ontology of Film* (New York: Viking Press, 1971), p. 103.

13   An odd situation, as Michel de Certeau wrote about Wittgenstein in relation to the ordinary in his influential book *The Practice of Everyday Life*, trans. Steven Rendall (Berkeley: University of California Press, 1984). For a different account of the ordinary in Venturi and Scott Brown's work, see Deborah Fausch, "Ugly and Ordinary: The Representation of the Everyday," in *Architecture of the Everyday*, ed. Steven Harris and Deborah Berke (Princeton: Princeton Architectural Press, 1997), pp. 75–106.

14 As Cavell has pointed out, since ancient times philosophy has felt a sense of intimacy between its aspirations and those of architecture, and vice versa. See "Epilogue: The *Investigations*' Everyday Aesthetics of Itself," in *The Cavell Reader*, ed. Stephen Mulhall (Cambridge, Mass.: Blackwell, 1996), p. 375.

15 See Walter Benjamin, "Rigorous Study of Art," *October* 47 (Winter 1988): 84–90; and Ludwig Wittgenstein, *Culture and Value*, ed. G. H. Von Wright, trans. Peter Winch (Oxford: Blackwell, 1990), 22e.

16 Jean-Luc Nancy, *Hegel: The Restlessness of the Negative*, trans. Jason Smith and Steven Miller (Minneapolis: University of Minnesota Press, 2002), p. 32.

17 With elements of Jean Baudrillard, Guy Debord, and Martin Heidegger, depending on the critic. These critics would include Tomás Maldonado, Kenneth Frampton, Manfredo Tafuri, Fred Koetter, Jürgen Habermas (in his brief references to the book), and most recently Neil Leach and Hal Foster.

18 Jacques Rancière, "La surface du *design*," in *Le destin des images* (Paris: Fabrique Editions, 2003), p. 105.

19 Stanley Cavell, *Pursuits of Happiness: The Hollywood Comedy of Remarriage* (Cambridge, Mass.: Harvard University Press, 1981), p. 39; and Cavell, *The Senses of Walden* (Chicago: University of Chicago Press, 1992), p. 33.

20 "To take an interest in an object is to take an interest in one's own experience of the object, so that to examine and defend my interest . . . is to examine and defend my interest in my own experience, in the moments and passages of my life I have spent with them." Cavell, *Pursuits of Happiness*, p. 7. One gets this sense of criticism in the work of art historian Michael Fried, when he notes of his book *Courbet's Realism* that it was not so much written chapter by chapter, but painting by painting—as if to say that his account emerged out of his intense conversations with these paintings. See Fried, *Courbet's Realism* (Chicago: University of Chicago Press, 1990), xvii.

21 Cavell, *Pursuits of Happiness*, pp. 34–40.

22 Stanley Cavell, *A Pitch of Philosophy: Autobiographical Exercises* (Cambridge, Mass.: Harvard University Press, 1994), p. 15. Derrida notes, "I continue to believe that that there is no reading that does not force things, the question of the *fitting* forcing of them remaining open for essential reasons." See Derrida, "Tense," in *The Path of Archaic Thinking: Unfolding the Work of John Sallis*, ed. Kenneth Maly (Albany: State University of New York Press, 1995), p. 63.

23 Cavell, *A Pitch of Philosophy*, p. 16.

24 Robert Venturi, preface to *Complexity and Contradiction in Architecture*, 2d ed. (New York: New York Graphic Society, 1977).

25 Henry David Thoreau, *Walden* (Oxford: Oxford University Press, 1999), p. 289.

26 Cavell, *Pursuits of Happiness*, p. 37.

27 Stanley Cavell, *In Quest of the Ordinary: Lines of Skepticism and Romanticism* (Chicago: University of Chicago Press, 1994), pp. 24–25.

28 Martin Heidegger, *What Is Called Thinking?*, trans. J. Glenn Gray (New York: Harper & Row, 1968), p. 76. Also see Nancy's discussion of "not-knowing" in *A Finite Thinking*, ed. Simon Sparks (Stanford: Stanford University Press, 2003), pp. 36–40.

29 Robert Venturi, "Mal Mots: Aphorisms—Sweet and Sour—by an Anti-Hero Architect," in *Iconography and Electronics upon a Generic Architecture: A View from the Drafting Room* (Cambridge, Mass.: MIT Press, 1996), pp. 304–305.

1.   *LLV*, p. 6. Their phrase "skyline of signs" was inspired by Tom Wolfe's "Las Vegas (What?) Las Vegas (Can't Hear You! Too Noisy) Las Vegas!!!," in *The Kandy-Kolored Tangerine-Flake Streamline Baby* (1965; rpt., London: Jonathan Cape, 1996), p. 8. This essay was one of the introductory readings for the Learning from Las Vegas studio.

2.   Quoted in David B. Brownlee, "Form and Content," in David B. Brownlee, David G. De Long, and Kathryn B. Hiesinger, *Out of the Ordinary* (Philadelphia: Philadelphia Museum of Art, 2001), p. 37. Venturi's first visit to Rome was another transformative moment. I am sure that many critics would use the word "stupefaction" rather than "wonder" to characterize their experience. In a sense this would not be incorrect, as long as it acknowledges that stupefaction is a risk *internal* to the experience of wonder. See Avital Ronell, *Stupidity* (Urbana: University of Illinois Press, 2002), p. 111. Needless to say, there has always been a close connection between the wondrous and commodification. See Lorraine Daston and Katharine Park, *Wonders and the Order of Nature* (New York: Zone Books, 1998), pp. 66–67.

3.   The phrase "melodramas of instruction" comes from Philip Fisher's *Wonder, the Rainbow, and the Aesthetics of Rare Experiences* (Cambridge, Mass.: Harvard University Press, 1998), p. 31. I was struck by Fisher's wording, as the melodramatic voice seems to permeate *LLV*. I return to the issue of melodrama in chapter 3, drawing on some thoughts in Stanley Cavell's book *Contesting Tears*.

4.   Martin Heidegger, *Basic Questions of Philosophy*, trans. Richard Rojcewicz and André Schuwer (Bloomington: Indiana University Press, 1994), p. 135. When one escapes from the "primordial need" of wonder, "the avidity for learning and calculation enters in" (p. 155).

5.   I grappled with the relation of repeatability to wonder in thinking about *LLV*, and about Venturi and Scott Brown's penchant for repeating themselves in their interviews and writings. I began to realize that being able to continue, to go on, to reaffirm, and, yes, to repeat, are all essential to the mood of wonder.

6   Stanley Cavell, *A Pitch of Philosophy: Autobiographical Exercises* (Cambridge, Mass.: Harvard University Press, 1994), p. 63. Plato, *Theaetetus*, trans. Myles Burnyeat (Indianapolis: Hackett, 1992), 155c–d. There is a long bibliography on the claim that philosophy begins in wonder; the following will have to stand in for the rest: John Sallis, "The Place of Wonder," in *Double Truth* (Albany: State University of New York Press, 1995), pp. 191–210; John Llewelyn, "On the Saying that Philosophy Begins in Wonder," in *Seeing through God: A Geophenomenology* (Bloomington: Indiana University Press, 2004), pp. 55–69; Fisher, *Wonder, the Rainbow, and the Aesthetics of Rare Experiences*; Martin Heidegger, *What Is Philosophy?* (New Haven: College and University Press, 1956), and *Basic Questions of Philosophy*; and the many passages on wonder permeating all of Stanley Cavell's writings.

7   Cavell, *A Pitch of Philosophy*, pp. 48–51, 55, 59. Cavell also describes his ecstatic experience of learning to hear the near perfect pitch of music at Berkeley from the composer Ernest Bloch. He also writes that he was "floored" by reading Wittgenstein's *Philosophical Investigations*. See "An Apology for Skepticism: Stanley Cavell," in Giovanna Borradori, *The American Philosopher: Conversations with Quine, Davidson, Putnam, Nozick, Danto, Rorty, Cavell, MacIntyre, and Kuhn* (Chicago: University of Chicago Press, 1994), p. 128.

8   Michael Fried, "An Introduction to My Art Criticism," in *Art and Objecthood: Essays and Reviews* (Chicago: University of Chicago Press, 1998), pp. 27–28.

9   Lacan uses the term "a-ha Erlebnis [experience]" in his mirror-stage essay. Jacques Lacan, "The Mirror-Phase as Formative of the Function of the I," in *Mapping Ideology*, ed. Slavoj Žižek (London: Verso, 1994), p. 93.

10 The locus classicus for any discussion of orientation, or for that matter disorientation, is Kant's essay "What Does It Mean to Orient Oneself in Thinking?," in *Religion within the Boundaries of Mere Reason and Other Writings*, trans. and ed. Allen Wood and George di Giovanni (Cambridge: Cambridge University Press, 1998), pp. 3–14.

11 Martin Heidegger, *Being and Time*, trans. Joan Stambaugh (Albany: State University of New York Press, 1996), §136. See chapter 3 for a further discussion of mood in relation to the deadpan.

12 Stanley Cavell, "Declining Decline: Wittgenstein as a Philosopher of Culture," *This New Yet Unapproachable America: Lectures after Emerson after Wittgenstein* (Albuquerque, New Mexico: Living Batch Press, 1989), p. 36. Cavell is providing a gloss on Wittgenstein's phrase: "A philosophical problem has the form: 'I don't know my way about.'" Ludwig Wittgenstein, *Philosophical Investigations*, trans. G. E. M. Anscombe (Oxford: Blackwell, 1976), §123.

13 In an interesting passage in his book on Adorno, J. M. Bernstein discusses how the thought that things we "suffer" are neutrally composed of things both pleasurable and awful gets transformed into the idea that anything suffered is wholly negative. See Bernstein, *Adorno: Disenchantment and Ethics* (Cambridge: Cambridge University Press, 2001), p. 404. Heidegger expresses exactly the same thought in *Basic Questions of Philosophy*. The biblical sense of the word—e.g., "suffer the little children to come unto me" (Luke 18:15–17)—captures the receptivity and vulnerability that Bernstein and Heidegger are trying to get at.

14 Sigmund Freud, *Totem and Taboo*, trans. and ed. James Strachey (New York: Norton, 1950), p. 194. Also see the definition of ambivalence in Jacques Laplanche and J. B. Pontalis, *The Language of Psycho-Analysis* (New York: Norton, 1977), p. 26. "[t]he simultaneous existence of contradictory tendencies, attitudes, or feelings in the relationship (to the same) object—especially the coexistence of love and hate." Bleuler introduced the term "ambivalence" into psychoanalytic thought in 1910. For Freud it became the most important characteristic of obsessional neurosis. More importantly, Freudian thought is fundamentally ambivalent. For a book that acknowledges this, see Samuel Weber, *The Legend of Freud* (Minneapolis: University of Minnesota Press, 1982).

15 Denise Scott Brown, "On Architectural Formalism and Social Concern: A Discourse for Social Planners and Radical Chic Architects," *Oppositions* 5 (1976): 103. We might also want to think of Venturi and Scott Brown's "loving and hating" in terms of "radical ambivalence," a phrase that commentators, such as John McCole, have used to describe the antinomic structure in Walter Benjamin's thought and writing. Miriam Hansen has made the astute comment that this ambivalence was Benjamin's response at the time to the "irresolvable contradictions in media culture itself"—conditions just as relevant now as then. See Miriam Hansen, "Benjamin and Cinema: Not a One-Way Street," in *Benjamin's Ghosts: Interventions in Contemporary Literary and Cultural Theory*, ed. Gerhard Richter (Stanford: Stanford University Press, 2002), pp. 43–44.

16 Robert Venturi, *Complexity and Contradiction in Architecture* (New York: Museum of Modern Art, 1966), p. 23 (and compare pp. 30–37): "I prefer 'both-and' to 'either-or,' black and white, and sometimes gray, to black or white."

17 Cleanth Brooks, *The Well Wrought Urn* (New York: Harcourt, Brace & World, 1947), p. 81.

18   Finkelpearl was an expert on the English mannerist playwright John Marston, an author Eliot had written on. The title for Venturi's first book was suggested by Finkelpearl, and is derived from a passage in *The Well Wrought Urn*: "In other words, the poet
wishes to indicate that his vision has been earned, that it can survive reference to the
complexities and contradictions of experience" (Brooks, *The Well Wrought Urn*, p. 212).
The specific word "ambivalence" comes up in William Empson's *Seven Types of Ambiguity*
(New York: Meridian Books, 1955) and comes increasingly to the fore in later editions
of his book, as does T. S. Eliot's criticism. In *The Well Wrought Urn* Brooks also draws on
Freud, noting that his work on dreams is closer to poetry than science. Stanley Edgar
Hyman, an important historian of the New Critics, acknowledges their attraction to
Freud in *The Armed Vision* (New York: Vintage Books, 1955).

     A close reading of Brooks's and Empson's work suggests that we really need to rethink
questions of irony as they have been raised in relationship to *Learning from Las Vegas* as an
exemplary text of postmodernism. Although Brooks at times defines irony fairly traditionally "as the recognition of incongruities" (*The Well Wrought Urn*, p. 209), it is clear that his
understanding of irony, and Venturi and Scott Brown's, is much closer to Schlegel's definition of it "as the clear consciousness of eternal agility, of an infinitely teeming chaos." See
Friedrich Schlegel, *Philosophical Fragments*, trans. Peter Firchow (Minneapolis: University of
Minnesota Press, 1991). In any case, I begin to rethink the issue of irony—and the fact that
it might not even look or sound like irony anymore—in terms of the two types of humor in
play in *Learning from Las Vegas*: the jester and the deadpan. On these issues I have benefited
from Paul de Man's essay "The Concept of Irony," in *Aesthetic Ideology*, ed. Andrzej Warminski (Minneapolis: University of Minnesota Press, 1996), pp. 163–184.

19   The following are all cited: William Empson's *Seven Types of Ambiguity*, Cleanth Brooks's
The Well Wrought Urn, Stanley Edgar Hyman's *The Armed Vision*, Kenneth Burke's *Perma-
nence and Change*, T. S. Eliot's *Selected Essays, 1917–1932*, and his *The Use of Poetry and the
Use of Criticism*.

20   *LLV*, p. 77 (p. 31 in the first edition). Venturi first met van Eyck in the spring of 1960
when he was a visiting professor at the University of Pennsylvania, where Venturi was
an assistant professor. Francis Strauven makes it clear that Venturi's understanding
of "twin phenomenon" is radically different from van Eyck's: "Venturi finds it unnec-
essary to bring the opposing poles into harmony. It is precisely their polarity, indeed
their contradictions, that interest him." See Francis Strauven, *Aldo van Eyck: The Shape
of Relativity* (Amsterdam: Architectura & Natura, 1998), p. 475. This strikes me as basically correct, but not nuanced enough to account for Venturi's take on the matter. I
would rather take the word "contradiction" literally as voices brushing up against each
other. Paul de Man's critique of the New Critics is particularly relevant for their role
in *Complexity and Contradiction*. See de Man, "The Dead-End of Formalist Criticism," in
Blindness and Insight: Essays in the Rhetoric of Contemporary Criticism, 2d ed. (Minneapolis:
University of Minnesota Press, 1983), pp. 229–245.

21   See Charles Jencks, *The Language of Post-Modern Architecture* (New York: Rizzoli, 1991).

22   I am in basic agreement with Geoffrey Bennington's evaluation of the limitations of
Jencks's approach to conceptualizing the postmodern, but I disagree with his implica-
tion that Venturi and Scott Brown are reading Eliot and the New Critics in a somewhat
naive and "metaphysical" way, particularly when it comes to the texture of *LLV*. See
Bennington, "The Rationality of Postmodern Relativity," in *Legislations: The Politics of
Deconstruction* (London: Verso, 1994), pp. 172–195.

23 I would also agree with Bennington that ambiguity remains within "the ambit of a notion of meaning as ideally unitary and recoverable" (ibid., p. 184). But *ambivalence* doesn't. Ambivalence is really a question of disposition and attunement. As Jean-François Lyotard notes, "The operator of disintensification is exclusion: either this, or not-this. Not both. The disjunctive bar." Lyotard, *Libidinal Economy*, trans. Iain Hamilton Grant (Bloomington: Indiana University Press, 1993), p. 14.

24 Cavell, writing on Emerson and Thoreau, was one of the earliest to emphasize the importance of mood in Heidegger's work. See, for example, "Thinking of Emerson" and "An Emerson Mood," in Stanley Cavell, *The Senses of Walden* (Chicago: University of Chicago Press, 1981), pp. 123–160. Cavell's phrase "attunement in criteria" also recalls the use of the word "attunement" in Heidegger's *Being and Time*. Cavell also links mood with wonder and urban life: "For Wittgenstein and Austin, as for the figures of Socrates or Descartes (in the *Meditations*) or Hume or Emerson or Thoreau, the mood of philosophy begins in the street, or in doorways, or closets, anywhere but in philosophical schools; it is philosophy's power to cause wonder, or to stun—to take one aside—that decides who is to become a philosopher." See Cavell, *A Pitch of Philosophy*, p. 63.

25 Despite Deleuze's apparent dislike of Heidegger—in whom he no doubt finds too many traces of the legacy of intentionality, despite Heidegger's radical critique of transcendental phenomenology—there are more thought-provoking resonances between the two than one might imagine. In a beautiful diagram, Giorgio Agamben lays out a genealogy of modern philosophy in terms of a "line of transcendence" and a "line of immanence." In this genealogy Heidegger is figured as *the* crucial transference between the two lines. See Giorgio Agamben, "Absolute Immanence," in *Potentialities: Collected Essays in Philosophy*, trans. Daniel Heller-Roazen (Stanford: Stanford University Press, 1999), p. 239. Alain Badiou is also acutely aware of how Deleuze's thought locates its limit in regard to Heidegger. See Alain Badiou, *Deleuze: The Clamor of Being*, trans. Louise Burchill (Minneapolis: University of Minnesota Press, 2000), pp. 20–23, 79–80, 101. To go the other way, Jean-Luc Nancy has been engaged at times in a Spinozan reading of Heidegger's *Being and Time*.

26 Heidegger, *Basic Questions of Philosophy*, p. 140.

27 Fredric Jameson, *Postmodernism, or, The Cultural Logic of Late Capitalism* (Durham: Duke University Press, 1991). Jameson shares Heidegger's critique of the psychology and anthropology of subjectivity. In an odd sense, Jameson prepared the way for a primarily Deleuzian interest in "affect," as he suggested that we think about "intensities" rather than psychological feelings as such (although his primary reference here is to Lyotard, not Deleuze).

28 Heidegger, *Being and Time*, §§134, 345. It is pertinent that the "they" is Heidegger's definition of the "inauthentic self" that is influenced by the crowd. But the "they" also means "us."

29 For Heidegger, it is a gray that consists of an odd mixture of fear, boredom, anxiety, hope, and confidence. See the excellent essay by Klaus Held that discusses Heidegger's moods in relation to their historical and transhistorical dimensions: "Fundamental Moods and Heidegger's Critique of Contemporary Culture," trans. Anthony J. Steinbeck, in *Reading Heidegger: Commemorations*, ed. John Sallis (Bloomington: Indiana University Press, 1993), pp. 286–303. In this essay, Held argues for the mood of wonder that can break through this "gray everyday" in its ability to see the extraordinary in the ordinary, the unfamiliar in the familiar. In this sense, wonder is not tethered to the

temporal beginning of philosophy (i.e., the ancient Greeks). It is interesting to note that Held seems to translate Heidegger's "pallid lack of mood" as "waning of nonmoodedness" (p. 293). I have also benefited from Michel Haar's groundbreaking essays on Heidegger and mood. See for example Michel Haar, "Attunement and Thinking," in *Heidegger: A Critical Reader*, ed. Hubert Dreyfus and Harrison Hall (Oxford: Basil Blackwell, 1992), pp. 159–172.

30   Heidegger, *Basic Questions of Philosophy*, p. 145 (my emphasis).

31   There are passages in Heidegger's work on mood that are strikingly close to Cavell's account of acknowledgment: "as moved by wonder, man must gain a foothold in the acknowledgment of what has erupted, and he must see it in a productive seeing of its inscrutable disclosure"; and "The basic disposition of *thaumazein* compels us to a pure acknowledgment of the unusualness of the usual." See Heidegger, *Basic Questions of Philosophy*, pp. 146, 148. Needless to say, all moods are ambivalent. Heidegger has parsed all the "inauthentic" dimensions of wonder, the main one being curiosity. In fact, Heidegger is at times inclined to think that the mood of wonder occurs only in its inauthentic dimensions in the present era.

32   Le Corbusier, *When the Cathedrals Were White: A Journey to the Country of Timid People* (New York: Reynal & Hitchcock, 1947), p. 91. An entire section of the book is entitled "The Fairy Catastrophe," pp. 83–91.

33   This despite Venturi and Scott Brown's continuous attempts to rectify the misconception in subsequent articles and interviews. Derrida has outlined the logic and details of such a predicament in his analysis of the Greek word *Pharmakon* in Plato's *Phaedrus*, which, in the medicine chest of philosophy, was labeled either as "remedy" or "poison," thus canceling out its ambivalent meaning. See Jacques Derrida, "Plato's Pharmacy," in *Dissemination*, trans. Barbara Johnson (Chicago: University of Chicago Press, 1981), pp. 61–177.

34   A sophisticated Adornian approach to *LLV* would have to be written with an attentive eye to the nuances found in the work of J. M. Bernstein and Miriam Hansen. In chapter 2, I try to outline where a different take on Adorno might intersect with my Cavellian account. Also see my and Michael Golec's discussion of the critical theory reception of *LLV* in our introduction to *Relearning from Las Vegas*, ed. Aron Vinegar and Michael Golec (Minneapolis: University of Minnesota Press, forthcoming 2009). Mary McLeod's account of the critical theory reception of the book can be found in her article "Architecture and Politics in the Reagan Era: From Postmodernism to Deconstructivism," in *Architecture Theory since 1968*, ed. K. Michael Hays (Cambridge, Mass.: MIT Press, 1998), pp. 678–703.

35   Of course my parsing of these three positions is a gross simplification of a range of critical responses that, more often than not, overlap. Nietzsche has come up with the best description of the occupation of both extreme positions: the "passive nihilist" and the "omni-satisfied" or "last men." For a discussion of the "last men," see chapter 4.

36   "A Conversation . . . Walter Hopps and Edward Ruscha," in *Edward Ruscha, Romance with Liquids: Paintings 1966–1969* (New York: Rizzoli, 1993), p. 106. See Stanley Cavell, "Postscript (1989): To Whom It May Concern," *Critical Inquiry* 16, no. 2 (Winter 1990): 250–253.

37   Wittgenstein notes that "[a] perspicuous representation produces just that understanding which consists in 'seeing connexions.' . . . It earmarks the form of account we give, the way we look at things." *Philosophical Investigations*, §122.

38 Stanley Cavell, "Ending the Waiting Game," in *Must We Mean What We Say?* (Cambridge: Cambridge University Press, 2002), p. 156. From this perspective, Baudrillard's apocalyptic sense of America as the accomplishment of skepticism is inaccurate here. For example: "the natural deserts tell me what I need to know about the deserts of the sign. . . . They induce in me an exalting vision of desertification of signs and men." See Jean Baudrillard, *America,* trans. Chris Turner (London: Verso, 1988), p. 63. I find Deleuze's phrase about "bring[ing] language slowly and progressively to the desert" more to the point. See Gilles Deleuze and Félix Guattari, *Kafka: Toward a Minor Literature,* trans. Dana Polan (Minneapolis: University of Minnesota Press, 1986), p. 26.

39 The following section is my way of thinking through the word "abandonment," as nuanced by Cavell in his numerous passages on the topic; for example, see Cavell, *The Senses of Walden.* In conjunction with "abandonment," I have found myself reflecting on the intricate section on the word "from" in Heidegger's *Being and Time,* §185, and his claim that "Mood does not disclose in the mode of looking at thrownness, but as turning toward and away from it" (§135).

40 Here I am paraphrasing Cavell's sentence: "Walden was always gone, from the beginning of the words of *Walden.*" See Cavell, *The Senses of Walden,* p. 119.

41 Venturi, *Complexity and Contradiction in Architecture,* p. 102.

42 One can't help agreeing with Friedrich Schlegel: "I'm disappointed in not finding in Kant's family tree of basic concepts the category 'almost,' a category that has surely accomplished, and spoiled, as much in the world and in literature as any other. In the mind of natural skeptics it colors all other concepts and intuitions." Schlegel, *Philosophical Fragments,* p. 10.

43 For a (partial) list of these connotations, see Cavell, *The Senses of Walden,* p. 136.

44 Heidegger, *What Is Philosophy?,* p. 85.

45 Denise Scott Brown, "Pop Off: Reply to Kenneth Frampton," *Casabella,* nos. 359–360 (May–June 1971): 73.

46 The concept of the "enigmatic signifier" is a psychoanalytic theory developed by Jacques Laplanche as a modified return to Freud's disavowed "seduction theory." At first reading, it seems that Laplanche is giving a stronger directionality to the "from"—that is, the "enigmatic signifier" is sent from the mother to the child—than I seem to be implying here as a kind of facing that is predicated on a turning back. I have also found Leo Bersani and Ulysse Dutoit's commentary on the "enigma" in Western culture helpful (they are drawing on the work of Laplanche). They suggest that the enigma is usually thought of as a provisional unreadability, that is, merely a spur to the extension of knowledge. In contrast, they talk about the "intractably enigmatic quality" of Caravaggio's paintings. See Leo Bersani and Ulysse Dutoit, "Caravaggio's Secrets," in *Aesthetic Subjects,* ed. Pamela R. Mathews and David McWhirter (Minneapolis: University of Minnesota Press, 2003), pp. 106–107. Jean-Luc Nancy has noted that "Wonder itself is a kind of sign without signification." See Jean-Luc Nancy, "On Wonder," in *The Gravity of Thought,* trans. François Raffoul and Gregory Recco (Atlantic Highlands, N.J.: Humanities Press, 1997), p. 67.

47 It seems to me that even intelligent writers and readers such as Rem Koolhaas and Mark Taylor fall into this trap. See Rem Koolhaas and Hans Ulrich Obrist, "Relearning from Las Vegas," *Harvard Design School Guide to Shopping,* vol. 2, ed. Chuihua Judy Chung, Jeffrey Inaba, Rem Koolhaas, and Sze Tsung Leong (Cologne: Taschen, 2001), pp. 590–617; and Mark Taylor, "Stripping Architecture," in *The Virtual Dimension: Architecture, Representation,*

and Crash Culture, ed. John Beckmann (New York: Princeton Architectural Press, 1998), pp. 194–203. This essay is a summation of a chapter on Las Vegas in Taylor's book *Hiding* (Chicago: University of Chicago Press, 1997). Venturi and Scott Brown always acknowledged that Las Vegas was the "archetype" or "exaggerated example" of what had been reiterated on Main Street throughout America.

48   Gilles Deleuze and Félix Guattari, "Introduction: Rhizome," in *A Thousand Plateaus*, trans. Brian Massumi (Minneapolis: University of Minnesota Press, 1987), pp. 24–25.

49   The impact of this pedagogical model is exemplified in Rem Koolhaas's Harvard design studios, which involve intensive group research resulting in publications. It was Koolhaas who characterized his book *Delirious Manhattan* as a manifesto with research.

50   Robert Venturi and Denise Scott Brown, preface to the first edition, *LLV*, p. xii. In interviews, Scott Brown and Venturi always emphasize that Las Vegas was "strongly affective and exciting" for them.

51   Here I think the first edition of *LLV* is very close to the ideas worked out in J. J. Gibson's *The Senses Considered as Perceptual Systems* (Boston: Houghton Mifflin, 1966), p. 26: "No symbol exists except as it is realized in sound, projected light, mechanical contact, or the like. All knowledge rests on sensitivity." This is what Gibson calls a "stimulus ecology," which, according to him, involves many disciplines, including architecture (pp. 29–30). Also see chapter 5.

52   Heidegger, *Basic Questions of Philosophy*, p. 141.

53   As I note in the introduction, a concentration on *LLV*'s pragmatic use in architectural schools, or on its trenchant empiricism, tends to ignore the skeptical voice in the text.

54   Denise Scott Brown, preface to the revised edition, *LLV*, p. xv.

55   I am alluding to Cavell's gloss on Thoreau's peculiar use of the word "interest" and "interested" with its emphasis on the condition of "being between," our capacity for concern and implication, and with issues of withholding and displacement. See *The Senses of Walden*, pp. 67, 102, 117; and Stanley Cavell, "Thoreau Thinks of Ponds, Heidegger of Rivers," in *Philosophy the Day after Tomorrow* (Cambridge, Mass.: Harvard University Press, 2005), p. 229.

56   Plato, *The Republic*, trans. Francis MacDonald Cornford (London: Oxford University Press, 1945), p. 591. See Stanley Cavell, "Introduction: Staying the Course," in *Conditions Handsome and Unhandsome: The Constitution of Emersonian Perfectionism* (Chicago: University of Chicago Press, 1990), pp. 1–32. It should be noted that the English translation "our city of words" is peculiar to Cavell. All the translations of *The Republic* that I have consulted usually translate this phrase as the realm of "discourse" or "theory." There is a similar sentiment and phrase expressed in Emerson's essay "Experience": "I know that the world I converse with in the city and in the farms, is not the world I *think*." See "Experience," in *Ralph Waldo Emerson: Selected Essays, Lectures, Poems*, ed. Robert D. Richardson (New York: Bantam Books, 1990), p. 246. And Cavell has recently used the term in the title of his book *Cities of Words: Pedagogical Letters on a Register of Moral Life* (Cambridge, Mass.: Belknap Press of Harvard University Press, 2004), on Emersonian perfectionism and film.

57   I want to make clear that I am not arguing for VSBI's work as an example of "post-analytic architecture," à la Richard Rorty, in the model of an ongoing conversation (rather than an analytic exercise). Alan Plattus has made the argument for this position in his essay "Toward a Post-Analytic Architecture: Recent Work of Venturi, Rauch, and Scott Brown," in *Thinking the Present: Recent American Architecture* (Princeton: Princeton University Press,

1990), pp. 45–60. This is not to say that "conversation" is not a fruitful way of approaching *LLV*; I just prefer other modes of thinking about what a conversation might entail and enact.

58 Here I am drawing on Cavell's linking of having a conversation and being interested in one's own experience as the unfolding of acknowledgment (or its avoidance) that might lead from the "actual" to the "eventual"—i.e., to change. In particular see Stanley Cavell, "Introduction: Words for a Conversation," in *Pursuits of Happiness: The Hollywood Comedy of Remarriage* (Cambridge, Mass.: Harvard University Press, 1981), pp. 1–42.

59 This is clearly how Cavell's writing works as well. See Arnold Davidson's review of Cavell's book *The Claim of Reason*, "Beginning Cavell," in *The Senses of Stanley Cavell*, ed. Richard Fleming and Michael Payne (Lewisburg: Bucknell University Press, 1989), pp. 230–241.

60 Stanley Cavell, "Moral Perfectionism," in *The Cavell Reader*, ed. Stephen Mulhall (Cambridge, Mass.: Blackwell, 1996), p. 360.

61 Richard Rorty, ed., *The Linguistic Turn: Recent Essays in Philosophical Method* (Chicago: University of Chicago Press, 1967); and Rorty, *Philosophy and the Mirror of Nature* (Princeton: Princeton University Press, 1979). Also see the section "A Linguistic Turn in Architecture?" in my and Golec's introduction to *Relearning from Las Vegas*. It is clear that theorists and practitioners such as Mario Gandelsonas, Diana Agrest, George Baird, and Hubert Damisch were much more systematic in their linguistic approaches to architecture at that time.

62 This is how the "linguistic turn" is interpreted in Dell Upton, "Signs Taken for Wonder," in *Relearing from Las Vegas*. Upton's essay obviously takes a different position on "wonder" in *Learning from Las Vegas* than I do.

63 It seems to me that theories of postmodernism and the arts are heavily reliant on the assumption of such a veil no matter how "material." This really struck home with me in reading a forthcoming book by Amanda Boetzkes on the ethics of earth art. I am referring to her nuanced critique of Craig Owens's interpretation of Robert Smithson's site/nonsite works in relation to issues of textuality. The relationship between text and architecture in *LLV* is more fully explored in chapters 2, 4, and 5.

64 Martin Heidegger, "Language," in *Poetry, Language, Thought*, trans. Albert Hofstadter (New York: Harper & Row, 1971), p. 189: "This statement ['Language is language'] does not lead us to something else in which language is grounded. Nor does it say anything about whether language itself may be a ground for something else. The sentence, 'Language is language,' leaves us to hover over an abyss as long as we endure what it says."

65 Cavell would say that problems are not to be solved but to be undone. I believe Derrida says something akin to this in *The Postcard: From Socrates to Freud and Beyond*, trans. Alan Bass (Chicago: University of Chicago Press, 1987): "what is it to *resolve* a problem? Whether a theoretical or a practical problem is in question, one is concerned with difficulties, obstacles, at least provisional blockages. To tend toward the solution is to accumulate and to bind, 'to band' the maximum of energy at the greatest proximity to the obstacle, to make the tension mount until the solution unknots not only the 'problem,' but also the bonds of energy accumulated around the problem. The solution resolves the physical and psychical drive tensions that the problem had accrued to itself. In their great banality, these schemas are Freudian" (p. 390). Wittgenstein's approach to solving, resolving, and dissolving is also relevant here: "What is your aim in philosophy?—To shew the fly the way out of the fly-bottle." *Philosophical Investigations*, §309.

66   Venturi and Scott Brown, *LLV* (1972), p. 4. This passage is worded differently in the 1977 edition: "There is a perversity in the learning process: We look backward at history and tradition to go forward; we can also look downward to go upward" (p. 3).

67   *LLV*, p. 4. T. S. Eliot, *Four Quartets* (London: Faber and Faber, 1944). Eliot quotes fragment 60 of Hermann Diels's *Die Fragmente der Vorsokratiker*. Similarly, as Cavell points out, Emerson uses an image of a staircase in the first lines of his essay "Experience" to answer the question "Where do we find ourselves?" and to suggest that we do not know the difference between up and down. Cavell, *Philosophical Passages: Wittgenstein, Emerson, Austin, Derrida* (Oxford: Blackwell, 1995), pp. 93–94. The first epigraph to the *Four Quartets*, Heraclitus's fragment 2, is also pertinent here, considering my argument throughout this book about the ordinary in relation to skepticism: "Though wisdom is common, yet the many live as if they had a wisdom of their own."

68   Denise Scott Brown, "The Meaningful City," *AIA Journal* (January 1965): 29. I believe Kevin Lynch was also talking about something similar in his concepts of "low image-ability" and "direction ambiguity." See Lynch, *The Image of the City* (Cambridge, Mass.: Technology Press, 1960).

69   Oliver Sacks, *The Man Who Mistook His Wife for a Hat and Other Clinical Tales* (New York: Summit Books, 1998), p. 83.

70   *LLV*, p. 9. Also see Rudolf Arnheim, "From Chaos to Wholeness," in *The Split and the Structure: Twenty-Eight Essays* (Berkeley: University of California Press, 1996), p. 160: "Such disorientations occur . . . on highways, when the constellation of roads does not clearly indicate which way to turn. Of course, one can intend to create confusion, but that may be dangerous or at least unproductive." It is dangerous, but hardly unproductive. Arnheim's critique is quite predictable, considering his desire to prescribe the *proper* temporal rhythm and dynamic of the conversion of chaos into cosmos, part into whole.

71   Robert Venturi and Denise Scott Brown, "A Significance for A&P Parking Lots, or Learning from Las Vegas," *Architectural Forum* (1968): 39, figure 1.

72   Wittgenstein, *Philosophical Investigations*, §185. Also see §85.

73   Karsten Harries makes this claim in *The Ethical Function of Architecture* (Cambridge, Mass.: MIT Press, 1997). Although Harries's book is by far the most extensive and detailed commentary on *LLV*, his fundamental mistrust of its tone is due, I believe, to his belief in the ethical truth of the need for "dwelling" in the Heideggerian sense of that word. What Cavell has to say about Emerson and Thoreau's differences of emphasis from Heidegger might well suggest what I am talking about: "The Substantive disagreement with Heidegger, shared by Emerson and Thoreau, is that the achievement of the human settlement is by abandonment, leaving." Cavell, "Thinking of Emerson," p. 138, and Cavell, *Philosophical Passages*, p. 103.

74   Heidegger, *Basic Questions of Philosophy*, pp. 135, 145.

75   Paul Klee, *Pedagogical Sketchbook*, trans. Sibyl Moholy-Nagy (London: Faber and Faber, 1968), p. 54.

76   Denise Scott Brown, "On Pop Art, Permissiveness, and Planning," *Journal of the American Institute of Planners* (May 1969): 184–186.

77   Lacan's commentary on and diagram of the circular movement of the drive consisting in the "curve of this rising and descending arrow" are also relevant here. Jacques Lacan, "The Partial Drive and Its Circuit," in *The Four Fundamental Concepts of Psycho-Analysis*, ed. Jacques-Alain Miller, trans. Alan Sheridan (New York: Norton, 1981), p. 178. For another account of the arrow in architectural work, see Peter Eisenman, "Moving Arrows,

Eros and Other Errors: An Architecture of Absence," in *Architecture Theory since 1968*, ed. Hays, pp. 582–585. To put this arrow business in tragic terms, one could characterize it as species of classical *hamartia* (the Greek verb *hamartanein* means "to miss the mark" or "to err").

78 On Emersonian "indirection," see his essay "Experience," and Cavell's commentary on this passage in "Henry James Returns to America and to Shakespeare," in *Philosophy the Day after Tomorrow*, p. 97.

79 *LLV*, p. xi.

80 Lynch, *The Image of the City*, p. 4. For a succinct analysis of Lynch's position in the debates about order and chaos in the American city, see Ann Reynolds, *Robert Smithson: Learning from New Jersey and Elsewhere* (Cambridge, Mass.: MIT Press, 2003), p. 26.

81 To put it in rhetorical terms, if in an unacknowledged instance of prosopopoeia we habitually say that streets "go" from here to there—or signs "say," "right lane must exit"—then the cloverleaf is really the allegorical figure of an "ambivalent rhetoric" always already "knotted" within the "simple" crossroads.

82 Gregory Cullen, *Townscape* (London: Architectural Press, 1961), p. 67. This image also appears as figure 223 in Venturi's *Complexity and Contradiction in Architecture*, where he calls it a "sconce." Venturi and Scott Brown had a great respect for this text. The risk explored in this image is what Heidegger pejoratively calls "entanglement" in the everyday.

83 Scott Brown, "The Meaningful City," p. 28.

84 Cavell, "Ending the Waiting Game," p. 127.

85 Scott Brown, "On Pop Art, Permissiveness, and Planning," p. 184.

86 *LLV*, p. 3.

87 Scott Brown, "On Pop Art, Permissiveness, and Planning," pp. 184–186.

88 Jean-François Lyotard, "Answering the Question: What Is Postmodernism?," in *The Postmodern Condition: A Report on Knowledge*, trans. Geoff Bennington and Brian Massumi (Minneapolis: University of Minnesota Press, 1984). He notes that the postmodern "refuses itself the consolation of good forms" (p. 81). Not surprisingly, Venturi's *Complexity and Contradiction* was directly criticized in Rudolf Arnheim's *The Dynamics of Architectural Form* (Berkeley: University of California Press, 1977). Arnheim is probably the best-known Gestalt-oriented art theorist.

89 *LLV*, p. 74.

90 *LLV*, p. 52. Also see pp. 148–150, and the table on p. 118 comparing the characteristics of "urban sprawl" with those of "Megastructure." Also see Venturi, *Complexity and Contradiction in Architecture*, p. 103: "Some of the vivid lessons of Pop Art . . . should have awakened architects from prim dreams of pure order, which, unfortunately, are imposed in the easy Gestalt unities of the urban renewal projects of establishment Modern architecture."

91 One can see that a certain notion of "criticism"—literally to cut out, and foreground, one element from a background—is closely dependant on something like a Gestalt-oriented approach. It seems to me that Venturi and Scott Brown have a different understanding of criticism, even though Venturi's early interest in Gestalt psychology was crucial for his emphasis on complex urban relationships. Also see chapter 5.

92 Sigmund Freud, "Recommendations for Physicians on the Psychoanalytic Method of Treatment" (1912), in *Therapy and Technique* (New York: Collier, 1963), pp. 117–126.

93 Amos Rapoport and Robert E. Kantor, "Complexity and Ambiguity in Environment Design," *Journal of the American Institute of Planners* 33, no. 4 (July 1967): 214 (my emphasis).

Some relevant texts by Ehrenzweig include: *The Psycho-Analysis of Artistic Vision and Hearing* (New York: Braziller, 1965); "Conscious Planning and Unconscious Scanning," in *The Education of Vision*, ed. Gyorgy Kepes (New York: Braziller, 1965); and *The Hidden Order of Art* (Berkeley: University of California Press, 1971).

94 Rapoport and Kantor, "Complexity and Ambiguity in Environment Design," p. 214.

95 See Ehrenzweig, *The Psycho-Analysis of Artistic Vision and Hearing*, p. xiii.

96 Max Horkheimer and Theodor W. Adorno, "The Culture Industry: Enlightenment as Mass Deception," in *Dialectic of Enlightenment*, trans. Edmund Jephcott (Stanford: Stanford University Press, 2002), p. 100. Significantly, "dispersion" is also the English translation of *Zerstreuung* in Heidegger's *Being and Time*, the word he uses to characterize the fallen state of the "they" of the everyday and the "inauthentic" mode of wonder as curiosity.

97 Heidegger, *Being and Time*, §371. Eliot's lines from "Burnt Norton," the first of the *Four Quartets*, capture this thought beautifully: "Only a flicker / Over the strained time-ridden faces / Distracted from distraction by distraction" (p. 10).

98 David Hume, *A Treatise of Human Nature*, ed. L. A. Selby-Bigge and P. H. Nidditch (Oxford: Oxford University Press, 1978), pp. 216, 268–269. Cavell makes numerous references to this passage in his work. See, for example, Cavell, "Postscript (1989)."

99 Scott Brown, "On Pop Art, Permissiveness, and Planning," p. 69. I return to the suppression of expression in the section "Deadpan and the Absorption of Skepticism," in chapter 3.

100 The word also connotes scattering, strewing, and straying. We hardly need to be reminded here that in the penultimate section of his essay "The Work of Art in the Era of Its Mechanical Reproducibility," Benjamin notes that we absorb architecture in a mode of distraction, which is thus a "precursor" to our mode of experiencing cinema. I see Miriam Hansen's essay "Benjamin and Cinema" as an illustration of how this kind of criticism can be helpful in thinking about architecture's relationship to the conditions of the contemporary city and new media.

101 Hansen, "Benjamin and Cinema," p. 63. This kind of reading of the script of the city can be read productively with and against Adorno's critique of our passive consumption of the products of the culture industry.

102 Walter Benjamin, "One-Way Street," in *Walter Benjamin, Selected Writings: 1927–34*, ed. Marcus Bullock and Michael W. Jennings, vol. 2 (Cambridge, Mass.: Belknap Press of Harvard University Press, 1996), p. 476.

103 *LLV*'s critique of "purity" reminds me of the following passage from Wittgenstein's *Philosophical Investigations*: "The *preconceived idea* of crystalline purity can only be removed by turning our whole examination around (One might say: the axis of reference of our examination must be rotated, but about the fixed point of our need" (§108). It is important to understand that the critique of space in *LLV* is not meant to discount the importance of space to architecture; rather it is part of their critique of using space to locate the medium specificity of architecture in relation to painting, sculpture, and literature. Venturi and Scott Brown are arguing for "mixed media" as opposed to "pure form" or "medium specificity," not against space as such. Anyway, what would it mean to argue against space? See *LLV*, pp. 7 and 75, and my introduction, note 12.

104 Sigmund Freud, "Inhibitions, Symptoms, and Anxiety," in *On Psychopathology*, trans. James Strachey, Penguin Freud Library 10 (London: Penguin, 1993), p. 276.

105 Scott Brown, "Pop Off," p. 73.

106 See Robert Venturi, "Context in Architectural Composition: M.F.A. Thesis, Princeton University," in *Iconography and Electronics upon a Generic Architecture: A View from the Drafting*

Room (Cambridge, Mass.: MIT Press, 1996), pp. 343–344. In a footnote, Venturi relates that his mother suggested this quotation from Emerson's "Each and All" as an appropriate analogy for his thesis. The complete quotation in the thesis is as follows (it is not, however, the complete poem, and the last two lines are quoted out of place; they appear earlier in Emerson's poem):

The delicate shells lay on the shore;
The bubbles of the latest wave
Fresh pearls to their enamel gave,

. . . .

I wiped away the weeds and foam,
I fetched my sea-born treasures home;
But the poor, unsightly, noisome things
Had left their beauty on the shore

. . . .

All are needed by each one;
Nothing is fair or good alone.

It is interesting to note that ten years after Venturi's M.F.A. thesis, Kevin Lynch also distilled the spirit of Emerson's poem into prose on the first page of *The Image of the City*: "Nothing is experienced by itself, but always in relation to its surroundings, the sequences of events leading up to it, the memory of past experiences." One can see why Lynch's work is of interest to Venturi and Scott Brown.

107 Jean-Luc Nancy, *La ville au loin* (Paris: Editions Mille et une nuits, 1999), p. 59.
108 Derrida, *The Postcard*, p. 127. Derrida's preoccupation with all forms of "autos" is clear in this book, and also in Geoffrey Bennington and Jacques Derrida, *Jacques Derrida* (Chicago: University of Chicago Press, 1993).

2 Our City of Words

1 Vincent Scully, *American Architecture and Urbanism*, rev. ed. (New York: Holt, 1988), p. 260. Karsten Harries says something similar about their work: "meaning is to triumph over what lacks meaning, as spirit triumphs over body." See Harries, *The Ethical Function of Architecture* (Cambridge, Mass.: MIT Press, 1997), p. 77.
2 *Meaning in Architecture*, ed. Charles Jencks and George Baird (New York: Braziller, 1970). This was the first sustained book of essays on the relationship of semiotics and structuralism in relationship to architecture. Also see Colin Rowe's influential introduction to *Five Architects: Eisenman, Graves, Gwathmey, Hejduk, Meier* (New York: Wittenborn, 1972) in relation to the contested ground of the meaning of meaning in architecture during this time. Needless to say, meaning was also a preoccupation of sixties and seventies art in its Wittgensteinian and poststructuralist configurations. One obvious example is Joseph Kosuth's *Titled (Art as Idea as Idea)* of 1967, consisting of a dictionary definition of the word "mean-ing" mounted on wood.
3 *LLV*, pp. 7–8. The conceptual background to this approach is drawn from Ernst Gombrich, via Alan Colquhoun. I return to the issues of meaning and expression in chapters 3 and 4.
4 Peter Blake, *God's Own Junkyard* (New York: Holt, Rinehart, and Winston, 1964), pp. 32–33. The debate about the chaotic nature of the American city was initiated, to a

great degree, by Blake himself. On these debates, see Ann Reynolds, *Robert Smithson: Learning from New Jersey and Elsewhere* (Cambridge, Mass.: MIT Press, 2003), pp. 83–93; and Louis Martin, "The Search for a Theory in Architecture: Anglo-American Debates, 1957–76" (Ph.D. diss., MIT, 2002), vol. 2, pp. 261–265. Alexander Tzonis and Liane Lefaivre introduce their history of American architecture from the 1960s to the present through the debates about "chaoticism" at this time; see *Architecture in North America since 1960* (New York: Thames & Hudson, 1995), pp. 10–13.

5   Robert Venturi, *Complexity and Contradiction in Architecture* (New York: Museum of Modern Art, 1966), pp. 102–103.

6   Quoted in Stanley Cavell, "What Did Derrida Want of Austin?," in *Philosophical Passages: Wittgenstein, Emerson, Austin, Derrida* (Oxford: Blackwell, 1995), pp. 56–58.

7   Robert Venturi and Denise Scott Brown, "Ugly and Ordinary Architecture, or the Decorated Shed," part II, *Architectural Forum* (December 1971): 53.

8   Plato, *The Republic*, trans. Francis MacDonald Cornford (London: Oxford University Press, 1945), p. 591. Also see chapter 1.

9   Peter Blake later modified his radical critique in response to Venturi and Scott Brown's critique of his reading of these images. For an intelligent account of the "Disneyland" issue, see Stanislaus von Moos, *Nicht Disneyland und andere Aufsätze über Modernität und Nostalgie* (Zurich: Scheidegger & Spiess, 2004).

10 *LLV*, p. 56. The quotation is taken from August Heckscher's *The Public Happiness* (New York: Atheneum, 1962). There are echoes of Nietzsche here: "I tell you: one must have chaos in one, to give birth to a dancing star." Friedrich Nietzsche, *Thus Spoke Zarathustra* (New York: Penguin, 1969), p. 46. In a much later interview, Venturi commented, "my favorite [city] is a city of no obvious unity, perhaps of chaos—Tokyo." "Interview: Denise Scott Brown and Robert Venturi on Art and Architecture," in *Dialogues in Public Art*, ed. Tom Finkelpearl (Cambridge, Mass.: MIT Press, 1990), p. 166.

11 Richard Poirier, "T. S. Eliot and the Literature of Waste," *New Republic* (May 20, 1967): 21, quoted in *LLV*, p. 72, n. 6. Three references are made to this article: one at the beginning of Part I, and two at the end of Part I.

12 Poirier, "T. S. Eliot and the Literature of Waste," 20; quoted in *LLV*, p. 72, n. 5.

13 Quoted in Teresa Reese, "Rude Graphics, or Learning to Love Las Vegas," *Print* 34, no. 5 (1980): 45.

14 Quoted in *LLV*, p. 72.

15 The issue of voice is also key in Cavell's work. In my reading of *LLV*, I have profited from Timothy Gould's take on these issues in his *Hearing Things: Voice and Method in the Writing of Stanley Cavell* (Chicago: University of Chicago Press, 1998). For this section, pp. 46, 53, 94, and 106 are particularly relevant.

16 Poirier, "T. S. Eliot and the Literature of Waste," p. 20. Poirier emphasizes Eliot's skepticism. For another account of it see Jeffrey M. Pearl, *Skepticism and Modern Enmity: Before and after Eliot* (Baltimore: Johns Hopkins University Press, 1989).

17 Ludwig Wittgenstein, *Philosophical Investigations*, trans. G. E. M. Anscombe (Oxford: Blackwell, 1976), §120.

18 *LLV*, p. 161.

19 *LLV*, pp. 53, 149, 162. I return to the issue of deadness and coldness toward the end of this chapter, and again in the following chapter.

20 *LLV*, p. 4.

21 Tom Wolfe's essay on Las Vegas had a profound influence on Venturi and Scott Brown, and it was required reading for the Las Vegas studio.

22 Peter Fenves, *"Chatter": Language and History in Kierkegaard* (Stanford: Stanford University Press, 1990), p. xi. Also the following passage: "Since everything in communication can lay claim under certain conditions to being "chatter," the word can hardly be used to describe anything determinate, not even a mode of language in which things somehow become insubstantial, unimportant, weightless." In *Being and Time*, Heidegger prefers to call chatter "idle-talk," and identifies its "noise" as one of the characteristics of the everyday. Martin Heidegger, *Being and Time*, trans. Joan Stambaugh (Albany: State University of New York Press, 1996), §271.

23 Today it is hard to obtain a copy of the first edition of *LLV* that still has a dust jacket.

24 The lettering on the glassine jacket that appears along the sides of the Tanya image not only frames it but also literally begins to invade its gold border along the right-hand margin.

25 On Wittgenstein's treatment of aphorism, see Stanley Cavell, "Epilogue: The *Investigations*' Everyday Aesthetics of Itself," in *The Cavell Reader*, ed. Stephen Mulhall (Cambridge, Mass.: Blackwell, 1996), pp. 385–389.

26 Stanley Cavell, *A Pitch of Philosophy: Autobiographical Exercises* (Cambridge, Mass.: Harvard University Press, 1994), p. 112.

27 Theodor W. Adorno, "The Schema of Mass Culture," in *The Culture Industry: Selected Essays on Mass Culture*, ed. J. M. Bernstein (London: Routledge, 2001), p. 85.

28 Christian Norberg-Schulz's review of *Complexity and Contradiction* shows that there is some continuity in terms of the erasure of context between it and *LLV*: "*Complexity and Contradiction* is a small book, crowded with stamp-like illustrations and with a text treated as a sequence of captions." Norberg-Schulz, "Less or More?," *Architectural Review* 143, no. 854 (April 1968): 257–258.

29 Robert Venturi, "Mal Mots: Aphorisms—Sweet and Sour—by an Anti-Hero Architect," in *Iconography and Electronics upon a Generic Architecture: A View from the Drafting Room* (Cambridge, Mass.: MIT Press, 1996), p. 322.

30 Denise Scott Brown, preface to the revised edition, *LLV*, p. xv. I take it she is critiquing the pursuit of modernist "total design" in the first edition, which Venturi and Scott Brown felt worked against their critique of this approach to urban and architectural thought and practice. Despite their disdain for the first edition, its "modern styling" often did not work against their subject matter despite their explicit "negation" of it. See chapter 5.

31 *LLV* (1972), p. 5. There are other examples of such neon sentences in Venturi and Scott Brown's work. In the second edition, the written sentence is found in the "Studio Notes," p. 73, and only the "Vacancy" image is reproduced on p. 63. For a good account of billboards and their relationship to concrete and found poetry, see Marjorie Perloff, "Signs Are Taken for Wonders: The Billboard Field as Poetic Space," in *Radical Artifice: Writing Poetry in the Age of Media* (Chicago: University of Chicago Press, 1991), pp. 93–133. She refers to *LLV* on pp. 93–100.

32 T. S. Eliot, *The Confidential Clerk*, quoted in Northrop Frye, *T. S. Eliot* (Edinburgh: Liver and Boyd, 1963), p. 31. Frye also notes that "[t]he new poem, like the new baby, is born into verbal society, an order of words already there" (p. 26).

33 Marshall McLuhan, *From Cliché to Archetype* (New York: Viking Press, 1970), p. 176. This is also a major point in all of Richard Poirier's criticism of twentieth-century American literature ranging from T. S. Eliot to Norman Mailer.

34 "Interview: Denise Scott Brown and Robert Venturi on Art and Architecture," p. 166. Eliot seems to have entered into architectural discourse through Julius Posener's article "Criticism in Architecture," *Architectural Design* 18 (July 1948): 154–155. But Venturi and Scott Brown are drawing on the sophisticated literary criticism on Eliot produced in the 1960s and 1970s by Richard Poirier and, indirectly, by Marshall McLuhan.

35 McLuhan emphasizes that "my study of media began and remains rooted in the work of these men"—meaning, of course, I. A. Richards, F. R. Leavis, Eliot, Ezra Pound, and Joyce. See McLuhan, foreword to *The Interior Landscape: The Literary Criticism of Marshall McLuhan, 1943–1962*, ed. Eugene McNamara (Toronto: McGraw-Hill, 1969), p. xiv. Deleuze also makes some very insightful comments about clichés in "The Painting before Painting," in *Francis Bacon: The Logic of Sensation*, trans. Daniel Smith (Minneapolis: University of Minnesota Press, 2003), pp. 71–80, and in the last few pages of *Cinema 1: The Movement-Image*, trans. Hugh Tomlinson and Barbara Habberjam (Minneapolis: University of Minnesota Press, 1996). We should also be reminded here of Adorno's discussion of the culture industry in terms of "ready-made clichés," "jargon," and the "stones of stereotype."

36 Here I am drawing on art historian Leo Steinberg's essay on Robert Rauschenberg (particularly the section entitled "The Flatbed Picture Plane") in his book *Other Criteria: Confrontations with Twentieth-Century Art* (New York: Oxford University Press, 1972), which came out in the same year as the first edition of *LLV*. Steinberg's analysis of Rauschenberg's work resonates with many of the issues raised in *LLV*. The logic of Steinberg's argument is extended by Deleuze's account of the English painter Francis Bacon, when Deleuze notes that clichés have always already filled Bacon's blank canvas as "prepictorial givens" even before the painter starts painting. I return to Steinberg's ideas in chapters 3 and 5.

37 Henry David Thoreau, *Walden* (Oxford: Oxford University Press, 1999), p. 38. See the comments on this passage in Cavell, *A Pitch of Philosophy*, pp. 44–45.

38 Richard Poirier, quoted in *LLV*, p. 1. As Deleuze makes clear in his writings on the cliché, parody is not a creative response to the cliché but merely its perpetuation.

39 Denise Scott Brown, "On Pop Art, Permissiveness, and Planning," *Journal of the American Institute of Planners* (May 1969): 186.

40 Max Horkheimer and Theodor W. Adorno, "The Culture Industry: Enlightenment as Mass Deception," in *Dialectic of Enlightenment*, trans. Edmund Jephcott (Stanford: Stanford University Press, 2002), p. 98. The predigested schema produced by the culture industry is characterized by Adorno as "ready-made clichés."

41 Tomás Maldonado, "Las Vegas and the Semiological Abuse," in *Design, Nature, and Revolution: Toward a Critical Ecology*, trans. Mario Domandi (New York: Harper & Row, 1972), p. 65.

42 Adorno, "The Schema of Mass Culture," p. 83. The ethics of this passage are of a piece with another sentence on p. 93: "But since as subjects men themselves still represent the ultimate limit of reification, mass culture must try and take hold of them again and again: the bad infinity involved in this hopeless effort of repetition is the only trace of hope that this repetition might be in vain, that men cannot wholly be grasped after all." The word I want to call attention to here is "grasped."

43 Denise Scott Brown, "The Meaningful City," *AIA Journal* (January 1965): 32.

44 I use "us" to mean both individuals *and* our fellow humans who speak with us in words we share or dispute.

45   Thoreau, *Walden*, p. 24. It is important to note that Thoreau says that he emphasizes each word separately (i.e., "they" and "me") in order to evaluate by what degree *They* are related to *me*.

46   Ed Ruscha, *Leave Any Information at the Signal: Writings, Interviews, Bits, Pages*, ed. Alexandra Schwarz (Cambridge, Mass.: MIT Press, 2002), p. 57. Ruscha continues: "Sometimes I have a dream that if a word gets too hot and too appealing, it will boil apart, and I won't be able to read or think of it. Usually I catch them before they get too hot."

47   The issue of coldness is a key element in Adorno's thought. Besides appearing in his description of advertising, it is, as Bernstein points out, the fundamental principle of bourgeois subjectivity in Adorno's writings. Interestingly, Bernstein suggests that coldness is a mood. (Considering Bernstein's interpretation of Adorno, it is hardly surprising that he is the only philosopher I am aware of who has attempted to think about Adorno and Cavell together.) See J. M. Bernstein, "Coldness," in *Adorno: Disenchantment and Ethics* (Cambridge: Cambridge University Press, 2001), pp. 396–414. The issue of coldness also appears in Heidegger as *Benommenheit* (numbness), which is a characteristic of the fallen everyday in *Being and Time*. It is also his characterization of "animality," a connection pursed by Derrida in his later work on the animal.

48   Horkheimer and Adorno, "The Culture Industry," p. 135.

49   Bernstein, *Adorno: Disenchantment and Ethics*, p. 414. This also holds true for Heidegger, Wittgenstein, and Cavell.

50   Cavell's comments on "subliming" our thought and language are found throughout his many books and articles. One place to start would be Cavell's wonderful gloss on the cold, lifeless region in Coleridge's "The Rime of the Ancient Mariner," in Stanley Cavell, *In Quest of the Ordinary: Lines of Skepticism and Romanticism* (Chicago: University of Chicago Press, 1994), pp. 50–75. Also see the following passages in Wittgenstein's *Philosophical Investigations*: "This queer conception springs from a tendency to sublime the logic of our language . . . " (§38, also §§47, 94); "What *we* do is to bring words back from their metaphysical to their everyday use" (§116); "Every sign *by itself* seems dead. *What* gives it life?—In use it is *alive*. Is life breathed into it there?—Or is the *use* its life?" (§432).

51   Wittgenstein, *Philosophical Investigations*, §107. Wittgenstein defines the term "language-game" as "to bring into prominence the fact that the *speaking* of a language is part of an activity, or of a form of life" (§23).

52   See Gould, *Hearing Things*, p. 220, n. 8.

53   Wittgenstein, *Philosophical Investigations*, §432.

54   This image is isolated in the second edition on p. 63, where it appears on a double page of small neon signs and/or sentences. It emphasizes and isolates the "Vacancy" sign from its context in the neon sentence even more than it does in the first edition. Similarly, the literary critic Northrop Frye has interpreted Heraclitus's fragment 60, the epigraph at the beginning of the *Four Quartets*, to suggest the extremes of plenitude and vacancy that are alluded to in the third quartet, "Burnt Norton." See Frye, *T. S. Eliot*, p. 44.

55   Here I am drawing on Cavell's frequent references to the multiple voices in Wittgenstein's *Philosophical Investigations*. Poirier also refers to the multiple voices in Eliot's *The Waste Land*, in "T. S. Eliot and the Literature of Waste," p. 20.

56   The notion of "stripping criteria" is explored throughout Cavell's work. It is the act of subliming our language out of the ordinary, and thus a manifestation of skepticism. Also see chapter 5.

57 Venturi, "Mal Mots," p. 299.

58 T. S. Eliot, "Philip Massinger," in *Selected Essays* (London: Faber, 1951), p. 206.

59 Adorno, "The Schema of Mass Culture," p. 96. The relationship between the telegram and architecture in the 1960s is embedded in the very word "Archigram." This collective's favored form of communication was the broadsheet and mimeographed letter/folder crammed with written and visual "information."

60 Venturi, "A Series of Responses for *Via*, the Journal of the School of Fine Arts, University of Pennsylvania," in *Iconography and Electronics*, p. 150.

61 Neil Leach, *The Anaesthetics of Architecture* (Cambridge, Mass.: MIT Press, 1998), p. 64. Leach's criticism is, in a sense, "biblical" in that for him images are considered ipso facto seductive: they lead us astray, and out of our critical senses, so to speak. Leach misses the essential point about seduction—the risks of seduction are intrinsic to interpretation as such. It is the very stuff that attracts us to a text, and puts us in the mood for it. The supposed avoidance of that seduction does not entail an enhancement of criticality, but rather risks not caring about the text at all. In other words, the text's seductiveness is intrinsic to its form of criticism.

62 Thoreau, *Walden*, p. 98. The sentence reads: "We are a race of tit-men, and soar but little higher in our intellectual flights than the columns of the daily paper."

63 Philip Johnson acknowledged the metaphoric relationship between prostitution and architectural practice in his words, "I am a whore, and I am paid very well for highrise buildings." This was supposedly voiced in a conference held in 1982 at the University of Virginia, in response to a comment by Rob Krier.

64 One might say that much of the criticism against *LLV* suffers from some tinges of this psychopathology. And to put it in rhetorical terms, why should we assume that Venturi and Scott Brown are any less attuned to "promiscuous" rhetorical figures or "im-proper names" than a theorist such as Paul de Man? See Paul de Man, "The Epistemology of Metaphor," in *Aesthetic Ideology*, ed. Andrzej Warminski (Minneapolis: University of Minnesota Press, 1996), pp. 34–50.

65 Horkheimer and Adorno, "The Culture Industry," p. 111.

66 *LLV,* p. 35.

67 Denise Scott Brown and Robert Venturi, "The Bicentennial Commemoration of 1976," *Architectural Forum* 131, no. 3 (October 1969): 69.

68 The *r* in "Souvenir" is also cut off by the image's outer frame.

69 *LLV*, p. 162. They go on, "Just as Lichtenstein has borrowed the techniques and images of the comics to convey satire, sorrow, and irony rather than violent high adventure, so may the architect's high reader suggest sorrow, irony, love, the human condition, happiness, or merely the purpose within, rather than the necessity to buy soap or the possibility of an orgy."

70 Stanley Cavell, "The Politics of Interpretation," in *Themes Out of School: Effects and Causes* (Chicago: University of Chicago Press, 1988), p. 55.

71 The impact of such slight changes was noted long ago by Lucretius: "A small transposition is sufficient for atoms to create igneous or ligneous bodies. Likewise, in the case of words, a slight alteration in the letters allows us to distinguish ligneous from igneous." See Lucretius, *De rerum natura*, trans. W. H. D. Rouse (Cambridge, Mass.: Harvard University Press, 1975), Book 1, verse 910, p. 46.

3 Of Ducks, Decorated Sheds, and Other Minds

1   Fredric Jameson, "Architecture and the Critique of Ideology," in *The Ideologies of Theory: Essays 1971–1986*, vol. 2 (Minneapolis: University of Minnesota Press, 1988), p. 59.

2   Rem Koolhaas, *Delirious New York: A Retroactive Manifesto for Manhattan* (New York: Monacelli Press, 1994), p. 100. Koolhaas attributes the break from this model, toward the deliberate discrepancy between container and contained, to issues of "bigness," in which "less and less surface has to represent more and more interior activity." This is worked out in more detail in his book *S, M, L, XL* (New York: Monacelli Press, 1996).

3   Stanley Cavell, "Knowing and Acknowledging," in *Must We Mean What We Say?* (Cambridge: Cambridge University Press, 2002), p. 254.

4   Walter Benjamin, "Surrealism: The Last Snapshot of the European Intelligentsia," in *Reflections: Essays, Aphorisms, Autobiographical Writings*, ed. Peter Demetz (New York: Schocken Books, 1986), p. 180.

5   Robert Venturi and Denise Scott Brown, "On Ducks and Decoration," *Architecture Canada* 10 (October 1968): 48.

6   *LLV*, p. 87. It should be noted that the term "Decorated Shed" was not worked out until Venturi and Scott Brown's article "Ugly and Ordinary Architecture, or the Decorated Shed," part I, published in *Architectural Forum* in 1971. Their early article "On Ducks and Decoration" reproduces a diagram of the Decorated Shed but, as the title indicates, there is no verbal articulation of it as such.

7   This fact is also noted in Joseph Masheck's "Tired Tropes: Cathedral versus Bicycle Shed; 'Duck' versus 'Decorated Shed,'" in *Building-Art: Modern Architecture under Cultural Construction* (Cambridge: Cambridge University Press, 1993), p. 217.

8   These sheds are actually adjacent buildings, and not directly connected to the Duck.

9   We might remind ourselves from time to time that it was Wittgenstein himself who said that one could see the "duck-rabbit" image not only in terms of a gestalt switch—*as a* duck "or" *as a* rabbit—but also simultaneously: "I *may* say 'It's a duck-rabbit.'" Ludwig Wittgenstein, *Philosophical Investigations*, trans. G. E. M. Anscombe (Oxford: Blackwell, 1976), part II, 195e. Wittgenstein's understanding of "seeing as" plays an important role in Cavell's writings on interpretation. Although Cavell does not, as far as I am aware, acknowledge Heidegger's work on the "as-structure" of interpretation in *Being and Time*, I am assuming that Heidegger lurks not too far in the background in relation to these questions.

10   The only images I have found that deviate from this "facing" are the images of the Duck and Decorated Shed in their early article "On Ducks and Decoration," p. 48, in which the door/mouth is placed to the right of the two windows (eyes).

11   Stanley Cavell, *The World Viewed: Reflections on the Ontology of Film* (New York: Viking Press, 1971), p. 129.

12   Stanley Cavell, "Reply to Four Chapters," in *Wittgenstein and Skepticism*, ed. Denis McManus (New York: Routledge, 2004), p. 286; and Cavell, "The Quest of Traditional Epistemology," in *The Claim of Reason: Wittgenstein, Skepticism, Morality, and Tragedy* (Oxford: Oxford University Press, 1979), pp. 191–243.

13   Cavell, *The World Viewed*, p. 85.

14   Cavell, "Knowing and Acknowledging," pp. 263–264. In other words, we might see the comparison between the Duck and the Decorated Shed as "indiscrete" as well as "indiscreet."

15 Nikolaus Pevsner, *An Outline of European Architecture* (London: Pelican, 1960), p. 1.

16 Cavell addresses the relationships between response, historicity, and ontology in relation to John Wisdom's essay "Gods," in which he discusses various responses to flowers. See Stanley Cavell, *In Quest of the Ordinary: Lines of Skepticism and Romanticism* (Chicago: University of Chicago Press, 1994), pp. 67–69; and Cavell, *The Claim of Reason*, pp. 441–442. A good commentary on these passages can be found in Espen Hammer, *Stanley Cavell: Skepticism, Subjectivity, and the Ordinary* (London: Polity Press, 2002), pp. 172–173. The other great instance of work in this vein would be Ian Hacking's remarkable writings on what he calls the "the looping effects of human kinds," which he has more recently termed "historical ontology." See Ian Hacking, *Historical Ontology* (Cambridge, Mass.: Harvard University Press, 2002).

17 Cavell, "Knowing and Acknowledging," pp. 263–264. The passage is worth quoting in full: "The point, however, is that the concept of acknowledgment is evidenced equally by its failure as by its success. It is not a description of a given response but a category in terms of which a given response is evaluated. . . . A 'failure to know' might just mean a piece of ignorance, an absence of something, a blank. A 'failure to acknowledge' is the presence of something, a confusion, an indifference, a callousness, an exhaustion, a coldness. Spiritual emptiness is not a blank." Cavell's discussion of the term "ugly duckling" in relation to lack of recognition, and the necessity for responsiveness and improvisation in order to recognize this lack of recognition—or better, numbness and unresponsiveness—has been important to me in thinking about the Duck and the Decorated Shed in *Learning from Las Vegas*. See Stanley Cavell, "Ugly Duckling, Funny Butterfly: Bette Davis and *Now, Voyager*," in *Contesting Tears: The Hollywood Melodrama of the Unknown Woman* (Chicago: University of Chicago Press, 1996), pp. 115–148.

18 Ernst Gombrich, "On Physiognomic Perception" and "Expression and Communication," in *Meditations on a Hobby Horse and Other Essays on the Theory of Art* (New York: Phaidon, 1963), pp. 45–69; and Alan Colquhoun, "Typology and Design Method," *Arena* 83, no. 913 (June 1967): 11–14. Colquhoun's article was republished in George Baird and Charles Jencks's *Meaning in Architecture* in 1970. Both Gombrich and Colquhoun are cited on *LLV*, p. 132. Colquhoun was also influenced by Lévi-Strauss's structural anthropology, particularly his work on the "arbitrary" system of representation in primitive kinship systems. We don't have to assume, however, that the only alternative to expressionist theories of art are simply "conventional" ones. We are often much too hasty in our assumptions about what is "natural" and what is "conventional." One of the most important lessons one can learn from Cavell's reading of Wittgenstein is the upsetting of any easy partition between the natural and conventional, and where one might want to place the stress in relation to these conditions.

19 Gombrich, "Expression and Communication," p. 57.

20 See *LLV*, pp. 131–134. I use the word "supposed" here to point out that this is their reading of the situation and not necessarily one I agree with.

21 All of these words and phrases are mobilized in *LLV*.

22 Vincent Scully, unpublished introduction to *LLV*, pp. 5–6, AAUP, box 453 (see the appendix of this book). The sentence ends by stating that they flatten these facades out "to make them speak as signs." I assume that Scully's writings on the sculptural qualities of certain types of historical architecture had an influence on VSBI. Needless to say, Hegel is the starting point for any philosophical account of the relationship between architecture and sculpture.

23   *LLV*, 116 and 137. Venturi and Scott Brown do not cite any specific edition of *Towards a New Architecture*. The political dimensions of punctuality and singularity as opposed to mass *in* light and space are explored below in chapter 4. In this regard, the wording of the more common translation for this sentence is very interesting: "the masterly, correct, and magnificent play of masses brought together in light." See Le Corbusier, *Towards a New Architecture*, trans. Frederick Etchells (New York: Dover, 1986), p. 37.

24   I won't cite each particular passage on Guild House and Crawford Manor in *LLV;* all of the following direct and indirect quotations can be found on pp. 90–103.

25   Venturi and Scott Brown acknowledge that Crawford Manor also has a sign, but it is modest and tasteful and not commercial. In other words, it is not an explicit, denotative, and heraldic sign; it is too small to be seen from the fast-moving cars on the Oak Street Connector (p. 100).

26   VSBI are well aware of the ability of viewpoint and cropping in photography to capture particular kinds of effects. In fact, that was precisely Venturi's claim about the beautiful photographs of sprawl in Blake's *God's Own Junkyard*. Ignoring their own "framing" devices in *LLV*, Venturi and Scott Brown critique architects and theorists of the modern movement for their "contrived cropping of photographs." See *LLV*, p. 135.

27   David Bourdon, "Ruscha as Publisher," in Ruscha, *Leave Any Information at the Signal: Writings, Interviews, Bits, Pages*, ed. Alexandra Schwarz (Cambridge, Mass.: MIT Press, 2002), p. 43: "Ruscha photographed the Strip in the harsh light of high noon, making it appear just as dull and tacky-looking as Midwestern Main Street. . . . 'All I was after was that store-front plane,' he says. 'It's like a Western town in a way. A store-front plane of a Western town is just paper, and everything behind it is just nothing.'" For a philosophical take on "high noon" in Nietzsche's writings, see Alenka Zupančič, *The Shortest Shadow: Nietzsche's Philosophy of the Two* (Cambridge, Mass.: MIT Press, 2003).

28   *LLV*, pp. 91, 93, and 104. The shopworn description of pop art's reaction against abstract expressionism is one of the duller moments in an otherwise exciting and exacting book.

29   Detlef Mertens, "The Shells of Architectural Thought," in *Hejduk's Chronotope*, ed. K. Michael Hays (Princeton: Princeton Architectural Press, 1996), p. 32. Joseph Masheck notes that the exhibition "Visionary Architects: Boullée, Ledoux, Lequeu" was circulating in the United States in 1967–1968. See Masheck, "Tired Tropes," p. 216 and p. 168 n.

30   Karsten Harries, *The Ethical Function of Architecture* (Cambridge, Mass.: MIT Press, 1997), p. 73.

31   Paul de Man, "The Rhetoric of Blindness," in *Blindness and Insight: Essays in the Rhetoric of Contemporary Criticism*, 2d ed. (Minneapolis: University of Minnesota Press, 1983), p. 114.

32   The issues of tethering and abandonment to our words are key to Cavell's criticism of Derrida's reading of John Austin's *How to Do Things with Words;* they also serve as a way of marking out an emphasis on Cavell's calling for or recalling of voice in contrast to Derrida's emphasis on the suppression of voice. See Stanley Cavell, "What Did Derrida Want of Austin?," in *Philosophical Passages: Wittgenstein, Emerson, Austin, Derrida* (Oxford: Blackwell, 1995),pp. 42–65; and Cavell, "Counter Philosophy and the Pawn of Voice," in *A Pitch of Philosophy: Autobiographical Exercises* (Cambridge, Mass.: Harvard University Press, 1994), pp. 55–127.

33   See Cavell, *Contesting Tears*, pp. 40 and 43; and *LLV*, p. 139. Much of what follows in this chapter entails an engagement with issues of melodrama, theatricality, unknowingness,

and other minds explored in *Contesting Tears*. Peter Brooks, drawing on Freud and Benveniste, has argued that "recourse to plastic figurability is basic to melodramatic mute expression." See Peter Brooks, *The Melodramatic Imagination: Balzac, Henry James, Melodrama, and the Mode of Excess* (New Haven: Yale University Press, 1976), p. 215, n. 39.

34 Cavell, *Contesting Tears*, p. 40; and *LLV*, p. 150.

35 Wittgenstein, *Philosophical Investigations*, §103. The passage continues: "Where does this idea come from? It is like a pair of glasses on our nose through which we see whatever we look at. It never occurs to us to take them off."

36 Ibid., §108.

37 *LLV*, p. 161.

38 Ibid., p. 101.

39 See Cavell, *Contesting Tears*, p. 40.

40 Ibid., p. 103.

41 Ibid., p. 116.

42 Hammer, *Stanley Cavell*, p. 173.

43 On all of this, see Gianni Vattimo, *The Transparent Society*, trans. David Webb (Baltimore: Johns Hopkins University Press, 1992).

44 Cavell writes in *The Claim of Reason* (p. 440), "To say that there is a skepticism which is produced not by a doubt about whether we can know but by a disappointment over knowledge itself, and to say that this skepticism is lived in our knowledge of others, is to say that this disappointment has a history. To trace the history would presumably require tracing the hopes placed upon knowledge in the Renaissance and by the Enlightenment; and of the fears of knowledge overcome by those hopes; and of the despair of knowledge produced by the dashing of those hopes."

45 The former analogy is theirs, and the latter is mine.

46 *LLV*, p. 103.

47 The first part of the quotation is from Giorgio Agamben, *The Coming Community*, trans. Michael Hardt (Minneapolis: University of Minnesota Press, 1993), p. 65. In this passage Agamben is talking about "removing the thin diaphragm that separates bad mediatized advertising from the perfect exteriority that communicates only itself." The second phrase is from Theodor W. Adorno, "The Schema of Mass Culture," in *The Culture Industry: Selected Essays on Mass Culture*, ed. J. M. Bernstein (London: Routledge, 2001), p. 82.

48 *LLV*, p. 162. Also see chapter 2, where I discuss "coldness" in relationship to Adorno and Cavell.

49 Cavell, *In Quest of the Ordinary*, p. 68.

50 Cavell, *The Claim of Reason*, pp. 481–496; and Stanley Cavell, "Othello and the Stake of the Other" and "Recounting Gains, Showing Losses: Reading *The Winter's Tale*," in *Disowning Knowledge in Six Plays of Shakespeare* (Cambridge: Cambridge University Press, 1987), pp. 125–142, 193–222.

51 See note 10 of my introduction.

52 They were married on July 23, 1967, and Denise Scott Brown became a partner in the firm in 1969.

53 See Denise Scott Brown, "Room at the Top? Sexism and the Star System in Architecture," in *Gender, Space, Architecture: An Interdisciplinary Introduction*, ed. Jane Rendell, Barbara Penner, and Iain Borden (London: Routledge, 2000), p. 261.

54 Cavell, *The Claim of Reason*, p. 492.

55 This ignoring of Scott Brown is in stark evidence on the back cover of the revised edition of *LLV*, in which a blurb from the *Ohio Review* begins: "Venturi has written a dangerous book. . . ." Scott Brown is still rightfully angry about this kind of treatment, which she characterized to me as bordering on primal, with alpha males apparently preferring to deal with other alpha males.

56 Jean-Luc Nancy, *The Inoperative Community*, trans. Peter Connor et al. (Minneapolis: University of Minnesota Press, 1991), p. 29. This is what Nancy calls "finitude compearing." For Nancy, this "compearance" implies not juxtaposition but "exposition." The connections between Nancy's understanding of "exposure" and Cavell's use of that same term in relation to acknowledgment in *The Claim of Reason* are well worth exploring. See *The Claim of Reason*, pp. 432–440. Also see chapter 4.

57 The exploration of popular "expression" in "media" was integral to the Learning from Levittown studio, which explored genres such as TV soap opera, melodrama, and comedy.

58 See Vattimo, *The Transparent Society*, p. 72.

59 In *LLV*, VSBI contrast urban sprawl and the Decorated Shed with total design, the megastructure, and the Duck. These comparisons are woven throughout the book, but a succinct formulation can be read in the section titled "Megastructures and Design Control" (pp. 148–150). My characterization (caricature?) of design here draws on Cavell's brief discussion of it in *The World Viewed*, 91. Cavell's account seems to resonate with Vattimo's understanding of design as the bourgeois form of "utopia"; see *The Transparent Society*, pp. 62–64. Both of these accounts come across as rather crude descriptions of design then and now.

60 *LLV*, p. 161. Also see chapter 2.

61 Cavell, *Contesting Tears*, p. 90.

62 Robert Venturi, *Complexity and Contradiction in Architecture* (New York: Museum of Modern Art, 1966), p. 84.

63 Koolhaas, *Delirious New York*, p. 100.

64 Jean-François Lyotard, "Gift of Organs," in *Driftworks*, ed. Roger McKeon (New York: Semiotext(e), 1984), p. 89.

65 See Derrida, *The Gift of Death*, trans. David Wills (Chicago: University of Chicago Press, 1995), pp. 20–21. After all, the secret is a social notion no matter how "discrete." Elsewhere Derrida notes, "In consensus, in possible transparency, the secret is never broached/breached [*entamé*]." See Derrida and Maurizio Ferraris, *A Taste for the Secret*, trans. Giacomo Donis, ed. Giacomo Donis and David Webb (Cambridge: Polity Press, 2001), p. 57.

66 Gilles Deleuze and Félix Guattari, *A Thousand Plateaus*, trans. Brian Massumi (Minneapolis: University of Minnesota Press, 1987), p. 287. Their discussion of the secret (pp. 286–290) also speaks directly to the issue of "bigness" in architecture as this has been worked out by Rem Koolhaas. For example, they note that in the secret, "The content is *too big* for its form . . . or else the contents themselves have a form, but that form is covered, doubled, or replaced by a simple container, envelope, or box whose role it is to suppress formal relations. These are contents it has been judged fitting to isolate or disguise for various reasons" (p. 286).

67 Jean-François Lyotard, *Discours, figure* (Paris: Klincksieck, 1974), p. 13 (my emphasis). This is my translation.

68 Denise Scott Brown had written about the use of the comic strip form and speech balloons in her commentary on Archigram's pamphlet number four. See Denise Scott Brown, "Little Magazines in Architecture and Urbanism," *AIP Journal* (July 1968): 228.

The speech balloon continued to play a prominent role in their subsequent exhibitions and articles, and in relation to the concept of the deadpan.

69   David Carrier, *The Aesthetics of Comics* (University Park: Pennsylvania State University Press, 2000), pp. 73–74.

70   Ibid., pp. 29–30. Also see Wittgenstein, *Philosophical Investigations*, §427: "'While I was speaking to him I did not know what was going on in his head.' In saying this, one is not thinking of brain-processes, but of thought-processes. The picture should be taken seriously. We should really like to see into his head."

71   Here I am thinking of the Duck and Decorated Shed image in Robert Venturi and Denise Scott Brown, "A Significance for A&P Parking Lots, or Learning from Las Vegas," *Architectural Forum* (1968): 39, figure 2.

72   Jameson, "Architecture and the Critique of Ideology," pp. 58–59.

73   For a history of ventriloquism, see Steven Connor, *Dumbstruck: A Cultural History of Ventriloquism* (Oxford: Oxford University Press, 2000); and more recently, David Goldblatt's *Art and Ventriloquism* (New York: Routledge, 2006).

74   Maurice Merleau-Ponty, *Phenomenology of Perception*, trans. Colin Smith (London: Routledge, 1996), p. 187; quoted in Connor, *Dumbstruck*, p. 11.

75   Here I am drawing on Cavell's use of the word "driven" to suggest our "naturalizing" the skeptical repudiation of our attunement with each other. For example, see Cavell, *In Quest of the Ordinary*, pp. 48–49 and 60.

76   Michel Foucault, "La folie, l'absence d'oeuvre," in *Dits et écrits: 1954–69*, vol. 1, ed. Daniel Defert and François Ewald (Paris: Gallimard, 1994), pp. 412–420.

77   If the "motivated sign" is usually associated with a literal reading and the arbitrary sign with an "ironic" reader, and the former speaks about a certain transparency while the latter speaks about ambivalence and ambiguity, then in my reading *LLV* gives a different valence to these terms in relation to one another.

78   Fredric Jameson, *Postmodernism, or, The Cultural Logic of Late Capitalism* (Durham: Duke University Press, 1991), pp. 97–129. This chapter, "Architecture: Spatial Equivalents in the World System," begins: "Postmodernism raises questions about the appetite for architecture which it then virtually at once redirects" (p. 97).

79   Bruce Nauman's *Eating My Words* comes to mind here.

80   Gertrude Stein, *Gertrude Stein's America by Gertrude Stein*, ed. Gilbert A. Harrison (New York: Liveright, 1996), p. 94.

81   Henry David Thoreau, *Walden* (Oxford: Oxford University Press, 1999), p. 13.

82   Max Horkheimer and Theodor W. Adorno, "The Culture Industry: Enlightenment as Mass Deception," in *Dialectic of Enlightenment*, trans. Edmund Jephcott (Stanford: Stanford University Press, 2002), p. 119.

83   Wittgenstein, *Philosophical Investigations*, §§2, 19.

84   John Austin, *How to Do Things with Words*, 2d ed., ed. J. O. Urmson and Marina Sbisà (Cambridge, Mass.: Harvard University Press, 1975), pp. 71–72.

85   Wittgenstein uses the German word *Rüfe*, which can be translated as "calls" or "barks."

86   Stanley Cavell, "Notes and Afterthoughts on the Opening of Wittgenstein's *Investigations*," in *Philosophical Passages*, pp. 158–159.

87   Why perform such extreme conditions in the first place? Sometimes that is simply what one has to do, as Thoreau claims in *Walden*: "I am convinced that I cannot exaggerate enough even to lay the foundation of a true expression" (p. 289).

88   Austin, *How to Do Things with Words*, p. 73.

89   Agamben makes clear that the question of the *infans* is not limited by chronology or any developmental schema. See Giorgio Agamben, *Infancy and History: Essays on the Destruction of Experience*, trans. Liz Heron (London: Verso, 1993), p. 4.

90   Oliver Sacks, *The Man Who Mistook His Wife for a Hat and Other Clinical Tales* (New York: Summit Books, 1998), p. 83. Also see my discussion of "urban agnosia" in chapter 1. This diremption of thought and emotion is raised by Koolhaas in his discussion of the discrepancy between the container and contained in the skyscraper. See Koolhaas, *Delirious New York*, p. 100.

91   Nancy characterizes this as psychoanalysis envisaging the world with a "cold eye" and "an insensitivity to the sense." See Jean-Luc Nancy, *The Sense of the World*, trans. Jeffrey S. Librett (Minneapolis: University of Minnesota Press, 1997), p. 48. Nancy's evaluation is not negative—far from it.

92   On the deadpan, see also Michael Golec's essay "'Doing it Deadpan': Venturi, Scott Brown, and Izenour's *Learning from Las Vegas*," in "Instruction as Provocation, or Relearning from Las Vegas," special issue of *Visible Language*, ed. Michael Golec and Aron Vinegar, 37, no. 3 (December 2003): 266–287.

93   Scott Brown was photographing vernacular architecture for some time before this in South Africa and Philadelphia. For the ubiquitous references to Ruscha throughout Venturi and Scott Brown's early work, see Katherine Smith, "Mobilizing Visions: Representing the American Landscape," in *Relearning from Las Vegas*, ed. Aron Vinegar and Michael Golec (University of Minnesota Press, forthcoming 2009). Venturi and Scott Brown were also involved with the photographers Stephen Shore and John Baeder, both of whom were included in their "Signs of Life" exhibition at the Renwick Gallery.

94   There are actually three references to Ruscha in the first edition of *Learning from Las Vegas* if we include the Philadelphia Crosstown Community project of 1968 in Part III, which includes an image titled "Piece of South Street 'Ruscha'" that is also inspired by his *Every Building on the Sunset Strip*. Scott Brown also refers to Michelangelo Antonioni in her article, a director Ruscha admired and who apparently visited his studio in Los Angeles.

95   Denise Scott Brown, "On Pop Art, Permissiveness, and Planning," *Journal of the American Institute of Planners* (May 1969): 185–186.

96   Denise Scott Brown, "Remedial Housing for Architects Studio," in *Venturi, Scott Brown & Associates: On Houses and Housing*, ed. James Steele (New York: St. Martin's Press, 1992), p. 56.

97   Scott Brown, "On Pop Art, Permissiveness, and Planning," p. 185.

98   Interviews with Ed Ruscha in Ruscha, *Leave Any Information at the Signal*, pp. 217 and 26.

99   Scott Brown, "On Pop Art, Permissiveness, and Planning," p. 186. Collecting facts might be an appropriate response if, as Wittgenstein says, "the world is the totality of facts, not of things." Wittgenstein, *Tractatus Logico-philosophicus*, trans. D. F. Pears and B. F. McGuinness (London: Routledge & Keegan Paul, 1961), §1.1. In Vincent Scully's unpublished introduction to *LLV*, he notes, "All the multiple facts of the present . . . become usable when reality rather than dream is the goal." Vincent Scully, introduction to *LLV*, p. 5, AAUP, box 453 (see the appendix of this book).

100 Scott Brown, "On Pop Art, Permissiveness, and Planning," p. 185.

101 I mean "transcendental" here in the Kantian sense of the condition of possibility of any particular experience. The exact wording of Scott Brown's sentence is, "judgment is

merely deferred a while in order to make it more sensitive." For a Goodmanian reading of this passage, see Ritu Bhatt, "Aesthetic or Anaesthetic: A Nelson Goodman Reading of the Las Vegas Strip," in *Relearning from Las Vegas*.

102 Scott Brown, "On Pop Art, Permissiveness, and Planning," p. 185 (my emphasis).

103 Jürgen Habermas uses this specific phrase ("stage-set architecture") in his brief discussion of *LLV* in "Modern and Postmodern Architecture," in *Rethinking Architecture: A Reader in Cultural Theory*, ed. Neil Leach (London: Routledge, 1997), p. 234. Jaleh Mansoor's article on Ruscha discusses flatness in his work, but in a different way from the one I am pursuing here. See Mansoor, "Ed Ruscha's One-Way Street," *October* 111 (Winter 2005): 127–142. Also see David Joselit, "Notes on Surface: Toward a Genealogy of Flatness," *Art History* 23, no. 1 (March 2000): 19–34, for a discussion of the centrality of flatness in the writings of Greenberg and Jameson, two major exponents of modernism and postmodernism.

104 For instance, see Randall Knoper, "'Funny Personations': Theater and the Popularity of the Deadpan Style," in *Acting Naturally: Mark Twain in the Culture of Performance* (Berkeley: University of California Press, 1995), pp. 55–73. For my purposes, sociohistorical accounts of the deadpan aren't particularly relevant, although there are obvious "analogies" to be made with *LLV*. As I mention in the introduction, this book is primarily a "reading" of *LLV*, and any sociohistorical dimension must strengthen that reading, not the other way around.

105 The three instances I will be discussing occur in the following publications by Cavell: "What Becomes of Things on Film?," in *Themes Out of School: Effects and Causes* (Chicago: University of Chicago Press, 1988), pp. 174–177; *The Claim of Reason*, p. 452; and *The World Viewed*, pp. 36–37. "Absorbing skepticism" is from "What Becomes of Things on Film?," p. 177; and "[Keaton's] refinement . . ." is from *The Claim of Reason*, p. 452. In that last quotation, Cavell uses the word "their" instead of "Keaton's," as he is referring to both Keaton and Chaplin. The chapter entitled "The Dandy" (pp. 55–59) in *The World Viewed* is also relevant here, as this figure seems to share a "family resemblance" with Keatonian deadpan humor. To be clear, Cavell never uses the word "deadpan" in his discussion of Buster Keaton.

106 This is neither the time nor the place to delve into the crucial role that "exemplarity" plays in Cavell's work, but I will simply say that it is deeply indebted to issues of Kantian aesthetic judgment that are woven throughout Cavell's writings on ordinary-language philosophy, criticism, modernism, skepticism, and Emersonian perfectionism.

107 Simon Critchley, *Infinitely Demanding: Ethics of Commitment, Politics of Resistance* (London: Verso, 2007), p. 78. Critchley claims that "comic acknowledgment" might be a better picture of human finitude than tragic affirmation. My sense is that *Learning from Las Vegas*'s odd amalgam of deadpan humor, tragedy, and melodrama is what makes it such a wonderful and important text.

108 Cavell, *The World Viewed*, p. 37.

109 Cavell, *The Claim of Reason*, p. 452.

110 Cavell, "What Becomes of Things on Film?," p. 174.

111 Robert Venturi and Denise Scott Brown, preface to the first edition, *LLV*, p. xi.

112 Cavell, *The World Viewed*, pp. 36–37, and "What Becomes of Things on Film?," p. 175.

113 Martin Heidegger, *Being and Time*, trans. Joan Stambaugh (Albany: State University of New York Press, 1996), §345. The issue of deadpan and its relation to "indifference" was first raised by Moira Roth in her essay "The Aesthetic of Indifference," in which

she suggests "neutrality of feeling" and "denial of commitment" as a condition and strategy for artistic production during the McCarthy period in America. Her particular references are to Duchamp, Cage, Cunningham, and Rauschenberg. It should be noted that Roth's views of pop art are generally harsh. See Moira Roth, "The Aesthetic of Indifference" (1977), in *Difference/Indifference: Musings on Postmodernism, Marcel Duchamp and John Cage*, commentary by Jonathan Katz (Amsterdam: G + B Arts International, 1998), pp. 33–48. My discussion of "indifference" is not fundamentally related to the issue of the "denial of commitment" implied in the "aesthetic of indifference," which is eventually linked to Ruscha and the deadpan through Benjamin Buchloh's brief account of Ruscha's work in "Conceptual Art 1962–69: From the Aesthetic of Administration to the Critique of Institutions," *October* 55 (Winter 1990): 121–122. Neither Roth nor Buchloh raises the issue of "indifference" in relation to Heidegger. Buchloh's essay seems to be the departure point for many of the essays in the recent issue of *October* (Winter 2005) devoted to Ruscha.

114 Heidegger, *Being and Time*, §345. The term "equanimity" is used sparingly in *Being and Time*.

115 Ibid., §135.

116 Ibid., §345.

117 Ibid., §137.

118 Ibid., §§137, 138.

119 Robert Venturi and Denise Scott Brown, *Architecture as Signs and Systems: For a Mannerist Time* (Cambridge, Mass.: Belknap Press of Harvard University Press, 2004), p. 40. For Heidegger, it is the mood of boredom that discloses "remarkable indifference" (perhaps another way of saying "equanimity"). Heidegger's belatedly published lecture course from 1929–1930, *The Fundamental Concepts of Metaphysics: World, Finitude, Solitude*, trans. William McNeill and Nicholas Walker (Bloomington: Indiana University Press, 1995), pp. 59–164, contains his most extensive writing on boredom. This text negates any attempt to tether one fundamental mood—that of anxiety—to Heidegger's disclosure of being and the "ontological difference." In *The Fundamental Concepts of Metaphysics*, Heidegger outlines three "levels" of boredom: "bored by"; "bored with"; and "it is boring for one." He relates three "concrete" situations to these levels of boredom: waiting at a train station; being at a dinner party; and walking through the streets on a Sunday afternoon. The beginning of Part II of *LLV* begins with three quotations, one of which is Andy Warhol's famous line, "I like boring things." Although it would appear that this comment corresponds to Heidegger's "first level" of boredom, "bored by," it is clear to me that Warhol, Ruscha, and Venturi and Scott Brown explore issues of boredom in a way that touches on all three levels.

120 Heidegger, *Being and Time*, §137.

121 Heidegger, "What Is Metaphysics?," in *Pathmarks*, ed. William McNeill (Cambridge: Cambridge University Press, 1998), p. 88. Agitation might mark anxiousness, but a "peculiar calm pervades it [anxiety]." And farther on: "The anxiety of those who are daring cannot be opposed to joy or even to the comfortable enjoyment of tranquilized bustle. It stands—outside all such opposition—in secret alliance with the cheerfulness and gentleness of creative longing" (p. 93). In "authentic" anxiety or boredom, "indifference" does not carry the negative connotations it does in his descriptions of it as the condition of the "fallen everyday." As I have indicated before, attunements are always ambivalent for Heidegger.

122 Heidegger, *Being and Time*, §337.

123 "A Kind of 'Huh': An Interview with Edward Ruscha" by Willoughby Sharp, in Ruscha, *Leave Any Information at the Signal*, pp. 65–66.

124 Nancy, *The Sense of the World*, p. 18.

125 Cavell, *The World Viewed*, pp. 35–36 and 72. The "ontological equality" of objects and human subjects is a condition that Cavell ascribes to what becomes of things and people in photography *as such*.

126 Sigmund Freud, "Negation" (1925), in *On Metapsychology*, trans. James Strachey, Penguin Freud Library 11 (London: Penguin, 1991), pp. 437–442.

127 Venturi and Scott Brown, *Architecture as Signs and Systems*, p. 109.

128 Denise Scott Brown, "Learning from Pop," *Casabella*, nos. 359–360 (December 1971): 23.

129 Stan Allen, "Artificial Ecology," in *Reading MVRDV*, ed. Véronique Patteeuw (Rotterdam: NAi Publishers, 2003), p. 83.

130 Heidegger, *Being and Time*, §§137, 138.

131 *LLV*, p. 100.

132 Cavell, *The World Viewed*, p. 132. Cavell is talking about a particular close-up shot in film.

133 Venturi and Scott Brown refer to Henry-Russell Hitchcock rather than Bel Geddes in *Architecture as Signs and Systems*, p. 35. See Norman Bel Geddes, *Horizon* (Boston: Little, Brown, 1932), p. 185: "In Coney Island and California we often see an entire shop built as a sign for its wares. An ice-cream cone is sold in a shop whose architectural form resembles a milk can."

134 Cavell makes references to Heidegger in relation to Buster Keaton in such a way. See "What Becomes of Things on Film?," pp. 174–175: "Buster Keaton is the silent comic figure whose extraordinary works and whose extraordinary gaze . . . illuminate and are illuminated by the consequent concept of the worldhood of the world announcing itself."

135 Thoreau, *Walden*, p. 88.

136 Bernard Tschumi, "The Pleasure of Architecture," in *What Is Architecture?*, ed. Andrew Ballantyne (New York: Routledge, 2002), p. 178.

137 Cavell, *The Claim of Reason*, p. 452; and Ruscha, *Leave Any Information at the Signal*, p. 245.

138 Ed Ruscha, "L.A. Suggested by the Art of Edward Ruscha," in *Leave Any Information at the Signal*, p. 223 (my emphasis).

139 Scott Brown is acutely aware that timing is everything, and that it can't be prescribed: "We have left the whole question of judgment and nonjudgment in the air since we have not defined *when* we defer judgment and when we reassert it." Denise Scott Brown, "Pop Off: Reply to Kenneth Frampton," *Casabella*, nos. 359–360 (December 1971): 45 (my emphasis).

140 Cavell, "What Becomes of Things on Film?," p. 174.

141 To pursue the work of McQueen in relationship to the deadpan would necessitate linking it to questions of race. David Joselit's discussion of the relationship of flatness to race in his essay "Notes on Surface" is a good place to start.

142 Ruscha, "L.A. Suggested by the Art of Edward Ruscha," p. 220.

143 Heidegger, *Being and Time*, trans. John Macquarrie and Edward Robinson (New York: Harper, 1962), §61.

144 I found the following passage on housing in Los Angeles in Nancy's *La ville au loin* particularly striking: "To build and inhabit are distanced from their sense: it shows [itself],

exposes, deposes." Jean-Luc Nancy, *La ville au loin* (Paris: Editions Mille et une nuits, 1999), p. 15 (my translation).

145 Leo Steinberg, "The Flatbed Picture Plane," in *Other Criteria*: *Confrontations with Twentieth-Century Art* (New York: Oxford University Press, 1972), pp. 82–91.

146 Ibid., 84.

147 Ibid., 90.

148 Ibid.

149 *LLV*, pp. 21–22. Owing to the economizing of images in the revised edition, this map is limited to a much smaller field of dispersion.

150 John Dos Passos, *Manhattan Transfer* (Boston: Houghton Mifflin, 2000), p. 351.

151 Sigmund Freud, "Notes upon a Case of Obsessional Neurosis" (1909), in *Three Case Histories* (New York: Collier, 1963), p. 48.

152 Quoted in Walter Benjamin, "On Some Motifs in Baudelaire," in *Illuminations: Essays and Reflections* (New York: Schocken Books, 1968), p. 164. The quotation is from Baudelaire's "Le soleil" in *Les fleurs du mal*.

153 I am thinking here of Cavell's analysis of Wittgenstein's "stumbling block" (Cavell's words) in a crucial scene of instruction in §217 of the *Philosophical Investigations*: "If I have exhausted the justifications I have reached bedrock, and my spade is turned. Then I am inclined to say: 'This is simply what I do.'" Cavell makes the important point that there are options in responding to this stumbling block: "if I discover resistance I might shift my ground, or take a new approach, or blast my way through, or exclude the site and this block from plans altogether. However I take it, the scene with its spade is going to remain for me . . . one of cultivation, of constraint." See Cavell, *Conditions Handsome and Unhandsome: The Constitution of Emersonian Perfectionism* (Chicago: University of Chicago Press, 1990), p. 82.

154 René Descartes, "Second Meditation," in *Descartes: Philosophical Writings*, trans. and ed. Elizabeth Anscombe and Peter Thomas Geach (Indianapolis: Bobbs-Merrill, 1971), p. 73.

155 Cavell, *A Pitch of Philosophy*, p. 111.

156 Gilles Deleuze, *The Fold*, trans. Tom Conley (Minneapolis: University of Minnesota Press, 1993), pp. 136–137 and 160, n. 4.

157 *LLV*, p. 13.

158 Meyer Schapiro, "On Some Problems in the Semiotics of Visual Art: Field and Vehicle in Image-Signs," in *Theory and Philosophy of Art: Style, Artist, and Society* (New York: George Braziller, 1994), pp. 1–32.

4   A Monument for Everyone and No One

1   M. Gottdiener et al., *Las Vegas: The Social Production of an All-American City* (Malden, Mass.: Blackwell, 1999), p. 67.

2   *LLV*, p. 131.

3   Ibid., p. 149.

4   Tom Wolfe, *From Bauhaus to Our House* (New York: Farrar, Straus, Giroux, 1981), p. 114.

5   Immanuel Kant, *Critique of Practical Reason*, trans. Werner Pluhar (Indianapolis: Hackett, 1996), AK 162. The passage in italics was inscribed on Kant's tombstone. The other critical passage about the "starry heavens" is found in the *Critique of Pure Judgment*. As Nancy has pointed out, Kant's passages operate as a "hinge" between the cosmic and acosmic, and thus the beginning of the end of what he calls *consideration*. See Jean-Luc Nancy, *The*

Sense of the World, trans. Jeffrey S. Librett (Minneapolis: University of Minnesota Press, 1997), pp. 42–43.

6 Theodor W. Adorno, "The Schema of Mass Culture," in *The Culture Industry: Selected Essays on Mass Culture*, ed. J. M. Bernstein (London: Routledge, 2001), pp. 96 and 83. Kant's passage on the "starry heavens" plays strongly in his discussion of the culture industry.

7 Joseph Rykwert, "Ornament Is No Crime" (1976), in *Theories and Manifestos of Contemporary Architecture*, ed. Charles Jencks and Karl Kropf (Chichester, West Sussex: Academy Editions, 1997), 97.

8 Friedrich Nietzsche, *Thus Spoke Zarathustra* (New York: Penguin, 1969), pp. 45–46. Heidegger clarifies the implications of the last man's "blink": "The last men blink. What does that mean? *Blink* is related to the Middle English *Blenchen*, which means deceive, and to *blenken*, *blinken*, which means gleam or glitter. To blink—that means to play up and set up a glittering deception which is then agreed upon as true and valid—with the mutual tacit understanding not to question the set up." See Martin Heidegger, *What Is Called Thinking?*, trans. J. Glenn Gray (New York: Harper & Row, 1968), p. 74. There are other challenging ways of thinking about the *Wink*—which can be translated into English as "blink" or "signs"—that are initiated by Heidegger and carried on in the work of Jean-Luc Nancy.

9 Jean-Luc Nancy, *La ville au loin* (Paris: Editions Mille et une nuits, 1999), p. 49.

10 *LLV*, p. 50.

11 George Santayana, *The Sense of Beauty: Being the Outline of Aesthetic Theory* (New York: Dover, 1955), p. 67 (my emphasis). As Corbusier said about his arrival in New York: "The sky is decked out. It is a Milky Way come down to earth; you are in it." See Le Corbusier, *When the Cathedrals Were White: A Journey to the Country of Timid People* (New York: Reynal & Hitchcock, 1947), p. 90.

12 *LLV*, p. 129.

13 Ibid., p. 130.

14 Ibid., p. 137

15 Ibid., p. 132. I believe Lévi-Strauss is critiquing the biological conception of the family that was dominant in Anglo-American anthropology. Venturi and Scott Brown are also drawing on George Hersey's essay "Replication Replicated," *Perspecta* 10 (1955): 211–248. This essay, which emphasized historical and perceptual association, is cited on *LLV*, p. 131.

16 *LLV*, p. 132.

17 Ibid.

18 Ibid., p. 133.

19 These ideas have been most thoroughly explored in the work of Jean-Luc Nancy, which I draw upon in this chapter.

20 We might note that the word "symbol" comes from the Greek *symbolon*, which was a broken potsherd in ancient Greece that marked the promise of a future reunion between friends.

21 Roland Barthes, "That Old Thing, Art . . . ," in *The Responsibility of Forms*, trans. Richard Howard (New York: Hill and Wang, 1985), pp. 201–202. It is unclear to me in what sense and from where Barthes is deriving his understanding of "facticity." The word is used in quite different ways by Sartre, Husserl, and Heidegger.

22 Martin Heidegger, *Being and Time*, trans. Joan Stambaugh (Albany: State University of New York Press, 1996); and Heidegger, *Ontology: The Hermeneutics of Facticity*, trans. John van Buren (Bloomington: Indiana University Press, 1999).

23   Jean-Luc Nancy, *L'évidence du film/The Evidence of Film,* trans. Christine Irizzary and Verena Andermatt Conley (Brussels: Yves Gevaert Editeur, 2001), pp. 42–46, 68–70, 76–78.

24   Roland Barthes, *Camera Lucida*, trans. Richard Howard (New York: Hill and Wang, 1981), 113. Another passage seems relevant here: "The photograph is an extended, loaded evidence . . ." (p. 115).

25   Nancy, *L'évidence du film/The Evidence of Film*, p. 42.

26   See the discussion of *kriterion* in Nancy, *A Finite Thinking*, ed. Simon Sparks (Stanford: Stanford University Press, 2003), pp. 159–160.

27   Stanley Cavell, *The Claim of Reason: Wittgenstein, Skepticism, Morality, and Tragedy* (Oxford: Oxford University Press, 1979), p. 433. The issue of criteria is central to both Cavell and Nancy.

28   Jean-Luc Nancy, "The Image, the Distinct," in *The Ground of the Image*, trans. Jeff Fort (New York: Fordham University Press, 2005), pp. 7–8.

29   Ibid., p. 7.

30   Nancy, *The Sense of the World*, p. 61.

31   AAUP, 225.II.A.27.5

32   Meyer Schapiro, "On Some Problems in the Semiotics of Visual Art: Field and Vehicle in Image-Signs," in *Theory and Philosophy of Art: Style, Artist, and Society* (New York: George Braziller, 1994), p. 1; Roland Barthes, "The Grain of the Voice," in *Image, Music, Text,* trans. Steven Heath (New York: Hill and Wang, 1977), pp. 179–189.

33   The participants in the Learning from Las Vegas studio were reading material on the detailed workings of advertising and neon signs. The following site is an excellent place to begin to explore the technical aspects of neon signs: http://gaming.unlv.edu/v_museum/neon_survey/neon_glossary.html.

34   Walter Benjamin, "One-Way Street," in *Walter Benjamin, Selected Writings: 1927–34*, ed. Marcus Bullock and Michael W. Jennings, vol. 2 (Cambridge, Mass.: Belknap Press of Harvard University Press, 1996), p. 476.

35   There are many other examples of photographs taken in Las Vegas, and projects such as Venturi and Rauch's "Bill-Ding-Board" proposal in their entry for the National Football Hall of Fame competition, that further explore these issues of framing and materiality within the image.

36   See chapter 3.

37   *LLV*, pp. 116–117.

38   The phrase "reciprocal supplementation" is used by Jean-Luc Nancy to describe the relationship between legibility and visibility in his important essay on the topic, "Catalogue," in *Multiple Arts: The Muses II*, ed. Simon Sparks (Stanford: Stanford University Press, 2006), p. 154.

39   *LLV*, pp. 130–131.

40   Nancy writes, "it is as relation that sense configures itself." See Nancy, *The Sense of the World*, p. 118.

41   Ludwig Wittgenstein, *Remarks on the Philosophy of Psychology*, ed. and trans. G. E. M. Anscombe and G. H. von Wright, vol. 1 (Oxford: Blackwell, 1980), §1100.

42   It should be noted that a "wink" in telecommunications is a brief interruption of a continuous signal.

43   Jean-Luc Nancy, "Distinct Oscillation," in *The Ground of the Image*, p. 75. For Nancy the opening and closing of the mouth (and the eye) negotiates issues of touching and detachment and the enunciation of singularity that articulate a nonplace in which freedom and commu-

nity are thought. The major work on these issues is his *Ego Sum* (Paris: Flammarion, 1979), individual chapters of which have been translated, but not the book as such. In any case, Nancy's *The Experience of Freedom* is a good place to begin an exploration of these ideas. See *The Experience of Freedom*, trans. Bridget McDonald (Stanford: Stanford University Press, 1993), pp. 90 and 145, and the chapter "Sharing Freedom," pp. 66–80.

44 Jean-Luc Nancy, "Why Are There Several Arts and Not Just One," in *The Muses*, trans. Peggy Kamuf (Stanford: Stanford University Press, 1996), p. 31.

45 Stanley Cavell, *The World Viewed: Reflections on the Ontology of Film* (New York: Viking Press, 1971), p. 103.

46 This word is raised in most of Nancy's work, but there are good discussions of it in *The Sense of the World* and *L'évidence du film/The Evidence of Film*.

47 Ian Balfour, *The Fragmentary Demand: An Introduction to the Philosophy of Jean-Luc Nancy* (Stanford: Stanford University Press, 2006), p. 149.

48 See Cavell, *The Claim of Reason*, pp. 3–36. A recent collection of essays attempts to explore the political dimensions of Cavell's thought in terms of this phrase; see *The Claim to Community: Essays on Stanley Cavell and Political Philosophy*, ed. Andrew Norris (Stanford: Stanford University Press, 2006).

49 Cavell, *The Claim of Reason*, p. 20.

50 I derive the word "unary" from Barthes's *Camera Lucida*, pp. 40–41. This is a grammatical term he uses to describe a widespread type of photograph dominated by the coded studium, as opposed to the uncoded aspects of the photograph exemplified by the punctum.

51 *LLV*, p. 50.

52 *LLV*, pp. 119 and 148–150.

53 Ibid.

54 Ibid.

55 See Nancy, *La ville au loin*; Nancy, *The Sense of the World*, p. 104. The issues of community are also explored in depth in Nancy's *The Inoperative Community*, trans. Peter Connor et al. (Minneapolis: University of Minnesota Press, 1991).

56 Nancy, *La ville au loin*, pp. 37, 43, and 49. These pages should be read in conjunction with the chapter "Space: Constellations" in *The Sense of the World*, pp. 42–45.

57 Cavell, *The Claim of Reason*, pp. 19, 26.

58 Stanley Cavell, "Philosophy and the Arrogation of Voice," in *A Pitch of Philosophy: Autobiographical Exercises* (Cambridge, Mass.: Harvard University Press, 1994), pp. 3–51.

59 Cavell, preface to *A Pitch of Philosophy*, p. vii.

60 Nancy, *The Sense of the World*, pp. 115–117.

61 Cavell, *The Claim of Reason*, p. 20. I already suggested this connection earlier in this chapter in bringing together Cavell's understanding of medium with Nancy's work on the distribution of the senses in relation to art, and how each art explores its particular way of touching on all the other arts.

62 Nancy, "Nous autre," in *The Ground of the Image*, p. 100. Thus, Nancy is able to state that "being-in-common is contemporaneous with singular existence." See *The Experience of Freedom*, p. 66.

63 Nancy, *Sense of the World*, p. 117.

64 Henry David Thoreau, *Walden* (Oxford: Oxford University Press, 1999), p. 11.

65 René Descartes, "Third Meditation," in *Descartes: Philosophical Writings*, trans. and ed. Elizabeth Anscombe and Peter Thomas Geach (Indianapolis: Bobbs-Merrill, 1971), p. 76.

66 Quoted in Louis Sass, *The Paradoxes of Delusion: Wittgenstein, Schreber, and the Schizophrenic Mind* (Ithaca: Cornell University Press, 1994), p. 43. This quotation is reminiscent of Adorno and Horkheimer's famous account of Ulysses' encounter with the Sirens as an allegory of the Enlightenment. See Max Horkheimer and Theodor W. Adorno, *Dialectic of Enlightenment*, trans. Edmund Jephcott (Stanford: Stanford University Press, 2002), pp. 25–28, and in particular, "Excursus I: Odysseus or Myth and Enlightenment," pp. 35–62.

67 Denise Scott Brown, "On Pop Art, Permissiveness, and Planning," *Journal of the American Institute of Planners* (May 1969): 185.

68 About this mode of intense looking, Wittgenstein wrote, "The phenomenon of *staring* is closely bound up with the whole puzzle of solipsism." Quoted in Rush Rhees, "Wittgenstein's Notes for Lectures on 'Private Experience' and 'Sense Data,'" *Philosophical Review* 77 (1968): 309.

69 T. S. Eliot, "Fragment of an Agon (Song by Klipstein and Krumpacker)," in *T. S. Eliot: Collected Poems, 1909–1962* (London: Faber and Faber, 2002), p. 123.

70 Cavell, *The Claim of Reason*, p. 354.

71 Ralph Waldo Emerson, "Experience," In *Ralph Waldo Emerson: Selected Essays, Lectures, Poems*, ed. Robert D. Richardson (New York: Bantam Books, 1990), p. 239. He continues: "I am ready to die out of nature and be born again into this new yet unapproachable America I have found in the West."

72 Vincent Scully, introduction to Robert Venturi, *Complexity and Contradiction in Architecture* (New York: Museum of Modern Art, 1966), p. 11. Scully's actual words are, "This is not an easy book. It requires professional commitment and close visual attention, and is not for those architects who, lest they offend them, pluck out their eyes."

5   Reducks, 1972, 1977

1 Here I want to acknowledge Michael Golec's essays "'Doing It Deadpan: Venturi, Scott Brown, and Izenour's *Learning from Las Vegas*" and "Format and Layout in Learning from Las Vegas," in "Instruction as Provocation, or Relearning from Las Vegas," special issue of *Visible Language*, ed. Michael Golec and Aron Vinegar, 37, no. 3 (December 2003), and *Relearning from Las Vegas*, ed. Aron Vinegar and Michael Golec (University of Minnesota Press, forthcoming 2009). These essays intersect with the issues raised in this chapter.

2 For a short but insightful book on books, see Jean-Luc Nancy, *Sur le commerce des pensées* (Paris: Editions Galilée, 2005).

3 Denise Scott Brown, preface to the revised edition, *LLV*, p. xv. Although the cost was a legitimate concern, and seems to be of a piece with Venturi and Scott Brown's populist stance, it really seems to have been more of an issue for Barbara Ankeny, the acquisitions editor for the revised edition. At various points, she reminded Venturi and Scott Brown that their desire for color photographs, and other interventions, would drive up the cost of the second edition.

4 There is no doubt that the cost of reprinting the first edition would have been prohibitive, as it was very expensive to produce in the first place, requiring external subventions to help pay for its numerous illustrations, including 182 that were in color. The first edition was typeset in house, on an IBM Composer, allowing the MIT Press to allocate more resources to the printing of color photographs in the book (Sylvia Steiner,

phone conversation with the author, April 29, 2007). The first edition originally sold for $25; it now sells on AbeBooks.com for approximately $5,000 to 6,000 in pristine condition with its glassine dust jacket. The revised edition sold for $9.95 in 1977; thirty years later it is listed in MIT's catalog for a reasonable $22.95.

5   Scott Brown, preface to the revised edition, *LLV*, p. xv (my emphasis).

6   The revised edition was also printed in a hardcover version. Its jacket is the same design as the revised edition's paperback cover.

7   The bibliography was meant, in part, to compensate for the deletion of Part III surveying their recent work since the publication of *Complexity and Contradiction in Architecture*.

8   Except for a "decorative" double-spread insert of 35mm color photographs that was, in turn, a reduction of a similar spread found in the first edition. Venturi and Scott Brown seemed to have approved this aspect of the first and revised editions.

9   In the first edition, the text in Part I is in 10-point Univers on a 30-point type body, with a text column 47 picas wide (the marginal column text is in 10 on 11 Univers Bold, 11 picas wide); see figure 5.1 for a sample. The text in Part II is in 10 on 30 Univers, the column 22.5 picas wide; the text for Part III is in 10 on 13 Univers, the column 15 picas wide. Sylvia Steiner, correspondence with the author, August 12, 2007. (The revised edition is set in 10 on 12 Baskerville throughout.)

10 The "Studio Notes" section of the revised edition is organized in two columns of text. The use of three-column text originated in Switzerland, in order to deal with trilingual publications in German, French, and Italian. I have seen books designed by Cooper with one, two, and three columns of text, but *LLV* is the only one I am aware of with all three kinds of text columns in the same book.

11 Scott Brown, preface to the revised edition, *LLV*, p. xv.

12 Ibid. Also see chapter 1 for a further discussion of the book's relationship to the city of Las Vegas in relationship to this quotation.

13 Scott Brown and Venturi requested that the subtitle be included on the front cover, but for marketing reasons, and in order to keep the connection to the first edition visible, the subtitle appeared only on the title page within the book. They also considered a couple of variations for the subtitle before coming up with "The Forgotten Symbolism of Architectural Form." The other variants were "An Essay on Symbolism in Architecture" and "Symbolism in Architecture."

14 Scott Brown, preface to the revised edition, *LLV*, p. xv.

15 William Drenttel, "*Learning from Las Vegas*: The Book That (Still) Takes My Breath Away," *Design Observer*, posted by William Drenttel on May 5, 2004, http://www.designobserver.com/archives/000146.html. In an earlier article in *Lingua Franca* ("Beautiful Books," *Lingua Franca* 9, no. 9 [December 1999/January 2000], http://linguafranca.mirror.theinfo.org/9912/brbooks.html), Drenttel had claimed, "Not since Robert Venturi [et al.]'s *Learning from Las Vegas* has the design of a book so eloquently expressed the point of view of its authors." Roger Conover, executive editor at the MIT Press and the editor who worked with Robert Venturi on a later book (*Iconography and Electronics upon a Generic Architecture: A View from the Drafting Room*) wrote back, informing Drenttel that in fact the opposite was true: the first edition had been designed not by the authors but by Muriel Cooper; and at least two of the authors found the design values it expressed so antithetical to their own that they insisted on redesigning the book as a precondition for reprinting it. Despite frequent requests from booksellers, the first edition has never been reprinted in its original format.

16   Roger Conover, telephone conversation with the author, April 28, 2007.

17   Robert Venturi, Denise Scott Brown, and Steven Izenour, *Learning from Las Vegas* (Cambridge, Mass.: MIT Press, 1972). The annotated copy, which I consulted, was given to Roger Conover by Muriel Cooper, and later inscribed to Conover by Robert Venturi and Denise Scott Brown. Conover lent it to the Canadian Centre for Architecture/Centre Canadien d'Architecture for the exhibition "Learning from . . . Ruscha and Venturi and Scott Brown, 1962–1977" (March 31–May 30, 2004), which examined the relationship between the books of artist Ed Ruscha and architects Robert Venturi and Denise Scott Brown dealing with the architecture and urbanism of the everyday in Los Angeles and Las Vegas during the 1960s and 1970s. Although I consulted the book while it was still in private hands, Conover later placed it and copies of related documents in the Avery Architectural & Fine Arts Library (referred to hereafter as AAFAL). Conover received queries from scholars who had viewed the materials during the CCA exhibition and wanted further access to them. The CCA exhibition was the first and only time that any of these materials had been viewed publicly.

18   Robert Venturi to Michael Connelly, February 11, 1972, AAUP, box 453. It should be noted that Venturi is referring not to the dust jacket for the first edition as published but, rather, to an earlier design that I discuss later in this chapter.

19   Denise Scott Brown to Michael Connelly, July 25, 1972, AAUP, box 453.

20   Quoted in Janet Abrams, "Muriel Cooper's Visible Wisdom," 1997, http://www.aiga.org/content.cfm/medalist-murielcooper.

21   Title page, annotated copy of *Learning from Las Vegas*, AAFAL.

22   Quoted in Abrams, "Muriel Cooper's Visible Wisdom."

23   Roland Barthes, "From Work to Text," in *Image, Music, Text*, trans. Steven Heath (New York: Hill and Wang, 1977), pp. 155–164.

24   Denise Scott Brown to Barbara H. Ankeny, April 16, 1976, AAFAL.

25   The process of "stripping" in graphic design is also called "image assembly." The analogies between stripping in film and book design became even more relevant with the introduction in the 1960s and 1970s of offset printing, which was replacing traditional typesetting. Muriel Cooper began to explore offset printing in the Visible Language Workshop in the early 1970s. Wendy Richmond recalled that the Visible Language Workshop had two large offset presses, which both directors and students were experimenting with. Wendy Richmond, telephone conversation with the author, April 28, 2007.

26   Quoted in Abrams, "Muriel Cooper's Visible Wisdom." Cooper also mentions the conflict over the cover in her conversation with Ellen Lupton, May 7, 1994, unpublished, http://www.elupton.com/index.php?id=29.

27   Robert Venturi to Michael Connelly, February 11, 1972.

28   Denise Scott Brown, "On Pop Art, Permissiveness, and Planning," *Journal of the American Institute of Planners* (May 1969): 185–186. See the section "Deadpan and the Absorption of Skepticism" in chapter 3.

29   This practice of picking out significant words, names, or titles is also typical of Josef Müller-Brockmann's and Jacqueline Casey's approach to poster design.

30   Robert Venturi to Barbara Ankeny, May 23, 1972, AAUP, box 453. During this period, some alternate designs for the cover were considered, including selected chapter headings printed directly on the cloth cover, a cloth cover without the Tanya image, and a version in which the words actually ran over the Tanya paste-down. No doubt some of

these were worked out more on one side than the other. Mario Furtado, telephone conversation with the author, April 24, 2007.

31 Or if we are willing to consider "tautology" as some kind of inexpressive expression. See the discussion of the dust jacket in chapter 2. In thinking about expression as "expression," I have found Nancy's essay "Res Extensa" quite informative. See Jean-Luc Nancy, "Res Extensa," in *Multiple Arts*, pp. 166–170.

32 The closely spaced words of the dust jacket also recall the decorative two-page spread of 35mm photographs included in the first and revised editions of *LLV*, which Venturi and Scott Brown liked. This decorative spread was also used in an expensive promotional brochure produced by the MIT Press to advertise the book.

33 Stanley Cavell, "The Wittgensteinian Event," in *Reading Cavell*, ed. Alice Crary and Sanford Shieh (New York: Routledge, 2006), p. 20 (my emphasis): "To possess criteria is also to possess the demonic power to strip them from ourselves, to turn language upon itself, to find that its criteria are, in relation to others, merely outer; in relation to certainty, simply blind; in relation to being able to go on with our concepts into new contexts, wholly ungrounded."

34 Stanley Cavell, *In Quest of the Ordinary: Lines of Skepticism and Romanticism* (Chicago: University of Chicago Press, 1994), p. 5.

35 Sigmund Freud, *Civilization and Its Discontents*, trans. James Strachey (New York: Norton, 1961), pp. 64–65.

36 Vincent Scully, unpublished introduction to *LLV*, AAUP, box 453 (see the appendix of this book).

37 In the preface to the first edition, John Rauch is also called their "Rauch of Gibraltar."

38 Here I am thinking of René Girard's essential work on the scapegoat in relationship to his theory of mimetic rivalry. See Girard, *The Scapegoat*, trans. Yvonne Freccero (Baltimore: Johns Hopkins University Press, 1986).

39 Denise Scott Brown to Steven Izenour, November 2, 1971, AAUP, box 6905.

40 Barbara Ankeny to Robert Venturi, November 9, 1971, AAUP, box 453.

41 The locus classicus for this material is John Austin's essay "A Plea for Excuses," in *Philosophical Papers*, 3rd ed., ed. J. O. Urmson and G. J. Warnock (Oxford: Clarendon Press, 1979), pp. 175–204.

42 Cynthia Ware to Denise Scott Brown, February 28, 1977, AAFAL.

43 Barbara Ankeny to Denise Scott Brown, August 1, 1972, AAUP, box 453. She goes on to note that "the inclusion of such a list can look 'cranky.'"

44 A letter from Barbara Ankeny to Scott Brown notes that Steve Izenour discovered that USIA in Washington, D.C., had around 50 to 75 undistributed copies of *LLV*, and might be willing to sell them back to the Press. It is likely that Venturi and Scott Brown bought these. See Barbara Ankeny to Denise Scott Brown, June 1, 1976, AAFAL. The erratum sheet is almost always missing in library copies, and seems to survive primarily in the pristine copies of the first edition, which Scott Brown and Venturi purchased. The first edition that I consulted in the AAUP was dedicated to some close friends and supporters of Venturi and Scott Brown, and it included the erratum sheet.

45 Cooper's design sensibility is also evident in her work for the *Simmons Review*.

46 "Swiss design" usually refers to the work produced, beginning in the 1940s, by the teachers and students from the Kunstgewerbeschule in Basel, led by Armin Hofmann and Emil Ruder, and in Zurich, led by Josef Müller-Brockmann. The Yale School of Design became an early center for Swiss design in the United States, due to its strong connections with the

Basel school. Also, Hofmann began teaching there as a visiting professor in 1956. For a recent overview of Swiss design, see Richard Hollis, *Swiss Graphic Design: The Origin and Growth of an International Style, 1920–1965* (New Haven: Yale University Press, 2006).

47 Max Bill also designed other seminal books in modern painting and architecture, in which his use of the typographic grid dovetailed with the material. For example, see Bill's design for *La nouvelle architecture/Die neue Architektur/The New Architecture*, ed. Albert Roth (Erlenbach, Zurich: Éditions d'Architecture, 1946), and the design for his own book on the bridge designer *Robert Maillart* (Erlenbach, Zurich: Verlag für Architektur, 1949).

48 Cooper might have been introduced to Kepes through Carl Zahn. She had a lifelong admiration for Kepes and considered his *The Language of Vision* a seminal work, one she continued to draw inspiration from.

49 Carl Zahn, telephone conversation with the author, April 28, 2007.

50 This brief history of the MIT Office of Publications has been derived from the author's phone conversations with John Matill, Dietmar Winkler, and Carl Zahn on May 19, April 27, and April 28, 2007, respectively.

51 Steven Heller, "Muriel Cooper: Introduction and Interview," in *Graphic Design in America: A Visual Language History* (New York: Harry N. Abrams, 1989), pp. 96–99.

52 Helvetica quickly became the preferred typeface for MIT's publicity material. It was ubiquitous in the design work of Jacqueline Casey, a colleague and friend of Cooper's in the Office of Design, and the designer for many of the posters and printed matter for MIT. A fine collection of her posters from 1963 to 1990 can be found in the Jacqueline Casey Poster Collection, in the Special Collections of the Rochester Institute of Technology library. This collection is digitized and available online at http://wally.rit.edu/special/JacquelineCasey.htm. Casey was a much stricter exponent of Swiss design than Muriel Cooper, and many of her posters recall the work of Josef Müller-Brockmann.

53 The two key texts that introduced the modular grid to an international audience were Josef Müller-Brockmann's *Gestaltungsprobleme des Graphikers/The Graphic Designer and His Design Problems* (Teufen: Niggli/London: Tiranti, 1961), and Emil Ruder, *Typographie/Typography* (Teufen: Niggli, 1967).

54 Sylvia Steiner, phone conversation with the author, July 7, 2007. Steiner, who worked on the first and revised editions of *Learning from Las Vegas*, confirmed that these layouts were indeed in Muriel Cooper's hand. This attribution is substantiated in a "to-do" list dated September 24, 1971, with the directive, "Give Steve Muriel's layout sheets I, II, III," AAUP, box 453. A schedule of drawings dated July 12, 1971, corresponds to Parts I, II, III, and suggests that Cooper's layout sheets were worked out between June and August 1971. Steiner asserted that the preliminary mock-up boards for Part I, dated to February 23, 1971, were not made by Cooper; this also seems to be confirmed by written material in the AAUP.

55 This is not exactly correct for Part III. There the three text columns abandon the earlier 11-pica columns, as the three together take up the width of four of the 11-pica columns from the five-column grid; thus they only coincide at the outside edge.

56 Quoted in Heller, "Muriel Cooper," p. 97. The format of the book is so large that it is beyond the capacities of a strict grid. Zahn, telephone conversation. In correspondence, Sylvia Steiner also confirmed that owing to the complicated nature of the images and their variations in size and importance, they do not always follow the grid.

57 Heller, "Muriel Cooper," pp. 97–98.

58 Both books have very similar formats: 10¼ x 14¼ inches for the *Bauhaus* book, and 10½ x 14 inches for *LLV*.

59   Rick Poynor, *No More Rules: Graphic Design and Postmodernism* (London: Laurence King Publishing, 2003). This is not to mention the work of Katherine and Michael McCoy at the Cranbrook Academy of Art, or the work done by Pushpin Studio. This list would have to include many of the designers that Cooper trained or influenced, such as Mario Furtado, Ellen Lupton, Michael McPherson, Wendy Richmond, David Small, Sylvia Steiner, and Cynthia Ware.

60   Muriel Cooper in conversation with Ellen Lupton, May 7, 1994.

61   "Author Questionnaire," MIT Press, November 2, 1971, AAUP, box 6905.

62   Muriel Cooper in conversation with Ellen Lupton, May 7, 1994.

63   Ibid. It is clear that Cooper saw many of her books as functional works of art, and enjoyed experimenting with them. No doubt this was also a source of conflict between her and some authors.

64   Another good example of a book set on the IBM Composer is Donis Dondis, *A Primer of Visual Literacy* (Cambridge, Mass.: MIT Press, 1973). Cooper's recognition early on that all book design would soon be done on computers was most likely a factor in her move to the Visible Language Workshop. Cooper was one of the first designers to set her own type, an approach that looked forward to the age of computer-aided design and self-publishing; she would help pioneer this approach while at the Visible Language Workshop. The Workshop was the milieu in which the long history of typography and book design entered the computer age, and it was the place where sophisticated research-based computer programming encountered the graphic design world and vice versa. See, for example, David Small, "Rethinking the Book," in *Graphic Design & Reading*, ed. Gunnar Swanson (New York: Allworth Press, 2000), pp. 189–200. Small reproduces an image from the first edition of *Learning from Las Vegas*, and makes clear that many of Cooper's interests, first worked out in her graphic design work at the MIT Press—such as layering and translucency, filmic approaches to layout and design, transformations of form and content across different media, an emphasis on dynamic type, and what she would later call "information landscapes"—were elaborated and intensified after her departure from the Press. Simply put, it is as insightful to look back from her work as director of the Visible Language Workshop to her approach to book design at the MIT Press as it is to look forward. Small applied to do his Ph.D. dissertation on "Rethinking the Book" with Cooper the year she died, and completed it under William Mitchell. In many ways, the spirit of Cooper's design and pedagogy is continued by John Maeda, who initially took over the Visible Language Workshop after her death. Wendy Richmond's trajectory is also interesting to consider, as she was hired by Cooper and began her career at the Press, before moving on to do much broader work in design. My conversations with Small and Richmond were very helpful in thinking about these issues. For an early history of the Media Lab at MIT see Stewart Brand, *The Media Lab: Inventing the Future at MIT* (Cambridge, Mass: MIT Press, 1989). Cooper's work at the Visible Language Workshop is barely acknowledged in this book. Although Cooper wrote little, see her "Computers and Design," *Design Quarterly* 142 (1989): 22–31.

65   See Ellen Lupton, "Women Graphic Designers," available at http://www.elupton.com/index.php?id=6.

66   Cooper was also involved with a half-dozen of Richard Saul Wurman's books published by the MIT Press from 1971 to 1976. The layout and design of two of these books—*Man-Made Philadelphia: A Guide to Its Physical and Cultural Environment* (1972) and *The Nature of Recreation: A Handbook in Honor of Fredrick Law Olmsted, Using Examples from His Work*

(1972)—demonstrate the same complex accumulation of information in photographs, diagrams, plans, and text that Cooper would be grappling with in her design for *Learning from Las Vegas*. It seems that Howard Brunner and Joel Katz, both working in Wurman's office, were the principal designers of these books. There was a great deal of mutual respect between Cooper and Wurman; in fact, Wurman dedicated his influential book *Information Architects* (New York: Graphis, 1997) to the memory of Cooper, who had died of an apparent heart attack in 1994. Their mutual interests must only have increased after Cooper's move to the Visible Language Workshop at the Media Lab, which operated as an intermediary between the computer culture at MIT and the design world. Cooper also introduced Wurman to Nicholas Negroponte, the director of the Media Lab. Cooper and David Small, a research associate at the Visible Language Workshop, would later make a presentation called "Information Landscapes" about their work at the TED 5 conference in 1994. These were a series of international conferences organized by Wurman, beginning in 1984, that explored issues related to technology, entertainment, and design.

67   Wolfgang Weingart, "How Can One Make Swiss Typography?" (1972), in *Looking Closer 3: Classic Writing on Graphic Design*, ed. Michael Bierut et al. (New York: Allworth Press, 1999), p. 221. Also see Keith Robertson, "On White Space/When Less Is More," in *Looking Closer: Critical Writings on Graphic Design*, ed. Michael Bierut et al. (New York: Allworth Press, 1994), pp. 63–65.

68   Two texts that I have found particularly helpful in thinking about these issues are Meyer Schapiro, "On Some Problems in the Semiotics of Visual Art: Field and Vehicle in Image-Signs," in *Theory and Philosophy of Art: Style, Artist, and Society* (New York: George Braziller, 1994), pp. 1–32; and Jean-Luc Nancy's discussion about figure and ground in "Why Are There Several Arts and Not Just One," in *The Muses*, trans. Peggy Kamuf (Stanford: Stanford University Press, 1996), pp. 1–40.

69   Quoted in Heller, "Muriel Cooper," pp. 98–99.

70   Nancy, "Why Are There Several Arts and Not Just One," p. 32.

71   *LLV,* 13. The precise phrases used are "expansive texture" and "megatexture."

72   Cooper went on to do pioneering work in "iconography and electronics" at the Visible Language Workshop, which she cofounded with Ron MacNeil in 1975. Some beautiful images produced in Carl Steinitz's studios at the Harvard Graduate School of Design exist in the VSBA archives. They are computer mappings of activity patterns that look remarkably like some of the material in Joseph R. Passonneau and Richard Saul Wurman's *Urban Atlas: 20 American Cities: A Communication Study Notating Selected Urban Data at a Scale of 1:48,000* (Cambridge, Mass.: MIT Press, 1966). Scott Brown wrote a review of Passonneau and Wurman's book, in which she expressed her admiration for its graphic representation of income and density data that recalled op art in its sensorial impact and oscillating figure-ground relationships. (It should be noted that Venturi and Scott Brown were drawing on Sheldon Nodelman's sophisticated writings on op art at this time.) See Scott Brown, "Mapping the City: Symbols and Systems," *Landscape* 17, no. 3 (1968): 22–25.

73   "Request for Grant in Aid for Combination of a Research Project Pertaining to the Form Analysis of the Commercial Strip, or *LLV*," Robert Venturi, Denise Scott Brown, Steven Izenour, AAUP, box 505.

74   "Studio LLV: Research Topics. Phase V: Deepening and Honing," AAUP, box, 505.

75   The event lasted from 10 a.m. to 10 p.m. The "schedules" are the large-scale grids of individual building parts for different building types and parts of the street, which are

then assembled into two-dimensional graphs with buildings on the x axis and parts of buildings on the y axis. Reading across one column of the graph, one sees all the parts for that building; reading down one column, one sees the same part for each building; and reading diagonally, one constructs a hybrid building. For example, see figures 42 and 43 in *LLV*. This was called compiling a "pattern book." See *LLV*, pp. 77–78; however, the "logic" of these schedules is poorly described in the "Studio Notes." If one looks closely at the images they are, at times, quite humorous, and they don't strictly adhere to the y axis headings. Needless to say, these schedules were drastically reduced for the first edition, and even more so for the revised edition.

76   Robert Venturi to Carroll Bowen, May 2, 1969, p. 2, AAUP, box 505. Similar letters were written to Yale University Press, Praeger Publishers, and the University of Pennsylvania Press.

77   Walter Murch, *In the Blink of an Eye: A Perspective on Film Editing*, 2d ed. (Los Angeles: Silman-James Press, 2001), p. 4. Also see Michael Ondaatje, *The Conversations: Walter Murch and the Editing of Film* (New York: Alfred A. Knopf, 2002).

78   We should always remember that the idea of the studio emerged from a publication, their 1968 article "A Significance for A&P Parking Lots, or Learning from Las Vegas," in *Architectural Forum*.

79   They received subsidies for *LLV* from the Edgar J. Kaufmann Foundation, the Celeste and Armand Bartos Foundation, and the National Endowment for the Arts.

80   See the letters in AAUP, boxes 505 and 453.

81   Quoted in Abrams, "Muriel Cooper's Visible Wisdom." Cooper continues, "Too often, the role of the designer is to clothe a set of messages they've had no participation in. Here is a book. You didn't write it. You don't change it except insofar as you present the information somebody else has generated. You're not really collaborating, either, because the stuff is here, and an accomplished fact. I decided I had to wash that out of my head and impose my own problems." Cooper is referring here to the reasons for her moving from the MIT Press to the Visible Language Workshop. It is not often that a real collaboration occurs, such as the one between Bruce Mau and Rem Koolhaas in *S, M, L, XL*.

82   Robert Venturi to Carroll Bowen, June 12, 1969, AAUP, box 505. Bowen resigned on December 1, 1969, and was subsequently replaced by Michael Connelly.

83   Letter from Anne Wilde, art editor, to Mr. Robert Venturi, September 19, 1969, AAUP, box 453. This was assuming a 12 x 9-inch format for the book.

84   Venturi to Bowen, June 12, 1969.

85   Robert Venturi to Michael Connelly, December 11, 1969, AAUP, box 505. From this letter it seems that the submission date for the manuscript was May 1, 1970; also, the book would include approximately 105 images and have a price between $12.50 and $15.00.

86   Peggy Scoville to Robert Venturi, January 21, 1970, AAUP, box 453.

87   From an internal note, it seems that Venturi and Scott Brown had consulted a lawyer about what paragraph six might mean in regard to MIT's legal obligation to them in terms of the book's design as well as the possibility of their breaking their contract with the Press. From the written record, it appears that the conflicts between Cooper and Venturi and Scott Brown began to intensify in fall 1971 and never abated. It would seem that much of this conflict was played out in letters, either to the director of the Press or to the design department. Sylvia Steiner recalled to me that Venturi and Scott Brown would fly in on weekends, meet with her and Cooper, approve everything, then return to Philadelphia, and send long letters critiquing the design. Steiner, telephone conversation.

88   As noted, Denise Scott Brown was the main "designer," with Sylvia Steiner supervising the design process, Mario Furtado working as one of the designers on the book, and Cynthia Ware copyediting. I have spoken to Steiner, Furtado, and Ware about their work on the project. Needless to say, all interpretations based on these conversations are my own.

89   Barbara H. Ankeny to Bob, Denise, and Steve, December 15, 1975, AAFAL. Between June and August 1976, Ankeny seems to have convinced them to check "mechanicals" in place of "blues," but only with the stipulation that the Press would consult them about any changes they might make after they had seen these. See Cynthia Ware to Denise Scott Brown, July 6, 1976, and Cynthia Ware to Denise Scott Brown, August 16, 1976, AAFAL. But then on September 14, 1976, Scott Brown wrote to Ankeny: "Yes, I agree we should see mechanicals, and hope we'd catch everything by that point, but I suggested that we see blues as well in order to catch the very last possible slips." See Scott Brown to Barbara Ankeny, September 14, 1976, AAFAL.

90   Mario Furtado to Barbara Ankeny, July 22, 1976, AAFAL.

91   Ibid. A letter to copyeditor Cynthia Ware written by Scott Brown exemplifies the kind of attention she demanded for the book during its production: "Enclosed are my corrections of the LLV proofs. I have read the text carefully for errors but I haven't made a two-person word-by-word check. I hope you have been able to do this." Denise Scott Brown to Cynthia Ware, November 10, 1976, AAFAL.

92   It is very unusual for authors to request, or be granted, the right to see "blues" as any changes to them are extremely expensive.

93   Even Barbara Ankeny, the acquisitions editor for the book, who played the "good cop" to Cooper's "bad cop" during the publication of the first edition, had her moments of frustration during the publication of both editions. In one letter of 1971 she writes to Scott Brown, "from this point on, do save corrections for galley stage, or we shall become muddled beyond hope." And after the publication of the revised edition, and Scott Brown's "final disappointment" with some design issues that were not resolved to their liking, she noted: "My eye—perhaps more objective—is pleased with the new book." Barbara Ankeny to Denise Scott Brown, May 20, 1977, AAFAL. Scott Brown remained dissatisfied with the pale blue cover and the tight margins in the revised edition of *Learning from Las Vegas*.

94   Denise Scott Brown to Barbara Ankeny, June 27, 1976, AAFAL.

95   Cynthia Ware, "Launching Report for Learning from Las Vegas," May 7, 1976, AAFAL.

96   Memorandum from Lee Ewing to Frank Urbanowski, "Re: Venturi/Learning from Las Vegas, Second Edition, " May 31, 1977, AAFAL.

97   See Freud, *Civilization and Its Discontents*, p. 72.

98   In a grant proposal seeking funds to prepare the Learning from Levittown studio material for publication, Venturi and Scott Brown felt the need to stress that "A book of this type needs close supervision in design by the authors as its essence lies in the relation of text and illustration." See "Learning from Levittown Project," AAUP, box 453.

99   For several years following her academic appointment, Muriel Cooper continued to collaborate on book projects with MIT Press editors and designers, notably with Roger Conover, who in 1977 left his position at The Architects' Collaborative to become the first full-time architecture and design editor at the MIT Press. The Architects' Collaborative (TAC) was founded by Walter Gropius in 1946, while he was teaching architec-

ture at Harvard, to promote and further the Bauhaus principles of modern design. The first project that Cooper and Conover discussed working on together was a biography of Walter Gropius by Reginald Isaacs.

100   Robert Venturi to Carroll Bowen, May 2, 1969, p. 3, AAUP, box 505.

101   These boards can still be seen in various states of preservation in the VSBA office in Manayunk, Pennsylvania.

102   Steven Izenour to Forrest Selvig, March 21, 1969, AAUP, box 505. They sent this material to Selvig at the New York Graphic Society in order to get estimates on production costs of the book based on different numbers and sizes of maps and illustrations on a 24 x 12-inch page format. They also wanted to see how much of the production costs would need to be subsidized. Selvig wrote back on April 9, 1969, noting that the cost would be astronomical, owing, in no small part, to the odd trim size, which meant that the book would open up to be 48 inches.

103   See AAUP, box 505. At the grandest dimension, it appears that Venturi and Scott Brown were looking for something along the lines of Passonneau and Wurman's massive *Urban Atlas*. This book had a print run of 3,000 copies, and sold for $100. It is usually stored or displayed in architecture libraries on a lecturn-like stand, or bookshelf, with other oversized atlases and reference books.

104   A letter from the MIT Press dated October 19, 1970, notes that the manuscript was due in June of that year, and asks them when the Press could expect to receive it. See Catherine Simpson to Robert Venturi, AAUP, box 453.

105   Part III was clearly modeled on the "Works" section of Venturi's *Complexity and Contradiction in Architecture*.

106   AAUP. This mock-up does not seem to have an archival number, and is stored in a glass vitrine.

107   There is also a rough early "typescript" of Part I on yellow lined paper with the "A&P" article and "Studio Notes" pasted onto it, and white stickers with figure numbers keyed to the text. It was probably produced around the same time as the mock-up boards. See AAUP, 225.II.A.22.15.

108   The boards themselves look as if have seen a bit of rearranging, as suggested by the tape abrasions, some missing images, and penciled-in question marks in their empty "slots." Many of the images have affixed orange or red sticky dots, which was a way for Muriel Cooper to indicate the relative importance and size of illustrations, corresponding to her lettering system of *a* (small), *b* (medium), or *c* (large). A separate list of images is keyed to the placement of each image on the panel, including an indication of their relative sizes in terms of Cooper's lettering system, and the kind of reproduction to be used: halftone, line, or color. See "Venturi/Las Vegas," April 15, 1971, AAUP, 225. II.A.22.15.

109   Steven Izenour to Michael Connelly, May 7, 1971, AAUP.

110   The manuscript was sent to the MIT editorial department on May 13, 1971.

111   This set of Photostats is located in the AAUP, box 6905.

112   To be clear, there don't seem to be any mock-up boards in the archives corresponding to these Photostats. This variant probably came before the preliminary mock-up dated February 1971. These Photostats exist in multiple copies in AAUP, 225.II.A. 26.16 and box 6905. The denser arrangement of images, however, and the inclusion of Loudon's dwelling with different stylistic "jackets" on the first board, which became figure 1 in the first edition, might suggest it came after the preliminary mock-up.

113 In the revised edition, only a snippet of this "deadpan" sequence is reproduced.

114 "Las Vegas Deadpan," 16mm film, transferred to VHS, approx. 21:45 minutes; VSBA Archive. There are two other films produced during the Las Vegas trip: "Las Vegas Strip (Day/Night)" by Dan Scully, 16mm film, transferred to VHS, approx. 14 minutes; "Las Vegas Electric," 16mm film, transferred to VHS, approx. 8:45 minutes. In the last video, the images have been reversed during transfer.

115 Robert Venturi to Alan Lapidus, Tom Wolfe, and Vince Scully, January 16, 1969, AAUP, 225.II.A.27.16.

116 "Feasibility Report for the Renwick Gallery," from Robert Venturi to Dr. Joshua C. Taylor, August 31, 1974, AAUP, 225.II.A.79.27.

117 Venturi and Scott Brown refer to the jester in relationship to the architect in *LLV*, p. 161.

118 Donald Lydon to Mr. and Mrs. Robert Venturi, January 23, 1969, AAUP, 225.II.A.26.14.

119 Muriel Cooper in conversation with Ellen Lupton, May 7, 1994. This variety was enabled by the IBM Composer, designed by Eliot Noyes, which had a type ball that allowed for changes in typeface. Scott Brown and Venturi used an IBM Elite typewriter in the "Signs of Life" exhibition, in which they employed Franklin Gothic for bold heads, owing to its ordinary styling; Times Roman and Caslon for institutional symbolism; and Futura for lobby signs, owing to its boldness and roundness. See "Print Casebooks Questionnaire: The Best in Exhibition/Display," AAUP, 225.II.A.80.06. This kind of typographic variety and accompanying sensory overload is also evident in their first exhibition, "From Rome to Las Vegas: An Exhibit of the Work of Venturi and Rauch at the Philadelphia Art Alliance, 1968." See the wonderful description of this exhibition in the first edition of *LLV*, p. 125. The use of an underlying typographic grid is conducive to either a deadpan or jester aesthetic; it is equally able to engage in minimal design—the "white-page aesthetic" that so disturbed Scott Brown—or to produce a "mise-en-page" of a noisy broadsheet, or newspaper-like, layout. In fact, isn't their "Bill-Ding-Board" project a giant columnar grid(iron)?

120 Muriel Cooper in conversation with Ellen Lupton, May 7, 1994.

121 In Muriel Cooper's two layouts for Part I, these elevations begin as a six-page spread and are then edited down to a four-page spread.

122 Denise Scott Brown and Robert Venturi, conversation with the author, Manayunk, Pennsylvania, June 16, 2007. Denise Scott Brown took the "Las Vegas Strip" photograph, which appeared as figure 39 and figure 111 in the first edition and was figure 1 in the revised edition.

123 Roland Barthes, *Writing Degree Zero*, trans. Annette Lavers and Colin Smith (New York: Hill and Wang, 1968).

124 Jean-Luc Nancy, "The Soun-Gui Experience," in *Multiple Arts: The Muses II*, ed. Simon Sparks (Stanford: Stanford University Press, 2006), pp. 207–211, and p. 260 n. 1.

125 Jean-Luc Nancy, "Forbidden Representation," in *The Ground of the Image*, trans. Jeff Fort (New York: Fordham University Press, 2005), pp. 35–36. Nancy provides a succinct "definition" of his way of thinking about this issue: "Representation is a presence that is presented, exposed, or exhibited" (p. 36).

126 See J. J. Gibson, *The Senses Considered as Perceptual Systems* (Boston: Houghton Mifflin, 1966), p. 26.

127 Barbara Ankeny to Robert Venturi, November 20, 1975, AAFAL: "The book will be redesigned as well, along the lines of your earlier desires. It will look like a book of ideas for students and professionals." See Nancy, "The Soun-Gui Experience," p. 209.

128 Here I am paraphrasing an idea in Nancy's essay "Catalogue," in *Multiple Arts: The Muses II*, p. 154, that I found quite relevant. Also see chapter 4.

129 The large presentation boards that explore the Las Vegas Strip's intensity utilize psychedelic Day-Glo colors to great effect; however, they are not nearly as striking when they appear in the first edition, owing either to their smaller scale or to the limitations of four-color reproduction.

130 In many ways the first edition recapitulates the studio, summarizing the *process* of its research and presentation of material, even as it further extends it into new configurations.

131 Although at one point the Press was considering including it as a numbered image, this idea seems to have dropped out sometime during the design and production of the revised edition.

132 Scott Brown, preface to the revised edition, p. xvi.

133 Robert Venturi, Denise Scott Brown, and Steven Izenour, "The 'Learning from Las Vegas' Studio, or Formal Analysis as Applied Design Research, Fall 1968," p. 3, AAUP, box 6905.

134 Ibid.: "Although at the end-of-term presentation neither instructors nor students could clearly answer the question 'What did you learn from Las Vegas?' (Can one answer the question 'What did you learn from the Parthenon?') students and faculty judged their efforts as worthwhile and relatively successful by two criteria: relevance and involvement."

135 Marshall McLuhan, "Decline of the Visual" (1966), in *Looking Closer 3*, ed. Bierut et al., p. 175. Significantly it was Marshall McLuhan who first declared the epochal importance of "suspended judgment": "the technique of suspended judgment is the discovery of the twentieth century as the technique of invention was the discovery of the nineteenth." See Marshall McLuhan and Quentin Fiore, *The Medium Is the Massage: An Inventory of Effects* (New York: Bantam Books, 1967), p. 69.

136 Michel Foucault, "The Masked Philosopher," in Foucault, *Ethics: Subjectivity and Truth*, vol. 3 of *The Essential Works of Michel Foucault* (Harmondsworth: Penguin and Allen Lane, 1997), p. 323.

137 Jacques Derrida, *The Postcard: From Socrates to Freud and Beyond*, trans. Alan Bass (Chicago: University of Chicago Press, 1987), p. 282.

138 See Kant, *Critique of Judgment*. The differences between reflective and determinate judgments are laid out in the introduction and in "Division I: Analytic of the Aesthetic Judgment." For an interesting way of thinking about Kant in relation to issues of judgment and pleasure in Freud, see Stanley Cavell, *A Pitch of Philosophy: Autobiographical Exercises* (Cambridge, Mass.: Harvard University Press, 1994), pp. 147–149. Cavell's understanding of Kant's "reflective judgment" and its "universal voice" is central to all of his writings on aesthetics, criticism, politics, ethics, skepticism, and the ordinary.

139 In 1972, Derrida had the following to say about the status of the book: "the form of the 'book' is now going through a period of general upheaval, and . . . that form now appears less natural, and its history less transparent, than ever." Jacques Derrida, *Dissemination*, trans. Barbara Johnson (Chicago: University of Chicago Press, 1981), p. 3.

140 Barthes, "From Work to Text," pp. 155–164. Derrida's writings about the relationship between oeuvre and text in the opening pages of *Of Grammatology* are also relevant here, but I have derived the most benefit from his discussion of that relationship in *The Postcard*, pp. 414–419, particularly as he relates them to issues of undressing, text, and

truth. An excellent overview of this moment in theory can be found in John Mowitt's *Text: The Genealogy of an Antidisciplinary Object* (Durham: Duke University Press, 1992).

141 Jean-Luc Nancy, "Distinct Oscillation," in *The Ground of the Image*, p. 66. This is an astute essay on the relationship between text and image.

142 See "Fallen Words Flat Out" in chapter 3, where I further elaborate on Leo Steinberg's notion of the flatbed picture plane in relation to the representational strategies in *LLV*.

143 Schapiro, "On Some Problems in the Semiotics of Visual Art," p. 26.

144 *LLV*, p. 20. Not to mention that Cooper's design is also an excellent typographic presentation of Ruscha's claim that "Streets are like ribbons. They're like ribbons and they're dotted with facts. Fact ribbons, I guess." "L.A. Suggested by the Art of Edward Ruscha," in Ruscha, *Leave Any Information at the Signal: Writings, Interviews, Bits, Pages*, ed. Alexandra Schwarz (Cambridge, Mass.: MIT Press, 2002), p. 224.

145 Denise Scott Brown to Barbara Ankeny, September 14, 1976, p. 4, AAFAL.

146 Denise Scott Brown to Barbara H. Ankeny, June 9, 1976, AAFAL.

147 The latter two phrases are used by Barbara Ankeny to describe the revised edition.

148 Another definition of a treatise is that it is shorter than a book, but longer than an essay.

149 *LLV*, p. 87.

150 Scott Brown to Barbara Ankeny, June 9, 1976, AAFAL.

151 From my perspective, there is no contradiction here with my claim in chapter 3 that the Duck and the Decorated Shed overlap with a vengeance.

152 Derrida, *The Postcard*, p. 343.

INDEX

Page numbers in boldface indicate illustrations.

Cartoon, 47, 67–68, 101. *See also* Carrier, David; Speech balloons

Cavell, Stanley, 3–6, 9–12, 14, 15, 17–18, 20, 27, 38, 44, 48, 50, 53, 58, 64–65, 67, 72, 78, 80–81, 83, 85, 91, 98, 105–107, 109, 122. *See also* Acknowledgment; Arrogation; Deadpan; Keaton, Buster; Melodrama; Ordinary; Skepticism; Subliming; Theatricality

Cloverleaf, 7, 24, 26. *See also* D'Arcangelo, Alan

Cold (coldness), 44, 46, 54, 64–65. *See also* Adorno, Theodor W.; Bernstein, J. M.; Cavell, Stanley

Colquhoun, Alan, 54, 97

Community, 3, 7, 9, 64–65, 105–107, 123–124, 147. *See also* "I Am a Monument"; *Learning from Las Vegas*; Nancy, Jean-Luc

Connelly, Michael, 117, 120–121, 126, 146, 148

Conover, Roger, 117

Consumer culture (commodity culture), 2, 5, 6, 9. *See also* Culture industry

Cooper, Muriel, 10, 38, 112–148, 153, 158–159, 166–167. *See also* Bauhaus design; Design; *Learning from Las Vegas*; MIT Press; Swiss design; White-page aesthetic

Architectural Space in Ancient Greece (Doxiadis), 136–**137**

Bauhaus (Wingler), 117, **118**, 134

Communication by Design, 121–**122**

File under Architecture (Muschamp), 139

layouts for *Learning from Las Vegas*, 112, **114**, 117, 126, 130–136, **131–133**, **135**, 139, 143–146, 153, 158, 167–168

The View from the Road (Lynch et al.), 136, **138**, 139, 160 (*see also* Lynch, Kevin)

Crawford Manor, 55, **56–57**, 93, 106, 168, **170**. *See also* Guild House; Rudolph, Paul

Critical theory, 6, 18, 30. *See also* Adorno, Theodor W.; Culture industry

Cullen, Gregory, 26

Culture industry, 6–7, 18, 30, 46, 71–72, 77, 95. *See also* Adorno, Theodor W.; Consumer culture; Critical theory

D'Arcangelo, Alan, 7, 24, **25**, 26. *See also* Cloverleaf; *Learning from Las Vegas*

Dead ducks, 64, 103. *See also* Duck and Decorated Shed

Deadpan, 8, 57–58, 66, 72–73, 77–78, 80–82, 86, 97, 103, 121, 157–160. *See also* Cavell, Stanley; Duck and Decorated Shed; Evenly distributed attention; Expression; Keaton, Buster; Ruscha, Ed

Deleuze, Gilles, 17, 21, 67, 91

De Man, Paul, 58

Derrida, Jacques, 111, 163, 171

Descartes, René, 5, 15, 91, 108

Design, 10–11, 21, 27, 29, 36–38, 54, 60, 64, 66, 77, 81, 97, 104, 106, 112–113, 116–**118**, 120–124, 126, 128–130, 134, 136–139, 141, 143–149, 153, 158–161, 166–168, 171. *See also* Cooper, Muriel; *Learning from Las Vegas*

Bauhaus design, 38, 94, 113, 117–**118**, 123, 134, 139, 159

Swiss design, 10, 117, 121, 129–130, 134, 136, 139, 160 (*see also* White-page aesthetic)

total design, 10, 27, 37, 66, 106, 123, 146–147

Diagram, 3, 8, 21–22, 52–53, 67–68, 136, 144

Donne, John, 15

Duck and Decorated Shed, 8, 10, 48, 50–55, 57, 58–73, **68**, 81–82, 93, 96, 99–100, 104, 106, 116, 118, 120–121, 147, 168. *See also* Dead ducks; Deadpan; "Eat" sign; Evenly distributed attention; Expression; *Learning from Las Vegas*; Modernism; Transparency

Dust jacket. *See Learning from Las Vegas*: dust jacket

"Eat" sign, 8, **52**, 67–**68**, 71–72, 77, 104. *See also* Duck and Decorated Shed

Ehrenzweig, Anton, 29, 30

Eisenman, Peter, 3

Eliot, T. S., 16, 24, 36, 42, 46, 109

Emerson, Ralph Waldo, 5, 13, 26, 32, 109

Empson, William, 16

Evenly distributed attention, 27, 73, 80. *See also* Deadpan; Duck and Decorated Shed; Expression; Freud, Sigmund; Melodrama

Expression (expressionism, inexpression), 5–6, 8–9, 33, 37–38, 49, 53, 54–55, 57–59, 64, 66–67, 70, 72–73, 80–82, 96–97, 99, 103–104, 106, 120, 139. *See also* Deadpan; Duck and Decorated Shed; Melodrama; Modernism; Transparency

Exscription, 101, 105. *See also* Nancy, Jean-Luc

Eyck, Aldo van, 16, 67

Fact (facticity), 11, 77–78, 97–98, 100. *See also* Barthes, Roland; Heidegger, Martin

Fenves, Peter, 37

Finkelpearl, Philip J., 15

Fire Station No. 4, 60, 82, 96. *See also* Rauch, John; Venturi, Robert

First edition. *See Learning from Las Vegas*: first edition

Frampton, Kenneth, 32, 35

Freud, Sigmund, 15–16, 21–22, 27, 31–32, 71, 73, 81, 91, 124, 148, 163, 166. *See also* Ambivalence; Evenly distributed attention

Fried, Michael, 14–15

Frye, Northrop, 16, 42

Gestalt, 27, 29–30, 141

Globalization, 2, 21

Gombrich, Ernst, 54, 97

Guild House, 55, **56–57**, 82, 96, 106, 168, **170**. *See also* Crawford Manor; Rauch, John; Venturi, Robert

Hansen, Miriam, 30

Harries, Karsten, 58

Heckscher, August, 35

Hegel, Georg Wilhelm Friedrich, 16, 49

Heidegger, Martin, 12, 15, 17, 23, 30, 78, 80–81, 98. *See also* Attunement; Fact; Mood

Heraclitus, 13, 24

Herzog and de Meuron, 3

Highway, 7, 24, 91, 167. *See also* Billboards

Hume, David, 5, 30

Huyssen, Andreas, 1–2

"I Am a Monument" (recommendation for a monument), 8–10, 82, 92, **94**–95, 97–110, 147. *See also* Blinking; Community

Ironic/Ionic column, 18–**19**

Irony, 6–7, 9, 18, 55, 95, 103, 109. *See also* Postmodernism

Izenour, Steven, 1, 36, 117, 123–124, 126, 145, 149

Jacobs, Jane, 29, 171

Jameson, Fredric, 1, 17, 67, 70–71

Jencks, Charles, 1, 16

Joyce, James, 16, 36, 42

Kant, Immanuel, 22, 43, 94, 163, 166

Kantor, Robert E., 29

Keaton, Buster, 78–**79**, 81, 83, **85**–86. *See also* Cavell, Stanley; Deadpan

Klee, Paul, 26, 30

Koolhaas, Rem, 3, 49, 67, 81

Kubrick, Stanley, 109, **110**

Las Vegas, city of, 2–4, 13, 15, 17–18, 20, 22–23, 26–27, 31–32, 35, 37, 42–43, 45–46, 48, 52, 72–73, 82, 87, 92–93, 106, 108, 113, 141, 143–144, 153, 158, 161

Las Vegas Strip, 3, 5, 18, 21–22, 27, 30–31, 37, 45, 47, 59, 60, **61**, 73, **84**, 87, **88–90**, 91–92, 102–103, 124, 136, **140**–141, 143, 153, **157**–160, 167. *See also Learning from Las Vegas*

Leach, Neil, 46

Learning from Las Vegas
cloth cover, 38, **40**, 120–122
cloverleaf, 7, 24, 26 (*see also* D'Arcangelo, Alan)
Crawford Manor, 55, **56–57**, 93, 106, 168, **170**

77, 94, 96–97, 103, 113, 136. *See also* Duck and Decorated Shed; Expression; Transparency
    modern architecture, 3, 5, 31, 33, 36, 49, 50, 52, 54, 58, 62, 64, 70, 129, 134, 136
Moll, Therese, 129
Mood, 3, 5, 7–8, 10, 15–18, 26, 44, 53, 78, 80, 86, 102. *See also* Attunement; Heidegger, Martin
Murch, Walter, 144
MVRDV, 3, 81

Nancy, Jean-Luc, 6, 9, 32, 49, 81, 98, 105, 107–108, 124, 141, 161, 166. *See also* Community; Exscription
New Critics, 16, 29
Nietzsche, Friedrich, 10, 71, 95
    Last Man, 10, 95, 108
Nihilism, 4, 18, 110
Noise, 7, 37–38, 72, 160
Nolli, Giovanni Battista, 27, **28**

Op art, 3, 100
Ordinary, 2–6, 8–10, 14, 18, 24, 36, 42, 44–45, 55, 59, 72–73, 91, 93, 95–96, 101, 106, 109, 149. *See also* Cavell, Stanley

Pevsner, Nikolaus, 54
Photo realism, 3
Plato, 15
Poirier, Richard, 16, 36, 42–43
Pollock, Jackson, 58. *See also* Expression
Pop art, 3, 18, 27, 31, 42, 58, 73, 81, 97–98, 100
Postmodernism, 1–3, 6–7, 9, 11, 16–18, 21, 71, 77, 95, 136, 171. *See also* Irony
    in architecture, 16, 77

Rapoport, Amos, 29, 30
Rauch, John, 55, **56–57**, 96, 112, 124, 126, 149, 168, **170**. *See also* Fire Station No. 4; Guild House; Venturi, Robert
Rauschenberg, Robert, 42, 87
Revised edition. *See Learning from Las Vegas*: revised edition

Rorty, Richard, 2, 23
Rudolph, Paul, 55, **56–57**, 93, 168, **170**. *See also* Crawford Manor
Ruscha, Ed, 18, 30, 44, 57, 71, 73–78, **75–76**, 80–81, 83, 85–86, 97, 121, 153, 157–158, 160. *See also* Deadpan

Sacks, Oliver, 24
Scene of instruction, 38, 47
Schapiro, Meyer, 92, 100, 139
Schema, 8, 43, 47, 53, 71, 81, 95, 100–102, 130
Scott Brown, Denise
    Architecture as Signs and Systems in a Mannerist World, 81
    in Las Vegas, **14**
    "The Meaningful City," 24, 27, 44
    "On Architectural Formalism and Social Concern: A Discourse for Social Planners and Radical Chic Architects," 15
    "On Pop Art, Permissiveness, and Planning," 27, 73, 81
    "Preface to the Revised Edition," 112, 120, 148 (*see also Learning from Las Vegas*)
    "Room at the Top? Sexism and the Star System in Architecture," 65
    "A Significance for A&P Parking Lots, or Learning from Las Vegas," 24, 52, 149, 153
Scully, Vincent, 7, 11, 33, 55, 110, 124
    unpublished introduction to *Learning from Las Vegas*, 11, 55, 124, 173, **174–180**
Semiotics, 8, 16, 23, 33, 92
Sexism, 2, 65, 124
"Signs of Life: Symbols in the American City" (exhibition), 45, 158–**159**
Skepticism, 3–8, 10, 16–18, 20, 30, 36, 38, 45–46, 48, 50, 53, 64–65, 67–68, 73, 78, 85, 101–103, 106, 109–110, 112, 122. *See also* Acknowledgment; Cavell, Stanley
    external world, 6, 102
    other minds, 6, 8, 49, 53, 65, 68, 102
Smith, Tony, 91–92

Socrates, 6, 23, 35
Southworth, Douglas, **22**
Speech balloons, 47, 67, 70. *See also* Carrier,
    David; Cartoon
Stein, Gertrude, 71
Steinberg, Leo, 87, 166
Steiner, Sylvia, 117, **135**, 146
Subliming, 5, 44. *See also* Cavell, Stanley;
    Wittgenstein, Ludwig
Swiss design, 10, 118, 121, 129–130, 134,
    136, 139, 160. *See also* Cooper, Muriel;
    Design; White-page aesthetic
Symbol (symbolism), 1, 22, 24, 42, 45,
    50, 52, 55, 66, 69, 91, 96–97, 102,
    105–106, 113, 124, 139, 158–159, 161,
    171

Tafuri, Manfredo, 18, 70
"Tan Hawaiian with Tanya," 7, 38, 46–**47**,
    101, 102, 111, 121. *See also* Billboards;
    Learning from Las Vegas
Theatricality, 50, 58–59, 82. *See also* Cavell,
    Stanley
Third, the, 123–124, 126, 128
Thoreau, Henry, 3, 12, 42, 44, 46, 71, 83,
    108
Total design, 10, 27, 37, 66, 106, 123,
    146–147. *See also* Design
Transparency, 5–6, 49–50, 59, 62, 66. *See
    also* Duck and Decorated Shed;
    Expression; Modernism
Typeface, 38, 46, 121, 136, 139, 159–160

Urban sprawl, 2–3, 21, 27, 34, 77, 106

Vasarely, Victor, 27, **29**, 141
Vattimo, Gianni, 62, 66
Venturi, Robert
    *Architecture as Signs and Systems in a
    Mannerist World*, 81
    Complexity and Contradiction in Architecture,
        2, 12, 15–16, 20, 34–35, 110, 124
    "Context in Architectural Composition"
        (MFA thesis), 32
    in Las Vegas, **14**
    "Mal Mots: Aphorisms—Sweet and
        Sour—by an Anti-Hero Architect," 12

"Note on Authorship and Attribution,"
    113, 124, 126 (*see also Learning from
    Las Vegas*: first edition)
    and Rauch, 55, **56–57**, 149, 168, **170** (*see
    also* Fire Station No. 4; Guild House;
    Rauch, John)
    "A Significance for A&P Parking Lots, or
    Learning from Las Vegas," 24, 52,
    149, 153
Venturi, Vanna, House, 82–**83**, 85
Vernacular architecture, 2, 5, 96
Virilio, Paul, 77

White-page aesthetic, 139, 141, 153, 160.
    See also Cooper, Muriel; Design; Swiss
    design
Wingler, Hans, 117–**118**, 134
Wittgenstein, Ludwig, 5–6, 24, 33, 36,
    44–45, 59, 71–72, 93, 103. *See also*
    Subliming
Wolfe, Tom, 37, 42, 72, 94–95, 103
Wonder, 7, 13–15, 17, 20, 24, 26, 27, 71, 80

Zahn, Carl, 121, **122**, 129
Zapf, Hermann, 129